Chasing the Beast

Also by George Greenfield

Desert Episode
This World is Wide Enough
At Bay
Scribblers for Bread
A Smattering of Monsters

Chasing the Beast

ONE MAN'S WAR

George Greenfield

RICHARD COHEN BOOKS · London

British Library Cataloguing in Publication Data:
A catalogue record for this book is available from the British Library

Copyright © 1998 by George Greenfield

ISBN 1 86066 128 9

First published in Great Britain in 1998 by
Richard Cohen Books
7 Manchester Square
London W1M 5RE

The right of George Greenfield to be identified as
the author of this work has been asserted by him in
accordance with the Copyright, Designs and
Patents Act 1988

Typeset in Galliard by MATS, Southend-on-Sea, Essex

Printed in Great Britain by T. J. Press International Ltd
Padstow, Cornwall

for Charles Daniels

a fellow Buff 1942–3
– and still a good friend

Contents

Acknowledgements

Warm thanks are due to Charles Daniels for supplying several of the photographs and for reminding me about the details of life with the war-time Buffs.

The photograph of the Battle of Alamein on p. 75 is reproduced by kind permission of the Imperial War Museum. All other photographs are from the author's personal collection.

All, all of a piece throughout:
Thy Chase had a Beast in View;
Thy Wars brought nothing about;
Thy Lovers were all untrue.

'Tis well an Old Age is out,
And time to begin a New.

Dryden, *The Secular Masque*

1

'The Little Victims Play'

A golden evening in early June 1939. The Foundation Dinner, attended by the fellows and scholars of Downing College, Cambridge, had come to a bibulous end with the last toast and the last drop of Chateau Yquem. I was strolling on the wide lawns – great privilege – with my tutor, Bill Cuttle. I had finished Part II of the English Tripos a few weeks earlier and had passed quite well. For a young man of twenty-two the world seemed an enchanted place. Every prospect pleased – except the long shadow cast by the Munich Crisis nine months earlier.

Bill, that owlish veteran who had devoted his adult life to Downing and its undergraduates, cut across my wine-enhanced reverie. He wanted to put my name forward for a vacant research fellowship. He was sure F. R. Leavis, my supervisor, would support the application and he had already had a quiet chat with the senior tutor. How did I feel?

I was, of course, immensely flattered. To be offered the keys of the cultural kingdom – almost on a plate, as it were – appealed to my vanity. But . . .

'I'm enormously grateful,' I said. 'Can't thank you enough. But surely there's going to be a war? My age and fairly fit, I'd be called up right away.'

'Nonsense,' Bill Cuttle said airily. 'That Hitler's all bluff. He can make a great speech and get those Brown Shirts cheering but when it comes to the crunch, you mark my words. He'll be very quiet then.'

I was living out of College that year in lodgings in Lensfield Road. Bill walked me to the porter's lodge by the great iron gates and we talked some more as we strolled, leaving it that I would think things over during the long vacation and consult my parents before coming to a decision. If I let him know by mid-September, three weeks before the Michaelmas Term started, there would still be plenty of time to apply, if I then wanted to become an academic. I thanked him warmly for the many hours of thoughtful help he had given me over my three years at Downing and then walked the short distance to my digs.

The decision was made for me. Twelve weeks later, I applied to join the Army.

Cambridge in the late 'thirties was another world. Public school boys from prosperous families strolled in and so did those good at sport. St Catherine's – 'Cat's' – was rumoured to give sporting scholarships; one year, the Scottish fly-half, R. B. Bruce-Lockhart, could not get into the Cat's rugby team in his usual playing position because the England fly-half, T. A. Kemp, already occupied it. He had to play as an inside-threequarter instead. Pass degrees were still part of the curriculum. Charlie Galloway, one of Downing's best rugby players and cricketers, did no work at all and knew he would fail even the minimal standards of his pass degree. So he consulted a local doctor, an old Downing man, who had been in Britain's Olympic team years before. Charlie had once been mildly concussed playing rugger and the doctor gave him a certificate stating he was liable to complete amnesia if put under the slightest mental stress. Thus the sportsman who had waltzed through Part I, having put in several mainly blank papers, was now entitled to an enjoyable third year at college and did not bother to attend the degree exams at the end of that year.

A friend of mine, Harry Roden, was an orphan. Under the terms of his parents' will, he could only inherit the substantial estate if he remained at a major university until he was twenty-five. He was then twenty-four, having spent three years at Oxford and now in his second year at Cambridge, reading agriculture. A rugger Blue, he played as my partner in the inter-college fives matches. He professed himself to be the most cowardly player who had ever won a Blue for rugger, let alone secured an England trial, preferring always to trip an opponent up rather than tackle him. But Harry milked his sporting stardom to great effect. Wearing his Varsity team blue and white striped vest with the red lion insignia – and with muddy knees, he would deliberately come on court late, manfully striving to disguise the bogus limp. He would apologise courteously to our opponents, saying that he had damaged his knee/thigh/calf – the ailment varied from week to week

– in the recent match against the Harlequins. But of course the game of fives must go on. If he collapsed suddenly with the pain, they must take no notice – just play round his prostrate form and then give him a moment to crawl off court.

It worked like magic. Harry would monopolise the front of the court, barging the opposition out of his way as he played drop shots and reverse angles. They would tiptoe delicately around the supposedly wounded rugger hero and, by the time they caught up with the ploy, Harry and I would be on the verge of winning.

He drove a Lagonda V-12 tourer. It was a long, low open two-seater which seemed to be all snout, with shiny exhaust pipes protruding from each side of the bonnet. The engine burbled away with a gruff note. He hâd palatial lodgings on the north side of Parker's Piece and on a summer morning I would call on him early and sit in the passenger seat as he drove along the Newmarket Road. There was almost no traffic and, approaching Six Mile Bottom – 'Zer – Boom', we called it – there was, no doubt still is, a long straight stretch for more than a mile. Harry would accelerate, the great engine roared and the wild air rushed in, over and around the narrow windscreen. Eighty, ninety – right up to and even a notch over a hundred miles an hour. Since then, I have driven an Aston Martin much faster and have been driven in an E type Jaguar at close on 150 mph but, apart from telegraph poles flicking past, there was little sensation of speed, compared to the thundering Lagonda.

But for many of us Cambridge life was not just a matter of fun and games. Sixty years ago there were really only three important universities in England – Oxford, Cambridge and Durham. The numbers in residence were then much smaller; at Cambridge something over 5,000 and at Oxford about 4,500. Durham, if anything, had fewer. Thus, there would be about 12,000 under-graduates at any given time, spread over an average three-year period. In other words, there were only some 4,000 places to be taken up at the three seats of learning each freshman year. For example, Downing, then a smallish and, of course, all-male, college, had fewer than 250 undergraduates at any one time, which meant that there were only about eighty places available to freshmen each year.

My father, a middle-grade civil servant, retired early through ill health in 1933, when I was sixteen years old. He was now on a half-pay pension. Whereas previously I was due to attend university in any event, provided I could amass six or seven 'O' Levels or two 'A' Levels in the Schools or Higher Schools Certificate respectively, now I would also have to get an open scholarship or exhibition at the college where I applied. The examinations were held in mid-March, just after the end of the Lent Term. Successful candidates had to be under the age of nineteen at the time of taking the exams. In March 1935, I entered for an English scholarship at Christ Church, Oxford, and failed. The following year, when I was only two weeks inside the qualifying age, Downing College, Cambridge, offered two scholarships of £100 and one exhibition of £40 in English Literature. Apparently, the examiners were unable to separate the third and fourth best examinees and so the college authorities decided to reduce one scholarship to £60 and offer two exhibitions each of £40. I scraped in as the fourth highest.

But it was a start. Coming from a minor public school. I was not eligible for a state scholarship, but the open exhibition proved to be a magic key. In those days, certain City livery companies gave annual contributions towards a 'poor scholar's' upkeep at university. I recall with gratitude the Fishmongers' Company's £15 donation. (It may seem ludicrously small in these inflated times but £15 in 1936 would be worth close on £400 today.) Topped up with a school-leaving scholarship of £50 a year for three years, the final total I managed to amass was £210.

I was quite pleased with myself until I read Downing College's notes for freshmen and saw that the minimum reasonable allowance per year was held to be £220. For the first year or so, counting pennies became essential. Dinner in hall at night was already covered as part of 'board and lodging' but throughout term-time lunch in my rooms was always the same, at a total cost of 6d (2½p): 3d for the smallest Walls individual pork pie and 3d for a small tin of Heinz baked beans. (It says much for the two famous firms that I can still enjoy their products.) Fortunately, towards the end of my second year I was awarded an internal college scholarship that brought in an additional £100 or so for the next two years; in one step I had gone from the penniless to the almost prosperous.

But, for lack of £2 a few months earlier, I had missed an artistic and financial scoop. In the Michaelmas and Easter terms, I played squash several times a week at the University courts in Portugal Place. Gordon Fraser had quite recently opened his art gallery and I often dropped in on my way back to my lodgings. He recognised that my close interest in his offerings was only matched by my ignorance and in free

4

moments he helped enlighten me. One day he showed me a set of Picasso etchings from his Blue period, which then was only twenty-five years earlier. He showed me how each one was numbered – out of ten – and said that the plate was always destroyed at the end of the run; although he added the rider that Picasso, even then, was considered a shade unscrupulous in keeping the plate secretly intact and running off more prints when he needed quick cash.

He offered to sell me one etching for £5. Try as I might, I could only scrape together £3, which would have meant cutting an already meagre regime even further for the rest of the term. He could not afford to drop the price, which was already a generous concession, so that was that. For a long time, whenever I recalled the economy of line, the power and yet the repose of the etched figures, I mourned my lack of funds at the right moment. The feeling returned, intensified, a year ago when the same etchings fetched £200,000 each in a big art auction.

Within a week of matriculating I met – and soon got to know, two great men: Sir Arthur Quiller-Couch, Q, as he was always known, and Doctor F. R. Leavis. Q must then have been in his early seventies, with long silvery-white hair and an abundant Victorian moustache of the same hue, but he was still Regius Professor of English. I had read with relish, and still re-read, his *The Art of Reading* and *The Art of Writing*. He carried his profound knowledge with such grace and lightness and, as a successful novelist in the 1890s, he had shown his practical understanding of the art of writing.

In the late 'thirties, he did not venture much into the lecture hall but used to hold *soirées* after dinner in his rooms at Jesus College. Always courteous and treating the rawest freshman as an equal, he insisted on pouring coffee from an exquisite eighteenth-century silver pot. One had to manoeuvre the delicate cup and saucer in time with the tremor in his elderly hand. Some idiot would blurt out, 'Do you believe that truth is beauty, sir?'

Q would answer with infinite politeness, 'Ah, that's always an interesting question. I remember discussing it with Matthew Arnold.'

Matthew Arnold! But he was a Victorian, a contemporary of Tennyson. 'And did you once see Shelley plain?' Arnold's life had its roots in the Romantic movement. And here in the up-to-date 'thirties was an elderly man who had shaken hands with History. It was a moment to savour.

Although they were so different in background and upbringing, Q much admired Leavis and indeed once saved his career. It happened like this. In the early 1930s, the English Faculty gave Leavis a temporary lectureship, subject to later ratification. His course of six lectures was on the Modern Novel and he included *Ulysses* as a seminal subject. James Joyce's novel was still on the banned list in the United Kingdom and copies could only be obtained in plain brown wrappers from places like Sylvia Beach's shop in Paris. The frumpish Faculty told Leavis to drop *Ulysses* and deal with a more innocuous novel but he insisted that his study of the development of modern fiction would be incomplete without it. And then he was informed that unless he toed the line, his lectureship would not be confirmed. But still he went ahead.

He was a terrible lecturer, talking in a monotone and in clotted sentences, heaping sub-clause upon sub-clause in his effort to pin down the elusive essence of his thoughts. Usually, only the hardy attended throughout his courses but, apparently, the lecture hall that day was packed with keen students, hoping to hear something 'dirty'. They would have been disappointed. Still, Leavis lost his lectureship and had to scrape by on his college stipend alone for the next few years. Things must have been very tough because he not only had a wife to support, the formidable Queenie, but an infant son as well.

Around 1934, a vacancy fell due for an English Faculty lectureship. Q as Regius Professor, never took up residence at Jesus College until the second week of term and always went back to his beloved Fowey in Cornwall at least a week before term ended. So, led by *flaneurs* like F. L. Lucas and George Rylands, a cabal at the Faculty decided to hold the crucial meeting in the first week of term. Leavis got wind of the plot and sent a telegram to Sir Arthur, begging him to do something.

The Faculty meeting was just about to start when in walked the silver-haired Regius Professor who sat down at the head of the table and said slowly and clearly, 'Good afternoon, gentlemen. I see there is only one item on today's agenda, the appointment of a lecturer. It's very simple. There is only one man outstandingly qualified – Doctor F. R. Leavis. All those in favour? I see we are unanimous. Doctor Leavis is hereby appointed. Thank you, gentlemen. I declare the meeting closed.'

He stood up, went out to the taxi that had been waiting for him and drove to the station on his way back to Cornwall.

Leavis was very shy, almost antisocial. He dined on high table at Downing as rarely as he could. In those days, of course, undergraduates all wore collars and ties in the daytime, with usually a sports jacket and grey flannel trousers. Supervisors and lecturers almost always wore a suit and waistcoat. But not Leavis. He had a grey open-necked shirt, a gingery tweed jacket and grey flannels a couple of inches too short so that his thin ankles were revealed. His bald pate, always sunburned, with long grey locks beneath and his pointed snipey nose made him a gnome-like figure. My first and abiding memory is of his riding into College on his clanking old bicycle, still with his shirt collar open and his gown bundled into a basket on the handlebars. As he walked jerkily across the lawns to the dining hall, he took out a grey-green woollen tie from a pocket and tied it round his neck. He never stayed chatting in the senior common room after dinner but went straight back to his cycle, tearing off the tie and opening his shirt collar as he went.

Three factors separated him from the rest of the English Faculty. First, he was passionate in his beliefs to the extent, as he proved, of jeopardising his whole career for them. The other members of the Faculty no doubt liked and admired Eng. Lit. but to him it was a superior substitute for religious belief. I think he really did believe that devotion to 'The Line of Wit' and the development of critical standards made a man or woman morally better, more rounded, more receptive to the *meliora*. Second, he was scathing about his colleagues, both in conversation and in *Scrutiny,* the severe critical magazine he and Queenie Leavis edited and ran. He never forgot a slight and he could demonstrate real pettiness and a mean spirit. The third factor during my time was his Tripos successes. In 1938, there were six Firsts in Part I out of the whole university, and three of them were from Downing. In 1939, there were six Firsts in Part II out of the 120 or so examinees, and again three were from Downing. The word got around and students from other colleges opted out from their college supervisor and applied to become Leavis's pupils. Which, as supervisors were then paid *per capita*, did not endear him to the rest of the Faculty.

In those happy days Cambridge University was still what a university had always been for over six hundred years, a place where poor scholars congregated to learn at the foot of the master. (The university terms are still based on an agrarian society. Young men worked on the farm and, when the harvest was safely in – by late September – they put away their scythes and spades and walked many miles to reach Oxford or Cambridge by the end of the first week in October, the start of the

Michaelmas Term.) Pupils reading English at Downing each spent two hours every week with the great Doctor. One of the hours was spent in a seminar with perhaps two other pupils present and the discussion subject(s) set in advance. The other hour was spent alone with him at his house on the far side of Midsummer Common, going through the weekly essay he had read beforehand. He was never dogmatic or forceful in those meetings, the reverse, indeed. He would listen patiently and, if he wanted to argue with the view expressed, do so with great modesty.

There was a story about Oxford current at 'the other place'. An undergraduate was being subjected to a *viva voce* for his finals by two dons. One said, 'What are your views on modern poets?' And the other one cut in with, 'Yes, what do you *really* think of Tennyson?'

Leavis was different. He believed so much in the importance of English literature that he made his pupils take it seriously. And not just as a subject to be studied under a glass case. It was a living, breathing subject. Sixty years ago he was discussing Eliot and Pound and Auden as poets and novelists like Dos Passos and Djuna Barnes – works that had appeared in the last twelve months.

And after all that time, I still recall vividly his textual criticism: how he would talk about the easy conversational rhythms in John Donne and his skill in placing the emphasis on the significant word, as in

> I wonder by my troth what thou and I
> *Did* till we loved? . . .

or his reading aloud, in that grating voice, Wordsworth's 'A slumber did my spirit seal', and then analysing it brilliantly ('She seemed a *thing* that could not feel . . .'). If I had not known Doctor Leavis and studied under him, I would have gone through life a poorer man, culturally speaking. I would never have read in detail and appreciated the Metaphysical poets, Dryden, Pope, the early Wordsworth – and I would have missed a great deal.

Downing was one of the most recently founded and, in my day, least regarded of the Cambridge colleges. Around the first quarter of the eighteenth century, Sir George Downing, who built the street that still bears his name and who must have been what we now call a property speculator – a slave trader as well, it was rumoured – died. What followed would make a kind of riproaring Restoration play or even a juicy historical novel.

He had been very wealthy. In his will, he decreed that, if none of his three vigorous sons left legitimate issue, his money was to be donated to the building of a new college. It seemed an extremely long shot and must have evoked chuckles in the London coffee-houses but, first, one son was killed in the hunting field and another died, leaving numerous bastards but no legitimate heirs. The third son, childless, fell ill and died. Plans for the building were drawn up. Downing College would have been highly ornate, with fountains all over the place, statues and temples, a cross between the Trevi Fountain and the courtyard of St. Peter's. By 1750, the college could have been ready for its first freshmen.

And then the law stepped in. Nearly ten months after the death of her husband, the last Lady Downing gave birth to a boy. She sued for the estate to remain in her possession. Two hundred years ago, the science of obstetrics was obviously less advanced than it now is. The battle waged on in the courts for year after year, with appeals against judgments and fresh appeals against the appeals, new medical witnesses appearing only to be rejected by the other side. The law suit lasted for over fifty years, a record in the history of English jurisprudence. And all the time the lawyers grew richer and richer, while the funds available for building a college grew smaller and smaller.

At last, the case was resolved. An old man, who had been a worker on the estate in his youth, made a solemn deathbed declaration. He said that, with the master still lying cold upstairs, Lady Downing had summoned all the staff in the Great Hall and ordered them to line up. She went down the line, looking closely for a young man with strong thighs and a light in his eyes. She had chosen him, made him accompany her to the main bedroom and there make love to her off and on for the next few days. The child she had given birth to was his, not the son of the late master.

So, after a delay of fifty years, Downing College came into being at the beginning of the nineteenth century. With the funds strictly circumscribed by the previous demands of lawyers – some things never change – gone were the grand avenues and 'cloud-capped palaces' of the original plans. Severe but symmetrical buildings on opposite sides of a large square were far more in keeping with the chaste endeavours of a community of learning. Unfortunately, potential endowments had also suffered and Downing spent the first 150 years of its life as one of the poorer colleges.

Part II of the English Tripos was a veritable Cook's tour of the cultural scene. At the end-of-year examinations, there would be a paper on Tragedy, ranging from Aeschylus to T. S. Eliot's *Murder in the Cathedral*. There were set books in French and Italian, concentrating on mediaeval works – François Villon's poems, Dante's *Divine Comedy*, Petrarch's sonnets, Boccacio's *Il Decamerone*. Most of the examinees knew some French but required a crash course in Italian, which was supplied by a refugee professor from Italy, whose liberal views clashed with the Blackshirt rule.

I went up to Cambridge a week early in 1938. It would be a crucial year, I knew, and I wanted to get a flying start. I walked into Bowes & Bowes bookshop on the corner of King's Parade and ordered a copy of the set book by Boccacio. In those days the assistants were better read than the undergraduates. On this occasion the bespectacled assistant, a man of middle years, frowned. He asked me to wait while he took advice. A few minutes later, he returned, with the manager in tow. The latter stared at me suspiciously and then summoned me to his office. There he asked me my purpose in ordering the book. I said it was a set book for Part II of the English Tripos. A likely tale – I could almost see the thought forming behind his hard stare.

'It really is,' I said. 'Look, why don't you ring up the English Faculty and check? Anyway, what's all the fuss about?'

It turned out that Mussolini, Savonarola-like in public but a private libertine, had banned those stories of frolicking friars and simple peasant girls. Reassured of my probity, the Bowes & Bowes manager unlocked his safe and took out a pink paperbacked copy for me to buy. I have it on my bookshelf today.

But Cambridge was not all reading late into the night, researching at the Faculty library, writing essays and arguing at tutorials. There were also the 'rags', some of them most ingenious. One student, studying Law, came across a fifteenth-century statute that had never been removed. It was to encourage undergraduates to practise archery, the long bow having successfully seen off the French at Agincourt and Crécy. As long as they dressed in Lincoln green and carried out certain arcane steps, they were entitled to set up a target at one end of Petty Cury and fire arrows at it from the other. Five hundred or more years ago Petty Cury (the little stable) had been an isolated track alongside stables. By the late 1930s it was a busy thoroughfare, housing Heffer's bookshop and many other well-known stores. And on Saturday morning, the day chosen, it was at its busiest. But undaunted, the raggers, all dressed in Lincoln green, started shooing the pedestrians aside as they set up their target practice. Motor cars were imperiously waved away and those already stationary in the narrow street were shoved to one side. There was chaos, confusion, mounting tempers. (There was then still a sharp division between Town and Gown.) The police were called.

But when the senior inspector tried to send the students packing, he was shown a copy of the statute and was told, courteously but firmly, that, with tension mounting in Europe, able-bodied young men in England must prepare to defend their country with the bow and arrows, just as their forebears had done centuries before. Luckily, the statute was still in force so that they could carry out their patriotic duties without let or hindrance.

The inspector, it seems, had a sense of humour. He proposed a happy compromise. Petty Cury would be temporarily cleared of pedestrians and traffic. Each of the students, properly attired, would be entitled to shoot one arrow at the target – 'And please try to aim straight. No broken windows, if you please.' Then would they kindly take their toys away and let the grown-ups get on with their Saturday shopping. A handshake and the day was saved.

Then there was the undergraduate, a member of the Footlights, who managed to steal some stationery from Claridge's during a vacation. He wrote to the Master of Trinity, his own college, claiming to be a wealthy Arab potentate who wished to send his six sons, all of the right academic age, to Cambridge. He wanted to inspect the college before coming to a decision. He had heard that King's and St. John's were also good centres of learning. The Master promptly invited him to lunch on the high table. Suitably made up, dressed in flowing robes and with two acolytes in tow, he arrived at Trinity to be welcomed by the Bursar, shown around the courts he knew all too well and given a sumptuous lunch by the Master and several senior dons. And no one spotted his true identity.

Another rag took place in Mays week. The University Madrigal Society, as darkness fell, was to float downstream in punts along the Backs, past King's and under the Bridge of Sighs, chanting Elizabethan melodies as they made their stately progress. It was to be an outside broadcast for the BBC. But, further upstream, a few members of Queen's had a different idea for background music. They amassed two or three dozen chamber pots – college sanitation then was still somewhat rudimentary – tied them together and put a night light in each one. Then they lowered the flotilla into the Cam fifty yards behind the convoy of singing madrigallers. Earnest music-lovers, listening to the broadcast on their wireless sets, must have been bemused by the clinking, clanking background noise as the chamber pots bumped together on the stream and by the roars of laughter from watchers on the banks.

The gauche young man from the provinces could find his aesthetic senses stretched at the Cosmopolitan Cinema (the old 'Cosmo') off Market Square. The programme changed twice weekly. The main feature would be a modern classic, usually foreign – *The Cabinet of Doctor Caligari*, Eisenstein's *The Battleship Potemkin* (I can still see in my mind's eye that pram bumping down the steps), *La Grande Illusion, Les Bas Fonds*. And the second feature was always a Marx Brothers film. I must have seen *Duck Soup, Horse Feathers, A Day at the Races* and *Night at the Opera* half a dozen times each. (Groucho, the horse doctor, taking the pulse of Margaret Dumont, always the female stooge, 'Either you're dead or my watch has stopped.' And to Harpo, 'I'd horsewhip you, if I had a horse.' The zany wisecracks can still raise a smile.)

Cheap – and not so cheap – music was indeed potent in the late 'thirties at Cambridge. On a summer afternoon, hiring a punt at Mill Lane and punting up to Grantchester for a swim in Byron's Pool, one could hear the portable gramophones on other punts blaring out Hoagy Carmichael's 'Deep Purple' or Artie Shaw's version of 'Begin the Béguine' or Louis Armstrong's trumpet sobbing away over 'St Louis Blues'. And one could never escape those three little fishes that 'swam and swam right over the dam'.

Bizarre things happened, too. Rooms in college had – still have, I believe – two doors. If the outer one were left open, visitors knew they would be welcome to enter. But if the occupant 'sported his oak' (closed the outer door), it was a sign that he was not to be disturbed. An elderly reclusive Regius Professor of Latin always sported his oak, except when he grudgingly left it open in the morning for his bedmaker to enter and tidy his rooms. On arrival early in the morning, she would leave a bottle of milk outside his closed door and then attend to other rooms on the staircase until she saw his door open. She was not a very bright woman and seven or eight bottles of milk had to mount up outside the closed door before she began to suspect all was not well with the professor. The head porter was called. He in turn had to send for a locksmith to deal with the door. Finally, it was open. The professor had been struck down by a heart attack. He was surrounded by some dozens of undergraduates living on the same staircase and walking past his door half a dozen times a day but no one had noticed. He died unaided, alone. His name was A. E. Housman. In his younger days he had been a great poet.

The second week of June 1939: my mother came to collect me in her old Morris open four-seater, as I had amassed an assortment of books, tennis and squash racquets and all the clobber, as we then called it, of three years at Cambridge. With the back of the car bulging with parcels, we drove sedately along the Trumpington Road. I felt serene, fulfilled. It had indeed been a liberal education. Now I felt ready to face anything. Bill Cuttle could be right. Hitler had huffed and puffed a year earlier but Munich and Chamberlain's 'peace in our time' had provided a breathing space. Perhaps I should take the long-term view and think seriously of that research fellowship. At least another two years at Cambridge – on a mellow summer morning, it seemed an ideal occupation for an ambitious young man.

2

❖❖❖

Short Back and Sides

❖❖❖❖❖❖

Sunday morning not three months later: my mother and father, my two sisters and I were listening to Chamberlain's sepulchral tones on the wireless. Despite his government's efforts to maintain peace – in the case of Czechoslovakia, some might think cowardly efforts – Herr Hitler had gone too far this time. It was war. And, just as Chamberlain finished speaking, the air raid siren began to wail. Our home had been an Elizabethan farmhouse in the village of Loose, two miles south of Maidstone. The quickest route for bombing London passed directly overhead. It was luckily a false alarm but a hard reminder of what war was all about.

Later that same day various notices issued from the radio. One was that recent graduates from Oxford and Cambridge who had qualified in their school OTC's (officer training corps) should register with their respective university to enlist and become officer cadets. I wrote the next day to the Cambridge Appointments Board and in a week or two was summoned to appear at the Senate House. On arrival, having rushed across London and only just caught the Cambridge train as it was pulling out of Liverpool Street, I went straight to the urinal and discharged my burden. Reporting to the main desk, I was handed a phial with the order to provide a specimen. I went back to my refuge and was vainly trying to squeeze out a few drops when a burly young man in an open white coat breezed in.

He spotted my predicament at once and said, 'Dried up? Why waste mine? They passed me OK, so you should be all right.'

This is going to be a good war, I thought, as I passed back the steaming full phial to the orderly on the desk. There followed the usual poking in the ribs and coughing and inspection of private parts, after

14

which I was passed fit. Then came the viva. Each candidate, having dressed again, was quizzed by a quorum of three dons to discover what arm of the services he should enter. When it came to my turn, the chief inquisitor was the senior tutor of Downing College, H. C. Whalley-Tooker. An old Etonian, tall and with an air of vagueness, he had devoted his life to Downing and, as he wandered round the fellows' rose garden communing with nature, always struck us undergraduates as other-worldly, almost ethereal.

'Ah, Greenfield,' he said, beaming, 'I've got just the job for you. Got a First or two, didn't you? The Intelligence service, that's the one. No question of charging around in uniform, you can wear your own clothes. And you won't risk being shot at. Join Intelligence and you'll be comfortable, safe and able to use your brains.'

'Thank you, sir, but I want to join the infantry.'

'The infantry?' I had seen Edith Evans as Lady Bracknell in *The Importance of Being Earnest*. My tutor's tone echoed her 'A handbag' in its uncomprehending horror.

'Yes, sir, the infantry.' I had, of course, read von Remarque and Robert Graves and Siegfried Sassoon. There was to my mind something romantic, if futile, about the infantry.

'But all those rough men . . . And the dirt. And marching all round the place. Are you sure about this, Greenfield?'

'Yes, sir, quite sure.'

'So be it.' He shrugged and made a note on the printed form. 'Let me know if you ever change your mind.'

I occasionally wonder what might have happened had he stressed the advantages of joining the infantry. Might I have opted for Intelligence instead? And would I have made it my career for life, as several others did? The true answer is that I was never cut out to be a secret backroom operator; I would have been far too indiscreet.

The Board was not a paragon of efficiency. My papers became lost among a myriad of folders and official forms. Weeks went by until at last I received orders along with a rail warrant to report to the Lincolnshire Regimental Depot in Lincoln on a certain date. There was another medical inspection and then we were issued with underwear, khaki shirts, battledress, thick socks and ammunition boots. The 'potential officers' were also issued with a white loop, to be secured to the epaulettes. It automatically made you a target for the envy of the other ranks and the opportunistic hate of the NCOs. Lance-corporals, corporals, sergeants and sergeant-majors would all be thinking, 'One day, if they don't find you out first, I'm gonna be standing to attention, saluting and calling you sir. Till then, I'll show you who's the master. Hup! hup! hup! – get those bloody knees up. You're marking time, not dancing the foxtrot!'

About half my squad of thirty were prospective officers, the other half a mixed bunch. There were several Cockneys, one of whom named Groombridge had been a secondhand car dealer in peacetime. We also had a gypsy, a short swarthy man with dark eyes that darted around all the time. He looked at his boots blankly and tried to pull the left boot on to his right foot. Someone had to show him which was which. He grunted in reply.

The barracks around the drill square had not expanded swiftly enough to cope with the regular new entries of recruits. We had to sleep in large bell tents, eight men to a tent, with feet to the pole and bodies radiating out like spokes. It was a revelation to me and the other potential officers, who were used to fresh air at night. The others insisted on securing the tent flap tightly. Most of them were heavy smokers. When 'Lights Out' sounded on the bugle, each of them took one last drag at his fag and stubbed it out. When we woke up next morning, you could write your initials on the heavy atmosphere. Then, with much coughing and hawking, the smokers lit up their 'doofers' – 'That'll do fer tomorrow' – took a deep drag and returned to a paroxysm of coughing.

For the next few weeks it was a case of drill, bull, more drill, more bull, sergeants screaming abuse, up and down the parade ground, at the double here, stand to attention, stand at ease – 'As you were, you horrible little men!' bellowed the drill sergeant. He could call you any name he liked except 'bastard'. That, the Army held with rigid courtesy, slandered your mother's reputation and a devoted son was entitled to defend his mother's good name i.e. by thumping the drill sergeant.

Of course, we white-tabbers already knew how to slope arms, order arms, present arms, fix bayonets and all the rifle drill we had learned in our school OTCs. And anyone who had been to a public school and a university was likely to be a trained survivor. The others in our squad had mostly lived a far more cushy life, doted on by grandparents, watching football matches, not lying at the bottom of a scrum with the other side kicking you rhythmically in the ribs, earning real money at an age when we were still scrimping and saving. The whole point of Army training is to brutalise the recruit, dehumanise him, if possible,

Private Greenfield at the Lincolnshire Regimental Depot, 1940

so that he becomes an automaton, ready to obey orders without thinking. The potential officers had come through their ordeal before this and had the brains to realise what was being attempted.

Once the recruits knew enough drill to appear in public, they were marched the mile or so to the cathedral behind the depot band and drums blaring away with the regimental march, 'The Lincolnshire Poacher'. It had a real swing to it and when the final chorus arrived –

> For – 'tis my delight
> On a shining night
> In the season of the year

– the big drum came thumping in. A great tune to march to, it put a swagger and a squaring of the shoulders into the meanest private soldier.

Arriving at the cathedral precinct, the band fell silent. We marched in file into the lofty nave, doffing our fore-and-aft caps as we went. Except for the gypsy. This was all new to him. He stood there gazing around, cap still firmly on his head. The RSM was standing a few yards to our rear, shepherding the troops into the cathedral.

'Tell that man to get his cap off,' he hissed in a whisper that must have penetrated to the altar at the far end. Our gypsy just stood there. 'Cap off!' shrieked the RSM *sotto voce*, which would be anybody else's full-blooded shout. Still no action. The RSM strode up to our mind-wandering gypsy and yelled, 'Get that fucking cap off. Don't you know you're in the House of God, you cunt!'

Twice a week, we had to undergo gymnastic drill, so many pull-ups on the parallel bars, leapfrogging over the vaulting horse and so forth. One of the sergeant-instructors was a pale-faced, slight but wiry Yorkshireman with expressionless eyes. His name was Hutton. Two years earlier, he had broken the Test Match record for the highest innings, 364 not out at the Oval in the Fifth Test against the Australians. Bradman, whose record he broke that day, was in the field to shake his hand. There was nothing glamorous or exciting about him – at least, not in the eyes of the private soldiers he drove without mercy up and down the gym.

The depot adjutant was Captain Welby-Everard, who went on to military heights before the war ended. He was a keen cricketer, who had represented the peacetime Army. It was a gloriously bright summer and he arranged several cricket matches to be played on the depot ground. The home team was mainly made up of potential officers; I was nominated to open the innings with Hutton. It should have been the high point of my sporting life, something that would have my son and in turn my grandsons listening in awe to the ancestral exploits. Alas, my son turned out to be a rowing man and the grandsons prefer golf and roller skating to the skills of cricket. In any event, I spent an infuriating hour or so. Staff-Sergeant Hutton, with that so correct batting style, would caress a couple of fours from the ragged bowling. Then he would tuck the last ball of every over round the corner, shout 'Come for one' and so monopolise the strike. We put on over 100 for the opening stand, of which my share was 12, three streaky fours I had slashed on the only occasions I had the chance to take guard. I thought the great man was behaving like a selfish shit and, although I was far too junior to tell him so. I did once hint between overs that there were supposed to be two opening batsmen.

He told me in that thick accent that he had learned his cricket the hard way. The great Herbert Sutcliffe had treated him just the same when, as a youth, he had first played for Yorkshire; not least, when there was a hostile fast bowler hurling the ball at the batsman. Sutcliffe would very quickly sneak a single and leave the beginner to be thumped in the ribs by a hard ball travelling at nearly a hundred miles an hour. The habit never died, it seemed, even in a so-called friendly match. Once a professional . . .

It was in the Lincolnshire Depot gymnasium that, a few weeks after that cricket match, Hutton fell off a parallel bar, smashing his left elbow. The arm healed but was permanently an inch shorter than the right one. After the war, he had to alter his style radically to cope with the problem; it says much for his fortitude and his innate skill that he adapted so successfully as to score many more centuries and become the first professional to captain England at cricket and receive a knighthood to crown a dour career.

The 'phoney war' had ended with Guderian's blitzkrieg through the Low Countries, the debacle of Dunkirk and, two weeks later, the fall of France and the German troops goose-stepping through the Arc de Triomphe. To my university generation, Paris had been the flower of culture, home of actors trained by the Comédie Française like Jean-Louis Barrault, Edwige Feuillère, Arletty, of impressionist painters, of Cocteau. I was feeling gloomy, as though I had lost something dear, when I went home on short leave.

My mother, a woman of great energy, who, although in her sixties, ran a sizeable house single-handed, an orchard, a largish fruit and vegetable garden, two 'Dig for Victory' allotments nearly a mile away, and my retired father, and in her spare time taught at a local Roman Catholic convent school, was in good form, almost gleeful.

'We're in the final now,' she said to me with real conviction. 'I never did trust those French. All smiles and bows and '*Merci bien*' to your face – but what were they saying behind your back? No, it's us against the Germans. We know just where we are.'

Yes, I thought. In a mess, if you want to know, dear mama. But then I thought, this woman's indomitable. With a few more stupidly brave citizens like her around, the country would be invincible. Three months later, when the Battle of Britain was in full swing and the Luftwaffe was still trying to bomb London by day, my mother was digging on her allotments when a Heinkel flew over on its way back to Occupied Europe. It had discharged its bomb load but had plenty of machine gun rounds aboard. The pilot thought he would have some fun. He circled round and then flew low over the solitary woman whose only weapon was a spade, firing a long machine gun burst. As the plane soared up again, the navigator must have spotted that the target had been missed. So round went the Heinkel in a long loop and took another raking dive at the lone digger with yet another machine gun burst. This time, my mother admitted later, she dived for cover between two rows of cabbages. As she apparently remarked afterwards to my father, it wasn't very sporting of the Boche.

In my last couple of months at Lincoln, Captain Welby-Everard was promoted and transferred to another unit. A new adjutant took his place, Captain Darwall. Where his predecessor had been large, bulky and hearty, he was slight, of medium height and saturnine, with dark hair and cold eyes. For some reason which I never fathomed, he seemed to take an instant dislike to me. I was keen to complete the initial training and be passed as fit to join an OCTU (Officer Cadets' Training Unit), where after twelve weeks' intensive further training, I would hope to earn my commission. So, however stupid I thought various rules and orders might be, I tried hard to keep my thoughts to myself and toe the line with everyone else. My fellow potential officers felt the same way and we were probably far more law-abiding than the average rookie.

At the first adjutant's weekly parade, Captain Darwall found fault with the blancoing of my equipment and the fact that I had not blacked and then polished the insteps of my boots. He discovered a single loose hair on the back of my battledress collar. I knew my rifle barrel was dazzlingly clean because our squad corporal had commented favourably on it when he did his own inspection prior to the adjutant's parade. All the same, Captain Darwall said there was dirt on the lands. He told the RSM to see that I was confined to barracks for the next week and be given three nights of extra sentry duty.

I was angry, both with the punishments and the unfairness of it all. When you have been cooped up for weeks on end in squalid huts or tents with a lot of other men, your only break a visit to the NAAFI where the wet rings of beer-glasses were soaking up the cigarette butts from the overflowing ashtrays and some would-be Jelly Roll Morton thumped away at the tinny piano, a visit to the outside world was bliss. Just to walk, not march, down the steep hill past the cathedral, to look at the shops in the town, to see men and women not in uniform strolling along, perhaps to drop into the Saracen's Head, the haunt of RAF officers, and to enjoy a pint in the public bar, was a reminder that private soldiers were still part of the human race. To be denied that chance to relax, and to be denied it unjustly, rankled.

Worse were the extra sentry duties. As a punishment, they meant being given the 'dead hours' of two in the morning till four, when will power and energy are at their lowest ebb. Winter was beginning to draw in and the depot is at a height above the city. A straight road runs north and south alongside one wall of the depot and the north wind comes off the sea and the stagnant fens to rip down the road. There was one sentry post outside the wall and that was the punishment area. Night after night, I stood there, bayonet fixed, rifle in the at ease position, stiff with the cold, aching for a cigarette, bored mindless and fighting to stay awake. The last late reveller had gone to bed, the street was deserted, the wind blew. There was always a risk that the sergeant of the guard or even the adjutant himself might sneak up in the hope of finding the sentry asleep at his post. Had Captain Darwall put in an appearance, I would happily have plunged my bayonet into his guts, I hated him so much.

But at last the course broke up a few days before Christmas. In spite of the adjutant's venom, I managed to pass, as did all of our potential officer intake. Thrown together from so many walks of life, we had become good friends and it was a wrench to say goodbye to so many in the squad. It did not take us long to learn that war is a matter of continual goodbyes. By chance, I was to be posted to 163 (Artists' Rifles) OCTU at an unpronounceable small seaside town, Pwllheli, in the north of Wales.

A book could be written about the problems and trials of wartime travel. The private soldier, being the lowest form of military life, was at the mercy of ticket clerks, wielding their little brief authority, station masters, military transport police and individual transport officers who went by the book, if they could only find an up to date edition. You were issued with a travel warrant on leaving the Lincolnshire Regimental Depot and the document stated that the transport authorities were to deliver you as soon as possible at your destination. Thus, loaded with a bulging kitbag. a full large pack on your back and a small pack, attached to the webbing belt and bumping off your buttocks, you marched to the railway station in Lincoln and produced the warrant. Then you waited – and waited. After an hour or two, or more, you were told to board the train that had just arrived at platform 2: destination London. You might be lucky first time or there might be a Luftwaffe bombing raid in progress on the City of London. So then you either went into a siding and waited a few more hours until the raid was over and the damage hastily repaired or you set off on a cross-country rail trek to stations that went back to Puffing Billy days. Luckily, there were usually splendid women doing their bit for the war effort at most of the stations. They would rustle up a hot mug of tea or a home-made Spam roll for the troops on board the creaking trains. Lincoln is about 150 miles from Pwllheli as the crow flies. It took me about a day and a half to reach my billet in a one-time boarding house on the rain-dripping front.

We were graded into squads alphabetically. I shared a dingy room with Robert Graves's son, a tall, glowing young man who was killed later in the Italian campaign. Also in the squad were Andrew Cruikshank, the actor who became synonymous with 'Doctor Finlay', and Jack Hawkins, star of many a British film. They were in the Royal Welch Fusiliers and wore the special bunch of black ribbons attached to the backs of their battledress jackets, the insignia of the Regiment. Being actors, they were able to throw themselves into the part more effectively than the rest of us. Jack Hawkins, with his eagle's beak of a nose and his broad black moustache, looked far more like a senior officer slumming it in a private's uniform than what he was, a mere squaddie.

We had scarcely sorted ourselves out and received an address of welcome from the commandant than we were granted a week's belated Christmas holiday. The news was far more welcome than the rest of his brief speech. The Artists' Rifles were, still are, the Territorial regiment associated with the City of London. The commandant, now a lieutenant-colonel, had been a major when he was wounded at Dunkirk. He had an unconscious habit, we noticed, of rubbing the outside of his damaged thigh when he sat down. What he said to the intake of potential officers was short and sharp. It went like this.

'Those of you who pass this course successfully – oh yes, there will be some who fail – will end up as infantry officers. I want each of you to look carefully at the comrades to his right and left. Memorise their features. For, by the time this war is ended, one in every three of you, two in every three perhaps, will be dead. Now go off and enjoy your Christmas leave. We have much work to do on your return.'

This time we did not have to lug all our kit and equipment with us on the home journey, only a pack, but there were thoughtful faces as the trucks ran us to the railway station. Damon Runyan had said that life was a case of six to four against and he did not even have a war to contend with.

The branch line ran along the north coast of Wales and linked up with the main line at Liverpool. The Luftwaffe decided to join in the festivities by launching their most ferocious bombing raids yet at the Liverpool Docks. My Christmas eve and the early hours of Christmas morning were spent in a twelve-hour wait in a siding outside Chester; the celebration consisted of a mug of over-sweet tea and a bun provided by the indomitable ladies of the Women's Volunteer Service.

Many hours later, we crept into London after further halts when bombing was in progress. Goering had switched his forces against the City and the London Docks, mingling incendiary bombs with the usual high explosive variety. I had to get to Victoria for the last leg of my journey and, as I did not then know London well and reckoned there would be no public transport, decided to strike south from Liverpool Street until I reached the Embankment and then walk westwards. Once I reached Westminster Bridge, I would know my bearings.

It was like a scene out of Dante. Over twelve hours after the raid, a blanket of thick black smoke lay across the Thames, so that you could not see the south side from the Embankment. There was more smoke billowing up from the East End. As I tramped along the north side, I was crunching broken glass under my ammunition boots. Looking round, I saw that the shards were the remnants of windows blown out by the blast from the Savoy Hotel and Shell Mex House. But these big buildings were set back perhaps fifty yards from the river. The fragments of window glass must have been whipped out with such force that God help any casual passer-by hit by one of those whirling missiles.

Two or three days of relaxation at home, listening to the local gossip and being overfed by my zealous mother, who was thrift itself in the way she stored her chickens' eggs in waterglass and bottled the plums, damsons and pears from her garden. Storing Cox's and Worcester Pearmain apples from the orchard was no problem and I had spent many an hour wrapping individual apples in paper and putting them into bushel baskets. This was long before the days of home refrigerators but at least the one-time farmhouse did have a kind of cold room for storage. Meat, bread and milk may have been strictly rationed but the Greenfield family could have survived on the fruit it grew.

And so back to Pwllheli for what with luck would be the last stage of learning to be an officer. The town then consisted of a promenade with small boarding houses, mainly requisitioned to house us, and a shopping centre where, we soon learned, even standard items like packets of razor blades or toothpaste tubes had three prices – the lowest for local purchasers, the mid price for Welsh people from other towns and the highest for the English 'invader'. We were looked on as brutal and licentious soldiery, who were liable to ravish the local maidens and to bring our foreign habits to pervert the traditions of the God-fearing locals. The Welsh had suffered more than most communities during the Depression and many of the more imaginative potential officers sympathised with them. But they were, we felt, a secretive, closed-in people, with the sea in front of them, the mountains behind and the rain clouds rolling in from the tip of the peninsula.

The OCTU's unofficial motto – a good one – was that a young officer should be better than his men at drill, marksmanship and endurance. My squad was to be rudely shaken when it came to drill. One of the men had been a regular sergeant-major in the Grenadier Guards and before that in peacetime a drill sergeant at Caterham Barracks, the Guards' centre for recruits. (All non-commissioned ranks had been dropped on joining the OCTU and those who had worn the insignia with pride now had bare sleeves on their battle dress.) I happened to be next to the ex-sergeant-major when we fell in for our first drill parade. I heard him mutter, 'Oh, Christ!' as the drill sergeant, a thin, scarlet-faced Coldstreamer stepped briskly up, swinging his pace stick in a practised hand.

We stood firmly to attention, eyes directly to the front, as this monster bore down on us. He was well over six feet and his custom was to draw himself up to his full height, glaring down from under his Guards peaked cap which came almost straight down over the nose. Then he would swoop and thrust his face within an inch or two of the squaddie's. You could smell the reek of tobacco fumes on his breath. He would scream, 'Stand still, you 'orrible little man! All of a tremble, are you? Been tossing off too much? You tremble now, I'll 'ave you weepin' and moanin' before you're finished. Don't try to look tough wi' me, laddie. I've eaten better men than you for breakfast.'

And so on. Then he came to the man on my left. Out of the corner of my eye, I have never seen a more malicious grin spread over a human face. He said softly, 'We've met before?'

'Yes.'

Scream: 'Yes-what?'

'Yes, sar'nt.'

'That's better. I'll make a soldier of you yet. You know where we met?'

'Yes, sarn't.'

'At Caterham parade ground, that's where. 1934. I was a rookie and you were the big, bad drill sergeant. Remember it? You marched me till I was fit to drop, you gave me sheer bloody hell. And now it's my turn.' He called out to the rest of the squad, 'Lads, you've got three months of hell ahead. I'm gonna march you and march you, up and down, down and up, with rifles at the slope the whole time until you either keel over or qualify for the Sovereign's Parade. And when you get back to your billets, take off your boots and pour the blood out, don't thank me. Thank your friend here. He's the one who taught me all the fiendish tricks – hah!'

He was as good, or as bad, as his word. The hours spent on the parade ground were indeed hell, marching and counter-marching, about turn, wheeling in columns, changing arms on the march. But at the end of it all, I could have drilled any infantry company anywhere. Even today, if watching the Queen's Birthday Parade at the Horseguards on television, I can spot a guardsman's rifle an inch out of line.

The course was not all foot drill. There were night exercises on the slopes of the Welsh mountains, survival tests, TEWTs (tactical exercises without troops), usually taking place in what had been the village hall, and driving instruction. There were no automatic gears or even synchromesh on the fifteen-hundredweight trucks, 1940 vintage. You had to double-declutch, either changing up or changing down. To double-declutch from top gear to middle gear meant pressing the heavy clutch in with your left foot, banging the gear lever up into neutral, giving the accelerator a flip with your right foot and when the revs sounded high enough, push the clutch in again and shove the gear lever home. If the revs were too low, there would be a scream of protest from the gearbox and the lever would not slip into its slot. At which point the corporal instructor would add his screams and yells of protest to the general cacophony. Having to do all this *and* steer the heavy truck round the winding Welsh country lanes made one feel like that well known one-armed paperhanger with the itch.

Worst of all was the crash course – the word has two meanings here – in riding a motor-bike. In twos and threes, we were shown how to kick-start the machine, which handlebar held the clutch and which the hand-brake, and how to change gear with the tip of the boot. Then a gentle ride up and down the promenade a few times, to show how easy it was to become an accomplished rider. Then, all in the same afternoon, a cross-country solo ride. It meant riding up a greasy slope, zigzagging down through pine trees and crossing a winding stream twice. I stalled the engine in the middle of the six-inch deep stream. Vainly, I tried to kick-start it back to life, while the chuckling stream lapped the exhaust pipe. My feet were getting wet and the damned machine refused to thrum again; but wetter still with streams of sweat were my forehead under the weight of a steel helmet and rivulets running down between my shoulder blades. I gave the starter one last desperate kick, the motor-bike skidded down on to its side in the shallow stream that still went burbling on. I was dressed in full battle order, a pack on my back, ammunition pouches attached to the webbing belt and a rifle slung across the pack – a walking military christmas tree. To lift the bike that weighed a ton by its handlebars and then push it for the engine had died beyond cure by my unskilful efforts up the side of a greasy and muddy slope used all the strength and swear words I could muster. It took the best part of an hour to cover the wet woodland, more slippery hills until at last the paradise of a tarmac lane, a journey which, if the engine had kept running, would have taken less than ten minutes.

The rest of the squad had dispersed and only the disgruntled instructor remained to take back the stubborn bike. He rocked it a few feet forward and back, then kicked the starter contemptuously. The engine coughed twice and throbbed into life. He gave me a sneering look as I stammered my excuses and he roared away. I made a secret but firm resolve never to ride a motor-bike again in my life, a resolve I have managed to maintain to this day.

Spring was slowly arriving, a watery sun shone now and then and even the scudding rain clouds lifted as they rolled in from the sea. The OCTU course was in its last few weeks and most of us were reasonably confident of getting a temporary commission. At last, we were ordered to put down the names of three different infantry regiments in descending order of preference. My three were the Buffs, the Black Watch and the Lincolnshire Regiment. In nominating the Black Watch, I had no Scottish blood in my veins but just liked the romantic-sounding name. As for the Lincolnshire Regiment, it was a case of the devil you know. But my main choice for many reasons and the one I was luckily granted was the Buffs.

The River Medway divides the county of Kent into two halves. East of the Medway live 'the men of Kent'; on the west bank and beyond live 'the Kentish men'. And if you ask me which is better, a man of Kent or a Kentish man, my answer will be the traditional one. 'Which do you prefer – a bottle of whisky or a whisky bottle?' My family home in Loose was a few miles east of the Medway. The Buffs had their regimental depot at the Cavalry Barracks on the outskirts of Canterbury. They were therefore in effect my local regiment. The fact that the Royal West Kent Regiment had its main barracks in Maidstone, two or three miles from my home *and*, oddly enough, also on the east bank of the Medway did not somehow enter my calculations.

The Buffs' cap badge is the Tudor dragon, a symbol of the regiment's descent from the trained bands of Elizabethan days. Indeed, the Buffs were one of only a very few regiments entitled to march through the City of London with bayonets fixed and drums beating. The name derived from the eighteenth century when two different colonels named Howard commanded infantry regiments. They were separated through the colour of the facings on their uniform. Those with green facings became and have remained the Green Howards. Those with buff facings became the Buff Howards. The second name was dropped during the Spanish battles under Wellington and for another 150 years they were known just as the Buffs. All infantry units had a number to denote precedence, usually based on the date of their formation. For example, the Lincolnshire Regiment was the 10th Foot. The Buffs, with battle honours going back to Marlborough a hundred years before Wellington, were the 3rd Foot, coming after the Royal Scots ('Pontius Pilate's Bodyguard') and the Queens'.

What finally turned the trick in my order of choice was that the colonel of the regiment was General Sir Bindon Blood. My father, who knew the old man slightly, had taken me to meet him at his home near Tunbridge Wells after war had broken out and I was still a civilian. The general, hunched up and arthritic, had an augur-like eye. He looked at me for a while without saying anything, then nodded and said in a low, husky voice that if I joined up and was offered a commission, he hoped I would settle on his old regiment.

For the last few days of the course, we all walked about as if on eggshells. There was that notorious story of the cadet who had fallen out with the RSM during the course. Once his commission came through, he confronted the RSM, told him to stand to attention and salute when he spoke to an officer and proceeded to tear the proverbial strip off him. The senior NCO took it all with a straight face but then reported the confrontation in detail to the course adjutant. Result: the new officer had his commission withdrawn, was reverted to the ranks and RTU-d (returned to unit) as a private soldier. All of us wanted to give the drill sergeant a taste of his own medicine but discretion took over in good time.

There was an end of term concert with the usual cross-dressing and bumping about, the local girls' choir sang with that special Welsh fervour and lyricism and the two professionals, Jack Hawkins and Andrew Cruikshank, gave a polished version of Leslie Henson's then famous spoof of 'On the road to Mandalay.' Next day, the commandant gave us a repeat of his welcoming speech with a morbid assessment of our chances of living to a ripe old age. It was over. I was now a temporary officer and gentleman, 176795 Second-Lieutenant Greenfield of the Buffs. I had two weeks' leave ahead; time enough to break my journey in London and get measured at Hawkes in Savile Row, the regimental tailors, for my service dress and peaked cap. Brown boots, a Sam Browne belt and one bronze pip in each epaulette – if manners maketh the man, a uniform maketh the officer.

3

. . . and the Long-Haired Boys

I arrived at the Buffs' Depot, the Cavalry Barracks on the eastern edge of Canterbury with all my brand-new officer's gear and was assigned a room of my own. After over a year spent huddled up with other men in tents, huts and barrack-rooms, at once I became a fervent disciple of Virginia Woolf.

Reality closed in at breakfast the next morning. When I found the mess and entered the dining room, there were two elderly (to my twenty-four-year-old gaze) majors sitting like two upright sea-lions at one end of the long table. Each had a luxuriant moustache, like a springtime hedge. I said good morning and took my place some seats away.

One put down his paper and snorted loudly to his companion sitting opposite, 'Subalterns only speak when they are spoken to, what?'

'Yes,' said the other, equally loudly. 'Must be a new boy, what?'

I thought, oh shit, what have I dropped into? 'The scarlet majors at the base' should have gone out with Sassoon's *Memoirs of an Infantry Officer*.

Fortunately, my stay at the Depot was only for a few days, when I was posted to the 70th (Young Soldiers) Battalion stationed at Hothfield, a village near Ashford. Indeed, we occupied Hothfield House, a splendid Georgian mansion with ornate gardens and acres of parkland. It seems that around 1850 the then Earl of Thanet died, leaving a bastard son but no legitimate issue. It was an ancient and influential line and, rather than see it disappear, Queen Victoria was persuaded to ennoble the illegitimate son by making him the first Baron Hothfield. He and his subsequent family occupied Hothfield House. By the time war broke out, it had been leased to a Mrs Mappin, a wealthy woman through the Mappin & Webb connection. When the Luftwaffe began to bomb London in the autumn of 1940, Ashford being roughly in direct line of the Dorniers' and Heinkels' flight path, Mrs Mappin and her husband departed in a hurry, leaving all the silver, the expensive crockery, vases and what-have-you in the house. There was a Vandyck on the main staircase and on the wall of the bedroom I occupied an exquisite Lely portrait. The Army requisitioned the house and the soldiery moved in.

It was desecration of a low order. The hobnailed boots scored the mahogany floors. Rifle oil was spilled on priceless Persian carpets. Worse still, the light-fingered troops – and by the law of averages there are always one or two thieves in every unit – slipped the odd silver spoon or fork into their knapsacks, reckoning quite rightly that they would not be missed when the somewhat casual handovers and takeovers took place between an outgoing and an incoming unit.

Mrs Mappin and her family fared none too well. They had apparently decamped to a small village in the wilds not far from Chester, the width of England away from the aerial blitz on London. They had not realised that the next most important strategic target would be the Liverpool Docks. Now, they were much closer to the bombing and more likely to be in the way of overshoots. After some months, long after I had left Hothfield, they decided to return and reclaim the property. They found a shell. Every moveable item apart from the large paintings had disappeared. Tens of thousands, if not hundreds of thousands, of pounds' worth of valuables had been stolen and the inside of the building would need redecorating from floor to ceiling. Naturally, they complained to the military authorities, who set up a court of enquiry. It ran for months, even years, I was told, the longest court of enquiry ever held by the War Office. Units had come and gone in short order, handovers had been cursory, key witnesses had dispersed into different theatres of war, some indeed had been killed in action. I never knew the outcome but the Mappin motto should have been, 'If you're a snail, take your house with you – don't emulate the slug.'

The 70th Battalion was a very mixed bunch, consisting of a sprinkling of public school youths, a large dash of Cockneys and a few hard boys. Borstals had been thrown open with the coming of war and the inmates were offered the option of enlisting in one of the services or remaining to serve out their time under strict supervision. Most of them opted for the Army. King's Regulations then permitted young men to enlist at the age of eighteen but they would not be eligible for posting over seas until they reached twenty. Thus, the young soldiers' battalions came into being as a two-year kind of military prep school.

I learned far more from my Cockney hard boys than they ever did from me. One thing was the real Cockney slang, not the genteelised rhyming version. Although, there again, not everyone realises that the term of abuse 'berk' derives from 'the Berkely (pronounced 'Birkley') 'Unt' I do not need to spell out the only swearword that rhymes with 'Hunt'. But phrases like 'a shiv on the mooey', meaning a knife slash or scar on the cheek must come from a mingling of gypsy words with French. It is perhaps too late for a dialectician to research the origins of London language, derived from centuries of foreign arrivals.

Within two or three days of my arrival, before I had really begun to get to know the platoon under my command, the sergeant said one morning, 'Private Brabourne wishes to speak to you, sir.'

'Any time,' I said.

'No, this is a formal request.'

'Well, we've got about quarter of an hour before rifle inspection. Round him up and march him in, will you, Sergeant?'

My platoon had a large outhouse near the stables as its quarters. A small space at one end, just big enough to accommodate a trestle table and a wooden chair, had been partitioned off as my little HQ. I sat down in the chair and wondered what all this was about. Someone had told me that Private Brabourne had recently left Eton. He must have been around nineteen, a slim young fellow with clear-cut features. The sergeant marched him in, barked 'Halt!' and then 'Officer salute – salute!'

'All right, Brabourne,' I said. 'At ease. Now what's this in aid of?'

'Sir, I wish to see the commanding officer.'

'What about?'

'I'm sorry, sir. It's a personal matter.'

'Look, that's all very well but we can't have every private soldier rushing off to see the colonel over something quite silly. I can't recommend your request unless I know what it's about.'

'I assure you, sir, it's not in any way a complaint about you.' He smiled.

That was something of a relief. Starting on the wrong foot in a new unit is no recipe for success. I questioned him further but could get nothing out of him, apart from the fact that he had no wish to make a formal complaint about his treatment by the officers, the NCOs or his comrades in the ranks. We left it that I would consult the adjutant and recommend Brabourne appeared on CO's parade next morning.

Lieutenant-Colonel 'Tug' Wilson commanded the 70th Battalion. A burly man with the build of a second row forward, he had lost an arm in the Great War and had gone on the Reserves until called into service for World War Two. He had the scaring habit of summoning young officers who had fallen short of his high standards to a pre-breakfast ticking off in his room. When his right arm had been amputated, the surgeon had left a few inches of bone and muscle, covered by a flap of skin. Stripped to the waist while he was washing or shaving from a bowl of hot water on the marble washstand in his bedroom, he would waggle his stump at the offender as he excoriated the recent past, the present and the limited future of the man. The performance, as I knew to my cost, had a devastating effect on an empty stomach.

Colonel Wilson was, in fact, eminently fair and an inspiring commander. He had largely overcome his handicap through ingenuity. His staff car had a kind of peg attached to the top of the steering wheel so that he could spin it with his one good hand. He changed gear, as usual, with his left hand but jammed his stump against the steering wheel to keep the car on course. He was a keen shot; his shotguns had been adapted for firing one-handed.

That evening, as I was drinking a pre-dinner beer in the mess, the adjutant, another Great War veteran, sat down and told me what had happened at CO's parade. Private Brabourne, it turned out, was indeed Lord Brabourne. He had inherited a large estate between Ashford and Folkestone, which before the war had been noted for its pheasant shoots. His tenants were happy to act as beaters and the pheasants really did need thinning out. Would the CO please do him the honour of coming as his guest on Saturday and Sunday for a spot of shooting?

It says much, I think, for Colonel Wilson that he accepted at once. The shooting party was a great success and we dined on game birds most nights for the next week or so, until we got bored with the delicacy. But afterwards, had Private Brabourne come up before the CO on a provable charge, there would have been no favouritism and he would be meted out the same punishment as any other offender. And he, I am sure, would have accepted his punishment without demur.

The story has a sad corollary. Not long afterwards, Brabourne was posted to an OCTU and was eventually commissioned into the Grenadier Guards. He served well in the Italian campaign but was taken prisoner when German forces overran his position. He escaped from the POW train, was recaptured and shot by his guards in September 1943. He was twenty-one years old. His younger brother inherited the title and, after the war, made a distinctive mark in film and royal circles, marrying into the Mountbatten family.

One of the tasks at Hothfield was to help train the Ashford Home Guard. Although Operation Sealion, Hitler's planned invasion had not taken place the previous September, there were German forces massed only twenty miles from Dover across the English Channel, and Ashford was a further twenty miles inland, on a direct route to London. The whole rough triangle of land east of the town was then a closed area; only residents, the services and people with a good reason to enter were allowed in. Eighteen months after the start of the war, there were still too few trained soldiers to stop the enemy in his tracks and so all reinforcements were welcome. Television-viewers may laugh now at the stupidities of *Dad's Army* but the Home Guard overall performed splendidly and relieved the troops of many duties.

It was sobering for a brand-new second-lieutenant with an empty space above his left breast pocket, who had not yet heard a shot fired in anger, to drill and train much older men with two or three rows of medal ribbons on their tunics, a few indeed sporting a DSO, a DCM or an MC. Things had changed, but not all that much since their day. The Lee Enfield .303 was still the standard issue rifle, although none of them had ever seen or fired a Bren gun or a Thompson sub-machine gun in their time. They might have lost some physical strength and vigour through age, although several were only about fifty and a few even younger, but they made up for it by their enthusiasm and, to use an old-fashioned word, patriotism.

One big problem emerged when it came to the practical side of teaching them to throw a Mills grenade, which is a very nasty contraption. Pineapple-shaped, the metal body has serrations to help the thrower's grasp. A lever, secured by a split steel pin, is shaped to lie along one side of the grenade. When the pin is pulled out, the weapon can still be secured by gripping the lever tightly in place but once the lever is released it springs up. Five seconds later, the grenade explodes. The interval is deliberately kept short so that an enemy cannot catch the grenade and toss it back. The Army training then was – presumably, still is – that, on the command to throw the Mills bomb, you pull out the pin with your left forefinger, swing your right arm back and bowl the missile in an overarm action, the safest and most effective way to despatch it. Deep slit trenches had been dug so that the thrower would be well under cover when there was a loud bang and shrapnel whizzed around. In addition, the troops had dug a pit, covered in soft sand, in the landing area, to minimise the spread of shrapnel.

The instructors, of whom I was one, had to accompany each thrower into the trench and help him with a last-minute run through of the drill and in a few cases to calm his nerves. A highly lethal lump of metal, packed with explosive, can easily cause a slight shake in a hand unused to gripping it. All went well on the first hour of training. The Home Guard members came into the deep trench one by one, took up their positions and on the command 'Grenade – throw!' plucked out the pin, released the lever, swung their arms back and bowled the bomb overarm into the pit beyond and above their line of sight. And then it happened.

A much older and much bemedalled veteran entered the trench. He had been a lieutenant-colonel in the Great War and had been wounded more than once. Apparently, although I did not then know it, a German bullet had damaged the main muscle in his right arm between elbow and wrist. Over the years since, he had undertaken special exercises to strengthen the arm, which never recaptured its full vigour. He nodded calmly as I ran through the simple drill, grasped the grenade and on the command, neatly pulled out the pin in one motion. Balancing the grenade in his clenched fist, he took a pace to the rear and swung his arm. The back of his hand struck the earthen wall of the trench behind him; the force jolted the grenade out of his hand. It rolled on the floor of the trench, lever out.

Five-four-three-two-one seconds to eternity. He started stooping painfully slowly to pick it up. I shoved him aside – he went sprawling on the ground – grabbed the grenade and flung it over the top. A couple of seconds later came the *crump* of the explosion and a cloud of sand drifted upwards. The old man, flat on the floor of the trench, gave a low whistle and then grinned. I made a gesture of apology for my rough handling but he shook his head as he scrambled to his feet.

My tyrannical mother in my Cambridge days had berated me for the hours I spent on the squash court when I could have been studying.

But those hours might well have sharpened my reflexes and helped to save a couple of lives when the grenade dropped.

Around this time, Lieutenant-General (as he then was) Montgomery began his impact on our lives. He was the corps commander responsible for throwing back the enemy, should they have the impudence to invade Kent and East Sussex while he was in command. Later, he was to be promoted to Army commander for the South-East area. Our poor little battalion were the only infantry who came directly under his command. The buffers of Division and Brigade were removed. The small man with the grating metallic voice could pick up a telephone and give Colonel Wilson his orders.

Monty – the vainest man I ever met, and in a long, chequered career I met many ardent self-lovers – was good at inventing slogans that might well attract publicity. One was 'Fighting fit and fit to fight.' It doesn't really mean anything if you analyse it but it sounds effective – and that was all that mattered to him. He decided to see just how fit his 70th Battalion was, starting with the CO. Apparently, one of his staff officers pointed out that Wilson was in his late forties with one arm and something of a belly. Monty decided to test him by walking him all round the Ashford defence perimeter, much of which our CO had himself planned. What the staff officer in his briefing had failed to point out was that when Wilson sunk his teeth into a project, he was indomitable. It was raining hard, the meadows were slippery and the ploughed fields a quagmire of mud. Every hundred yards or so, the pair came to a gate or a stile which the CO impatiently vaulted over. Monty, the little man, kept up with the other's long-ranging strides for the first mile or two. Halfway round the perimeter, he was trailing by fifty yards or more and, when they had to cross a convenient tarmac road decided to call it a day, much to the silent amusement of the junior officers who had traipsed along in the great man's footsteps.

To be fair to him, he decreed that our CO was more than fit to fight. But then he turned a beady eye on to the supporting officers. Many of them in their late thirties and forties, patriots to a man, had volunteered when war broke out, some had found the going with an adult battalion too much and all had ended up with the 70th. The most obvious square peg in the round hole was a forty-year-old who had lived in Paris for over five years as an engineer with a French car manufacturer. When war was declared, he gave up his well-paid job, returned to England and volunteered. He not only spoke French with complete fluency but was well versed in all the technical terms. Not many scholars, for example, know the French for 'carburettor' or 'reciprocating valve'. He should have been given an immediate commission and then attached to a French armoured division as a British liaison officer. After Dunkirk, he could have carried out the same duties with the Free French forces back in Britain. As it was, the Army had squandered his special skills and had posted him to the least suitable of military tasks.

In his clipped tones, Monty said to Colonel Wilson, 'Yours is a bad battalion. There are no bad soldiers, only bad officers. We must get rid of them. You will select twelve names. I shall be here next Saturday between eleven a.m. and twelve noon. I will see each man in turn. He will have five minutes, no more, no less, to state his case. I will then adjudicate. That is all. Any questions?'

It was hard on Colonel Wilson, who had come to know his officers and the sacrifices, financial and domestic, some of them had made for their country. It was harder still on the ten, as I recall, who got the ignominious chop; they had done their best. Their places were taken by recently commissioned officers in my own age group but whether the battalion became a better unit would be hard to evaluate. Shortly after this, the four companies split up. Mine, under a new company commander, a regular officer, was sent to carry out airfield defence at Manston in the tip of North Foreland.

But first there was to be one last strange interlude.

During the Mappins' absence, the Honourable Peter Tufton, the younger son of Lord Hothfield, had occupied a small suite of rooms in the mansion. A Rifle Brigade officer, he had been badly wounded in the retreat to Dunkirk and had been invalided out of the Army. I had met him a few times, strolling round the ornate garden and we enjoyed our chats.

He asked me once, 'You interested in books?'

'I'll say.'

'Good. You ought to look at the library. Rather special, I hear. I'm not a great reader meself. But if you'd like the keys, say the word.'

I did and he walked away, coming back with a bunch of keys which he pressed on me. I had at least an hour to spare before dinner in the mess and decided to inspect the library right away. There was an airless, musty smell as I unlocked the main door but as I approached the bookcases there arose that booky odour bibliophiles know so well. Apart from one wing of modern, fairly popular titles and reference books, the other two walls contained leatherbound, ancient copies. It was difficult to pick them out as they were behind strong metal grilles, each with its own lock. Hunting through the bunch of keys, I finally selected the right one and swung back a grille. I picked out a book at random. It was a mid-nineteenth century edition of Byron's secret erotic poems. 'Right through the centre of the rose' – my glance fell on one line. Alongside was an unexpurgated edition of *The Satyricon* and a copy of *Daphnis and Chlöe* with enchanting obscene drawings. These had been printed and bound in full calf in the eighteenth century. There were obscene Victorian works and even a paperback unexpurgated edition of D. H. Lawrence's *Lady Chatterley's Lover*, printed, as I remember, in Amsterdam.

One of the Hothfields had obviously been an ardent collector of what the book trade defines as 'curiosa'. No wonder the collection had been kept so rigorously under lock and key. I was looking forward to what Daniel George entitled in his anthology *Solitary Pleasures* when the order came through for our move to Manston. Sadly, I handed the keys back to Peter Tufton.

The RAF airfield at Manston was little more than twenty miles across the English Channel from the enemy, the nearest fighter base to Occupied France. The fact that a squadron of ME 109s could take off from the Pas de Calais and be buzzing like hornets over us in six minutes or so helped to concentrate the mind. For the first time, I began to get the feeling of being on active service, even though the infantry's role was ground defence only. Operation Sealion, Hitler's proposed invasion of Britain, had not in fact taken place the previous autumn but there was always the risk of hit-and-run raids, ground attacks to smash the effectiveness of the Manston defensive shield.

The main runway ran roughly east and west, the direction of the prevailing wind, and the airfield itself was largely grass. There was nothing more stirring than to watch a squadron of Spitfires scrambling. Drawn up in a V spread across the width of the field, with the leader at the apex, each aircraft kept formation as it first taxied across the grass, then accelerated and finally took off, to soar over our craned necks and regroup into battle formation. On the north side of the airfield lay the officers' mess, a brick building, and alongside it huts for the pilots' sleeping quarters. The watchtower and outbuildings for stores and aircraft repairs were on the eastern end. We infantry – the 'brown jobs' or 'coolies', as the RAF called us – occupied tents and a wooden hut in the gap between the two. I was lucky enough to have a small wooden hut on my own, just outside the perimeter fence, which consisted of rolls of double dannert barbed wire.

When we inspected the trenches that had been dug on the outside of the airfield as a line of defence, it was clear that the officer who had sited them was no countryman. He had done so in winter when the fields were bare; he had forgotten or had not been told that Thanet was known as the granary of England. Already in early spring, the green shoots of wheat were a foot high. The line of fire from the trenches was about five yards; when the wheat was a little higher, a persistent foe could wriggle on his belly undetected to within grenade-throwing distance. The whole trench system had to be filled in – by us – and resited to greater effect.

We had hardly settled in when there was an urgent alarm. The night before, there had been suspicious movements in the channel, a few miles off North Foreland, and a hit-and-run raid on Margate was considered likely. It was my platoon's job to hold the Margate beaches almost as far as Birchington. It was a 'last man, last round' situation, I was told by a grave company commander. The odds were that the last round would be reached well before the last man, for we were short of ammunition – short, indeed, of almost everything required for a stout defence. I had a Great War Webley pistol with five rounds. All of my men had rifles and bayonets with about ten rounds apiece. We also had three or four hand grenades. One scenario was that when the Panzer tanks came rolling off their landing craft to hit the beach, they would be held at bay by a flourish of the bayonets while one brave soldier stepped up and dropped a primed grenade down the barrels of their 88mm guns. Fortunately, it turned out to be a false alarm but we earned the gratitude of the local shopkeepers for our devotion to duty. That gratitude swiftly turned first to suspicion and then strong dislike when the Borstal boys in my platoon swarmed into Margate on their off-duty hours. Metal ashtrays in pubs and cafes had to be nailed down to stop my lads from pinching them. The slot machines that used to stand outside tobacconists' shops when the latter were closed had to be chained to a solid support after one nicotine addict removed the machine and pushed it the two or three miles back to camp. Even with the chains on there were still problems. One of my fellows, Private Bedworth, stole some bolt-cutters from the RAF stores and was apprehended by the Military Police, about to attack the chain holding a cigarette slot machine in place. The OC company gave him seven days' CB and, having seen him for the first time at close quarters with his cap off, ordered him first to get a hair cut.

I had had lunch at the RAF mess and was on my way back to our lines when a corporal came rushing over, panting that there was trouble in the barber's tent. Would I come at once and sort it out? The scene that hit me was not catered for in King's Regulations. Bedworth, I learned later, always carried a cut-throat razor in his hip pocket. The left half of his head was as bald as a baby's bottom; the right half still carried his thick and greasy locks. The barber, a Jew from east of the Aldgate Pump, was an old enemy and had grasped the opportunity to give him the ultimate short back and sides. Bedworth was crouched low with the back of the blade up against his knuckles. He was making little sparring movements with both hands, like a boxer warming up. The barber, too, had opened his razor back across his knuckles. I was told afterwards by one of the cockneys that the technique allowed for fairly shallow slashes to face or hands but no deep, penetrating wounds that might even be fatal. They were swearing at each other; you could almost smell the rising anger in the confines of the barber's tent.

I had to do something fast. Remembering the old story of the man trying to separate two dogs from fighting over a bone, I was certainly not going to step between them. Being blessed – or cursed – with a very loud voice, I bellowed 'Stop' with the full force of my lungs. It worked. They pulled up and looked at me.

'Bedworth,' I shouted, 'put that razor down! You're in enough trouble already.'

'Look what that bleeder done to me,' he said.

'I know.' I turned to the barber. 'I'm going to count to three. If you haven't put that razor down by three, I'll have you before the company commander for attempted grievous bodily harm! You hear me?'

On hearing a loud 'One', he dropped the razor on to his instruments table. I said, 'Now you'll give Bedworth a proper haircut with the rest of his hair. Corporal, I want you to watch, and put that man on a charge if he as much as cuts one hair wrong. Bedworth, you have permission to wear a cap the whole time until the hair grows out. From now on, both of you, act like men, not babies.'

When I was fifty yards from the tent, I stopped and let out a rush of breath. It was not a particularly hot day but the sweat was running down the back of my ears and from my shoulder blades to the small of my back. It could have been very nasty.

But we, the infantry, were really spectators at the match. 601 (City of London) Squadron was the resident fighting unit at Manston. They were mainly young men in their early twenties. They wore their hair long in revolt against standing orders and the top button of their uniforms undone, to show they were fighter pilots. Many of them had the purple and white diagonal stripes of the Distinguished Flying Cross above their breast pockets, some with a silver rosette on the ribbon to signify the Bar, a second award of the medal. When they were off duty, a group would drive up to London in a Lea Francis sports car or an MG and go dancing at the Four Hundred or the Café de Paris, where 'Snakehips' Johnson and his band played hot jazz. Later in the year, the Luftwaffe scored a direct hit on the Café de Paris in Leicester Square, killing 'Snakehips' and, it seems, half the Brigade of Guards.

They had grown up fast, risking quick death high in the skies above the English Channel in dogfights with Messerschmidts. One of them, a pink-cheeked youth who looked as though he should still be at school, was known as 'Two-score'. It was not a reference to his age, hardly more than a single score. In his very first encounter with a tight bunch of ME 109s, he had dived in, firing bursts to no real purpose until he suddenly realised he was about to smash into the opposition. At the last moment, he tilted his wings diagonally and felt a loud double bang that shook his Spitfire from propeller to tail. And then he was out and descending. His plane was now more of a boat than an aircraft because both wings had been sheared off through the impact. But he had also damaged the two close formation enemy aircraft by slicing the port wing off one and the starboard wing off the other. They were spinning down towards the Channel like sycamore seeds, completely out of control. Our man baled out, as did the Luftwaffe pilots, and all three were picked up by the watchful AirSea Rescue unit from Broadstairs. The Germans were debriefed and sent to POW camp, and Two-score, as he became, was credited with downing two enemy aircraft.

The pilots were brave and they had style. When they listened to Churchill on the radio and heard that lisping growl say, 'Never in the field of human conflict was so much owed by so many to so few', one of them turned and said, 'He must be talking about our mess bills.' The Buffs officers who were allowed to use the RAF mess at times felt embarrassed and in a strange way envious. They were the knights of the sky, we looked after the stables.

But there was a severe penalty to be paid by many of the brave volunteers. It was brought home to me when a new squadron moved in for a short stay. I recognised the squadron leader, who had been a contemporary of mine at Cambridge and a useful squash player. Squash helped to keep people fit and sharpen their reflexes; Manston possessed a couple of courts. He and I arranged a game which both of us enjoyed. After a shower, we sat drinking beer in a quiet corner of the mess and I suggested, in view of the demand, we should book another court for early the following week. He smiled and shook his head.

'Why not?' I asked. 'Won't the squadron be here?'

'The squadron will be here all right,' he said. 'The point is – will I?'

'Oh, come on.'

'No, listen, George. Let's be serious for a minute. I learned to fly when I went up, at the Duxford airfield. When I qualified, I joined the Volunteer Reserve. So when war was declared, I was called up at once. I was then number thirteen, first reserve, in the squadron. That was – what? – eighteen months ago. We didn't see much action over Dunkirk, not really before the Battle of Britain, less than nine months back. Now I'm leading the squadron. So what happened to the twelve ahead of me? They haven't all bought it. One went on the staff and another is training pilots in Canada. And we know two others are alive in POW camps. They baled out over France. But that leaves eight out of the dozen killed in action or missing, believed killed in action. Could be my turn tomorrow or next week or the week after that.'

'Oh, balls,' I said.

'Well, it makes you think.'

A few days later, a new squadron leader arrived to command his flight. We infantry had learned that you did not go around asking what had happened to X. If a pilot was missing, believed killed, he instantly became a non-person. His belongings were packed up by his batman and sent to his next of kin. No one in the squadron ever referred to him again, at least for several months. We had thought it a terribly hard-hearted attitude but eventually realised the long-term wisdom behind it. To be continually mourning the dead in public could quickly turn into the worst kind of inquest and a sentimental splurge enough to weaken the toughest resolve. The only send-off given to a dead comrade – shades of 'Poor Butterfly' in *The Dawn Patrol* – was to put a special Cole Porter record on the mess gramophone:

I get no kick from a plane,
Flying too high
With some guy in the sky
Is my i–
dea of nothing to do,
But I get a kick out of you.

It took me, therefore, some eavesdropping on conversations at the bar and catching the odd hint to learn that my squash-playing friend had 'dreed his own weird'. He went out on a sortie, was attacked by three Messerschmidts and had been shot down in flames. How might Britain have fared if all those hundreds of courageous and positive young men had survived into the peace?

At the officers' mess there was a fairly wide porch and to one side, a lavatory. A young pilot who had taken off from Tangmere on a routine flight, run into the enemy, and fought an avoiding action, had brought his badly damaged plane into Manston as the nearest airfield. Now I watched him striding up and down in the porch with his parachute harness still on. The lavatory door was half open and he could see the hunched up back of an elderly man in a dark suit in the gap. Someone asked the pilot what was the matter. He said, 'I'm bursting for a pee but there's a bloody old civilian in the lats.'

Churchill turned and stepped out, buttoning his flies, 'It's all right, m'boy,' he said with a broad grin, 'the bloody old civilian's finished.'

Churchill, who had charged the foe at Omdurman, loved to get away from Downing Street and Whitehall to refresh his spirits in the front line. He visited Manston on several occasions.

That night, as I got ready for bed, I had the warm feeling that with a prime minister of such understanding and a strong sense of humour, we would never be defeated.

Not to be outdone by Churchill, Monty decided he would come and inspect his Buffs at Manston. The troops would be drawn up by platoons, with the platoon commander in each case standing three paces in front of his men. Monty would stop at least ten yards away, so that the reply to a question could be heard by all the men, and then ask the platoon commander in that clipped, metallic voice, 'What did you do before you joined up?' What the hell did it matter to him or to anyone else what one had done before the war? Whatever the response, he would invariably reply in his stiff way, 'Very good. Carry on,' and move along to the next victim.

On the second or third of these occasions, a friend named Arnold who commanded the next-door platoon decided enough was enough. When Monty asked the usual leading question, he answered brightly and loudly, 'Sir, my mother ran a brothel and I used to play the piano there.'

The great man's thoughts must have been far away. 'Very good. Carry on,' he said.

But his Quartermaster-General was something else again. A tall, sandy-haired man with pale eyes, Brigadier Hansen had won the Victoria Cross in the previous world war. He was the toughest inspector of troops I ever encountered in six years' service. A soldier had to lay out his bed exactly so, with each blanket folded neatly, the palliasse or bolster lined up to the same limits, the spare pair of boots, polished to a dazzle, side by side in the exact middle of the space at the foot of the bed. The huzif had to be washed clean and its contents laid out to the right formula, starting from the left: 'Knife, fork, spoon, a razor, comb and a lather brush.' Any Buff should always have got that right because as a recruit he would have learned to chant the words in tune with the opening of the regimental march. But Brigadier Hansen did not just check the layout by eye. He would pick out the folded middle blanket from a bed, hold it up and beat it vigorously with his swagger stick. Woe to the soldier if clouds of dust rose.

He once caught out our keen and efficient company commander. The whole company was drawn up on parade; Hansen asked him, 'Do all your men wear socks?'

'Of course, sir.'

'You're positive?'

'Yes, sir.'

'Right,' said the Brigadier. 'You see that shortish fellow in the middle of the rear rank?' He pointed with his swagger cane. 'Order him to fall out and remove his left boot.'

It was a case of 'Private X, three paces to the rear, march! Ground arms. Stand at ease. On the command "Remove", you will take off your left gaiter and left boot. Understood? Right, remove!'

The soldier, who was not a youngster but a man of long service, a mechanic with the battalion, bent down, unbuckled his gaiter and unlaced his boot, which he removed. He stood there with his left foot bare.

The company commander went scarlet. 'I don't know what to say,' he stuttered, 'I would have sworn . . .'

Brigadier Hansen gave a wolfish grin. 'It's all right,' he said. 'He was my batman in India pre-war. He never wore socks then.'

The Luftwaffe had the nasty little trick of sending a solitary aircraft to circle the field with its wheels down, as though it were preparing to land. Both the RAF and the infantry had become so used to aircraft landing and taking off that few bothered to look up when yet another plane was circling overhead. In any case, at a vague glance, a Messerschmidt did not look unlike a Spitfire. The enemy plane would come in low as if about to land and then either drop two or three delayed-action bombs on the runway or fire long raking bursts at anyone wandering round the perimeter immediately ahead. The bombs were the greater nuisance because they made the main runway unusable until the tractors with great loads of earth had filled the holes and a local steamroller had flattened out the surfaces.

On one occasion when the sneak-invader had only fired machine-gun bursts, a petrol bowser had been sprayed. The petrol was pouring out of four or five holes low down on one side. The RAF quarter-master on the spot telephoned the adjutant with the bad news but suggested he and his men should catch the petrol in buckets and transfer it to a sound bowser. The adjutant vetoed his idea. A new squadron that had been involved in a series of dogfights over the Channel was due to land any minute. They would need re-arming, possible engine overhauls and the patching of fabric where bullet holes had appeared. The quartermaster and his men would have all those jobs to do, so the hell with the petrol. Write it off and let it run away into the ground. Leave one man to keep cigarette-smokers well clear but, otherwise, forget it.

It seemed crazy to the quartermaster to waste good petrol like that, but that was the order he had been given. But if it was going to waste, he might as well fill one bucket and pour it into the tank of his own car. Which he did. Petrol supplied to the Forces – WD fuel, as it was known – was coloured red. It was a crime for a civilian car to have any of it in the tank. The civil and the military police had the nasty habit of stopping private cars at random and extracting with a pipette an ounce or two of petrol from the top of the filler. Woe betide anyone if the contents of the pipette looked reddish. A few nights later, the quartermaster was driving his private car to meet some mates in a pub near Broadstairs, when he was stopped at a Military Police roadblock and the fuel pipe tested. The specimen showed dark red and he was arrested. The irony was that he could have driven himself there in an RAF pick-up and claimed he was on duty. The MPs would have flung him a smart salute and waved him on his way.

He was court-martialled. It was considered an important matter of legal principle and the Judge Advocate General's department sent a barrister to assist the court in its findings. Laymen like myself would only have their view confirmed that the law was indeed an ass. The barrister claimed that when the petrol had been inside the bowser, it was WD property. Yes, we would all accept that notion. When it had left the bowser but had not yet hit the ground, it was still WD property. Only when it had reached the ground and had run into the earth could it be considered as written off. Thus the official legal opinion was that by interposing a bucket between the dropping petrol and the ground, the quartermaster was guilty of stealing WD property – to wit, a gallon or two of RAF petrol. A man of long and conscientious service, he was, I believe, stripped of his rank and cashiered in disgrace.

We had an engaging Cockney mechanic and fitter with my Buffs company known everywhere as Smithie. He had a little black Ford car, which he was always keen to lend to officers and senior NCOs. Indeed, I borrowed it twice to run home and see my family when I had a day's leave, a round journey of at least a hundred miles. When I asked him where he got the petrol coupons from, he said with an engaging grin that his uncle ran a garage 'up in the Smoke' and 'helped people out' one way or the other. They showed their gratitude by handing over spare petrol coupons. Awright, sir?

One day, Private Bedworth, who now looked on me as a pal, told me the truth. Smithie had cut away the pipe that runs from the petrol filler cap to the main tank. He had soldered in a cocoa tin, which he had filled with a pint of harmless coupon petrol. He had rejigged the opening to the tank, which was full of the red WD variety. Any MP using his pipette on the petrol filler would be fooled.

I was left with a moral dilemma. I could borrow Smithie's car at any time – it never hurts to keep in with the officer commanding you – but doing so in these conditions was not only illegal but, indeed, immoral. Merchant ships bringing the essential fuel into the country were being sunk by the ravaging U-boats and their crews stood little chance of rescue. Even the gallon or two of petrol I might use in an occasional visit to my family was petrol denied a fighting vehicle. So, once I knew the score, I refused Smithie's offers, although I did not have the heart to shop him. That ingenuity in tackling problems could, indeed should, have been put to better use.

A Polish fighter-bomber squadron flew into Manston for a temporary assignment. There was a flourish about them, even in the air encircling the field and in their close-packed landing skills. They were young men, mainly dark-haired and with a spark of devilry in their eyes. In spite of the Ribbentrop-Molotov Pact, when war broke out the Germans and the Russians had both invaded Poland. The Poles fought ferociously but, without international backing and without enough tanks, guns and shells, they were doomed from the start. When all was lost, several fighter and bomber squadrons had made a dash westwards to France and ultimately to England and Scotland. Here we were, nearly two years later. In all that time, they had heard nothing from their families, who might have been dragged into forced labour or tortured or killed or, at the best, be scraping through in penury. Beneath the jokes and the laughing in the mess, there seemed to be a deadly intent. Their object was to kill Germans and Russians, as many as possible, in whatever order they turned up.

Although 601 Squadron and the permanent RAF Manston staff had treated us Buffs with great courtesy, making us full members of their mess, the fact that we brown jobs were carrying out defence on the ground, while they were attacking in the air, made for a psychological gap. And it was the same, somehow, in their treatment of the Polish squadron. There is usually an edge between fighters and bombers; besides, these dashing young men were *foreign* and they had a great and merited reputation for wooing the girls, supposedly allocated to the equally dashing long-haired boys.

As a result, several Buffs officers, Arnold and myself much to the fore, struck up friendships with new arrivals. It was late at night, the drinks had flowed all too freely and we were receptive to any suggestion. A flight leader named Wolf had to put in some training and testing next day. Why didn't Arnold and I come and fly with him as passengers? It could be quite an experience.

Neither of us had been up in an aircraft. Tourist flying to the Costa Brava or Florida or Los Angeles is such a modern development that one forgets how undeveloped the air services were in the 1930s. We were delighted to get the chance. In a quick oral huddle, we decided that formally approaching the keen company commander for per-mission would be the wrong tactic. If we were caught, our cover story would be that, being thoroughly professional soldiers, we had grasped eagerly the one chance to study our ground defences from the air. Both of us had competent sergeants in our respective detachments and they were quite capable of looking after the troops on a set exercise during the hour we were absent.

Next morning, a pick-up truck dropped us off in the far corner of the airfield where the Polish squadron's Blenheims were drawn up. Wolf greeted us with a broad smile.

'Today,' he said, striking a theatrical pose, 'you will make history as part-time members of the squadron!'

He went on to explain that his crew had gone drinking in Broadstairs the previous evening. Two had got embroiled in a pub fight and were now untangling things with the help of the adjutant and the local police. The other had induced a girl away from her boy friend, who fortunately caught up with them before inducing flowered into seducing. The Pole ended with a broken jaw and he was now in the RAF infirmary. Apart from the pilot himself, the Blenheim required a mid-gunner and a tail-gunner. A pure formality, Wolf told us.

'All very safe,' he said. 'I go up, I make a few passes over that pretty little town down there, I check what must be checked, then we land. What you call a piece of cake, no?'

Arnold and I were thrilled. To have been given a role while airborne doubled the excitement. The specially adapted Blenheim had two plastic bubbles protruding; the one amidships so that the mid-gunner could respond to an attack from above or from either side. The tail bubble, which was my position, gave an unlimited view from behind. As Wolf helped to strap me in and showed me how to operate the twin heavy machine guns – 'emergency use, but no emergency,' he said I thought of emulating the Great Ooflum bird, that legendary creature that flew backwards because it was not interested in where it was going, it wanted to know where it had been.

The plane taxied to the edge of the runway, the engines revved and Wolf was off. We climbed in a gentle incline and it was fascinating to watch Manston retreating between my legs which were dangling in space. Still climbing, he flew in a gentle arc to 5,000 feet or more. My ears clicked to conform with the altitude. So far, so good. Flying was fun. Then . . .

Wolf started to toss the Blenheim around the sky as if it were a paper dart. He dived almost vertically down, down towards Broadstairs. My back and shoulders were thrust against the rear of the bubble and my legs were above my head. It was like whirling in space on one's own. At the last moment he levelled out and then climbed as steeply as he had dived. My guts, which had been forced almost into my throat by the downward G forces, now lurched back again, matching the plane's ascent. A wave of nausea swept over me. It would have served Wolf right if I had thrown up all over the floor of his shiny bubble but somehow, achingly, I managed to contain it for the next ten or fifteen minutes, while the Blenheim bucked and swooped and the fuselage vibrated as he 'tested' his aircraft. At last, he was finished and, gradually descending, returned to land at the base. I tottered down from the bubble and breathed a quiet sigh as I felt firm earth under both feet after being 'thrown with restless violence round about the pendent world'. Fornicate that for a bird that sings as it flies – to bowdlerise a military expression. If that was flying, they could keep it.

Arnold also looked a little green as he left the aircraft but, not having flown at the extremity of the plane, he had missed the worst up and down swings. Wolf climbed down and pulled off his flying helmet. 'Good?' he asked. 'You enjoyed?'

We managed a stiff smile each and a nod of thanks as we walked wearily towards the waiting pick-up truck. On the drive back to the mess, it slowly dawned on us that we had been had – in a big way. All that talk of his crew being caught up with the police or in hospital was merely a device to put a couple of brown jobs through their paces.

The theory was soon proved. Arnold agreed to have another go when Wolf invited him to replace the Blenheim's tail-gunner who was nursing a sprained wrist. This time Wolf decided to fly a mile or two over the Channel and try his dry-run dive bombing from the angle the Luftwaffe would take. He was about to start his run when a Messerschmidt, lurking behind a cloud, pounced on the solitary aircraft, attacking from the rear with guns blazing. As Arnold heard the rounds crashing into the fuselage alongside him, he shut his eyes, pressed the double buttons of the twin machine guns and returned the fire. When he peeped out again, there was an ME 109 spinning down towards the Channel with a column of smoke pouring out. He had shot it down.

Which put an end to the Buffs as auxiliary flyers. Our keen company commander had Arnold on parade. He was, he said, in two minds: uncertain whether to recommend him for the DFC or for court-martial. In the end, he did neither but he did extract from all of us a firm promise to keep away from the Poles and their wiles.

70th Battalion reassembled as a complete unit at the Old Deer Park Barracks in Dover for several weeks. The Germans had a long-range gun stationed on the far edge of the Channel, near Calais; its shells could just carry the twenty or so miles to land with a roar in the Old Deer Park itself. Apparently, the recoil was so great that the gun and its chassis on rails reversed many yards back into the tunnel that normally hid it By the time it had been hauled back into position, reloaded and the sights checked, many minutes had elapsed. So the methodical Wehrmacht fixed it for one round to be fired each half-hour on the half-hour. The beleaguered people of Dover and we soldiers in the Barracks went about our normal duties for twenty-five minutes, glanced at our watches, went slowly into the nearest shelter, waited for the distant crump and then went about our duties again for the next twenty-five minutes. The firing stopped punctually in mid-afternoon. If the 'service' was erratic, the psychological pressure was considerable – but most German generals, in spite of Freud, Jung and Adler, must have had little knowledge of and no interest in psychology.

I genuinely liked and admired Tug Wilson, our indomitable CO, and had been able to help him when he told me that his teenage son was having problems in securing an university entrance. I wrote at once to the languid Hubert Whalley-Tooker, my old senior tutor at Downing, who had urged me to do a nice clean job in Intelligence, and a place was found for the young man. For many years after the war, he was the influential defence correspondent at the *Observer*.

One evening before dinner, Colonel Wilson sent for me to have a drink in his room. The 2nd Battalion, he told me, was preparing to go overseas, to Egypt and then the Western Desert. There were one or two vacancies for junior officers and he wanted to recommend me for a slot. Was I interested? Knowing very well that he could just have ordered me to go, I was touched and, I suppose, flattered; I accepted at once. It would be sad to leave my platoon and I would miss him and a few other seniors, but it was more than time to see really active service. Tug warned me that Colonel Nicholson, who had left the General Staff to command the 2nd Battalion, still had the last word. I was to visit Linton Park, three miles from my home, where 2nd Buffs were stationed, to be interviewed by the CO and the redoubtable RSM Vaughan.

In imperial peacetime regular infantry regiments consisted of two battalions. One would be stationed at home for several years, the other probably in India or perhaps Egypt or Palestine. Every now and then, they swapped over. The Buffs, as one of the oldest (we claimed to be *the* oldest) regiments, from the Tudor trained band days, and somewhat fashionable, showed its snobbish differences in many small ways. For example, regular officers in hot climates did not wear khaki shirts but a mauvish smooth variety specially produced by Hawkes, the regimental tailors in Savile Row. On the drive to Linton, I wondered how much the impact of war and the shake-up of Dunkirk had fractured the mould.

Regimental-Sergeant-Major Vaughan had done a valiant job at Dunkirk, bringing back many troops unscathed. He had then been posted to assist Lord Lovat, who was forming his No. 4 Commando in the Highlands. He had seen every kind of man under the pressures of Army life and war itself and, apparently, he could spot at a glance the skiver, the bullshitter, the one who would not get going when the going got tough. He saved Lord Lovat hours of useless field exercises in spotting right off who would be the drop-outs in any selection of volunteers.

He looked at me across the desk. He was a big man, thick trunk, arms and legs beginning to run to fat, his head was poised on his shoulders, almost lacking a neck, and his pale eyes that had gazed on most things levelled on me. He exuded a male power: I was glad he was on our side.

We chatted about No. 4 Commando and I asked him how David Niven was getting on with the assault course. (Thirty years later, when David Niven was a friend and a client, I told him about this encounter and he regaled me with those polished anecdotes about Vaughan and commando training.) Private Niven was doing all right, he said with a twisted smile. After about ten minutes, in which this vastly experienced soldier called me 'Sir' with each sentence, he asked to be excused and left the room. On returning, he said, 'Colonel Nicholson will see you now.' I had, it seems, passed the first obstacle on the assault course of joining the 2nd Battalion.

The CO had an aquiline nose, a thick moustache with upturned ends and a sarcastic, grating voice. A brilliant staff officer, he needed a spell overseas in an active command to keep his career on its upward path. He talked most of the time – he was good at talking – and I nodded dutifully and respectfully. In the end, he stretched across the desk, shook hands and welcomed me to 2nd Buffs.

The battalion was about to move to Sutton, Surrey, where it would complete training and await embarkation. I had to return to Dover, get my things together, say goodbye to comrades of the past year, snatch a few days' leave at home and then join my new unit.

Uppermost in my mind were the memories of Manston, memories that are still vivid. If I close my eyes, I can visualise the aces who came and went – Whitney Straight, who before the War and late at night had driven from Marble Arch to Cambridge Market Place in under one hour in his Maserati, 'Jimbo' Gracie, 'Cocky' Dundas, the quiet Stanford Tuck, H.M. Stephen and his partner 'Mungo' Park, Max Aitken, Dennis Gillam, always known as 'Downwind' Gillam, as he had broken a flying speed record with a strong following wind, and Douglas Bader stumping and shouting around the place. Then, it was *their* war. If they had not fought off the Luftwaffe and commanded the English Channel in its narrowest stretch, at great cost in lives and machines, the ground forces four years later would never have rolled forwards across across the sea and into Occupied France.

I waved them a metaphoric goodbye, as I took my first steps towards battle.

4

✦✦✦

Dust to Dust

✦✦✦✦✦✦

At first, it was a relief to land in Egypt in the late summer of 1942 after two months of huddled life aboard ship. The liner we were on had been a North Atlantic ship with small portholes – boarded up in wartime, of course, so as not to betray the convoy to lurking U-boats – and covered passages, quite unsuitable for life when, after zigzagging southwards in mid-Atlantic, we approached warmer latitudes. With five large males and all their gear sharing what in happier times had been a cabin for a single passenger, it was pleasanter at night to take a bedroll and sleep on deck under the stars. There had been a week anchored off Freetown for re-fuelling in the humid sweating atmosphere where prickly heat rashes affected almost all on board. We sweated, fumed, swore – and scratched; no breeze stirred the blanket-like hot damp air around us.

Then a week in Cape Town, regaining our land legs in aimless marching up and down the waterfront. The typical warm and generous approach of local people to passing strangers was dimmed by the recent fall of Tobruk; several thousand South African troops, including the GOC Tobruk, had been 'put in the bag'.

Off again northwards, hugging the East African coast, as the weather grew hotter and hotter. As we entered the Red Sea, it was impossible to touch the ship's railings for more than a second or two; they were virtually red-hot with the dominating sun. Solar topees had been issued to all ranks before leaving a drizzling Liverpool two months earlier. We wore them self-consciously as we trooped down the gangplank, carrying our gear, but the hardened rank and file we encountered, most of them bare-headed, jeered raucously and shouted, 'Get your fucking knees brown.' The topees were promptly dumped.

52

From Port Suez by rail to Alexandria, where the battalion transport section picked up its trucks, and then by the coastal road to Burg-el-Arab and southward along dusty tracks to a training camp for a few days of intensive acclimatising – long route marches in the yielding sand, when water bottles were not carried, and night exercises.

I learned something new. Most of my platoon were Londoners with a smattering from rural Kent. The townees were afraid of the dark. I had been brought up in a country village; we lived in what had been an Elizabethan farmhouse and there was no artificial light of any kind in my bedroom. So from the age of five onwards, I looked on the darkness and the light as interchangeable – even when at the age of nine or ten I was awoken by a scratching noise on my small window. In the hard, bright light of a winter full moon, the shadow cast on the opposite wall was like a skeleton hand and fingers and a skeleton forearm. It turned out to be an unpruned shoot from climbing roses that screened part of the low, timbered upper floor.

But in the short time available, I had to try to train my men into believing that darkness could indeed be their friend. Just as it was difficult for them to spot Germans when night fell, so it was equally difficult for the enemy to spot them. And the one thing they must never do at night, I said, was to keep a fixed gaze on a particular object, a bush, for example, or a patch of camel-thorn. If you looked long and hard enough, your eyes would play tricks. You would swear that the bush got up and stealthily moved a yard or two to one side. The best thing was to keep your eyes moving slowly from left to right and back again.

Again, there were simple rules for knowing where you were. Whether there was a moon or not, the desert nights were always clear of clouds and the stars sparkled crisply. There was the Plough, impossible to miss when you knew the shape of the handle and the four main stars that made up the blade. Look at the far edge, starting at the bottom, and let your eye run upwards past it. There, twinkling on its own, was the North Star. Once you knew which direction was north, everything else fell into place. The Eighth Army occupied the eastern side and the Afrika Korps with its Italian allies the western side. If you were lost at night, it was best to check the North Star, face it, do a half-right turn and, with it always on your left side, keep going until you bumped into friendly forces – or got shot at by a nervous British sentry. The other way might find you spending the rest of hostilities in a POW camp.

These men were not cowards. Many behaved bravely when it came to battle. But they had been reared in a big city where street lamps stayed on all night. Except for those few who might have gone hop-picking in Kent as youngsters, they had no experience at all of the dark.

After all too few days of training, 2nd Buffs and the rest of 142 Brigade were rushed forward to the bony southern slopes of Ruweisat Ridge. Rommel had routed the Eighth Army at the Battle of 'Knightsbridge' a month or so earlier. General Ritchie, the Army Commander, had been summarily dismissed and General Auchinleck, 'the Auk', GOC Middle East Forces, had taken personal command. The Army had been flung reeling back towards Alamein, fifty miles from Cairo, where it was going to have to stand and fight. We, the fresh troops, had to hold, fortify and, if possible, extend the southern end of the defensive line. The twin pillars of Himeimat on the horizon a few miles away marked off the edge of the Qattara Depression, impassable to heavy tracked vehicles, which meant that Rommel could not bypass the defensive line. He would have to attack and break us before sweeping on to Cairo and beyond in triumph.

And we were, literally, digging for our lives. Without deep slit trenches and a wide field of fire, we would be ducks in a shooting gallery for the Afrika Korps. Their breakthrough and tempestuous dash eastward after 'Knightsbridge' had stretched their lines of communication to the limit but Rommel was capable of a gambler's throw. The unctuous voice of Richard Dimbleby, broadcasting from the still complete safety of Cairo, spoke of the Eighth Army withdrawing to 'previously prepared positions', as though it were a clever move in a game of chess. It was utter nonsense. All was scrabble and dabble as, stripped to the waist under the blazing sun, we scraped at the rocky surface of Ruweisat Ridge with short-handled picks and almost useless shovels. Everyone worked all the hours of daylight, officers and NCOs included. As an officer, you couldn't expect your batman or another private to dig your trench and neglect his own safety. But it was gruelling, thirsty work, rationed as we were to two pints of water a day for all purposes. In the course of two weeks' navvying, I lost over twenty pounds in weight.

At first, it seemed unreal, almost as though we were extras on location for a film about desert warfare. I had been bombed at home by the Luftwaffe, machine gunned by a marauding Messerschmidt at RAF Manston, and shelled by the German long-range artillery at the Old Deer Park Barracks in Dover, but all that was long distance, impersonal. Now, after close on three years of war, we were really on active service. The enemy was a few hundred yards away, on the other side of a wide minefield. Sounds carry in the desert at night and the strains of 'Lili Marlene' would come floating across the gap, sung by a dozen strong baritone voices. They were other young men, the enemy. At any moment now, we could be fighting and killing them – or being killed ourselves. And yet reality had not quite broken in.

The sand was all-pervading. When men stripped, they found the sand had blown up inside their shorts and was caked in small ridges against the hair on their thighs. It had worked inside the woollen hose-tops, had rimmed their eyes and ears and matted the short hair on their necks. No breech-cover could protect a rifle from the insidious sand that clogged the bolt and jammed the magazine.

The sand could never be kept in place because it had no permanent place. It spread in a thin film on paper, on tents and on food. The sand had no properties of its own. It took in the heat of the sun so that at midday bare flesh could not stand its painful contact. The cold night air chilled it, the winds moulded it into heaps. It bore the imprint of the feet that marched across it and of the bodies that lay on it and of the spades that dug trenches in it. But not for long. It was always being patterned by passing events until the wind again shifted it and smeared out the footprint and the tyre track and slowly filled in the abandoned slit trench.

Sometimes the *khamsin* blew, a hot fierce wind that plucked up the sand in a mad dance so that the whirling dust obscured the sun and blotted out the day. Nothing could stand against the onrush of sand that choked everything in its way, whipping under tents and blankets and, when it subsided, leaving every object; covered inches deep.

My platoon in B Company happened to be the northernmost unit in the whole of 44th Division and we were brigaded alongside the southern flank of the New Zealand Division. They had seen fierce action in Greece, Crete and the Western Desert, commanded by the fearsome General Freyberg, VC, who in two world wars had been wounded in battle seventeen times. There was a famous story about him, which went like this.

Although well over six feet in height and of an imposing bulk, he had a squeaky high-pitched voice. One day, he was reviewing his men at an official parade and stopped to chat with a company commander.

He asked, 'You been in action?'

'Yes, sir.'

'In Greece?'

'Yes, sir.'

'Crete?'

'Yes, sir.'

'The Desert?'

'Yes, sir.'

'Ever been wounded?'

'No, sir.'

'Why the bloody hell not?'

Thanks to Freyberg, and not only his pugnacious but also his caring spirit for his men, the New Zealand Division was held, not only by the British forces but by the Germans as well, to be the finest fighting formation on either side. We were soon to learn how battle-hardened troops dealt with things.

One hot morning, shirtless, I was scratching away vigorously with a pickaxe that made little impression on the sun-baked slabs of rock, when I spotted a couple of men in Boy Scout hats approaching from the New Zealand side. I went on working when a squeaky voice from above me asked, 'Is there an officer, here?' Although he was wearing no badges of rank, one look at the big man was enough. General Freyberg had come to call, along with his military assistant.

I scrambled up, said, 'Yes, sir' and was trying to shove my head and shoulders, pouring with sweat, into my shirt, when he made a gesture with his hand to leave it. He said, 'Tough work. Are you short of anything?'

The thirty of us in the platoon were the furthest unit away from our brigade headquarters and the lines of communication were working none too well. I said, 'We've run out of beer and cigarettes, sir.'

He turned to his MA and told him to arrange for a case of beer and two boxes of Victory V cigarettes to be sent up to us after dark that day from *New Zealand* supplies. (The welcome beer and fags duly arrived without fuss.) Then Freyberg cast an experienced eye over our puny efforts to dig in.

He said, 'You'll never get done that way.' Again, he turned to his MA and told him to get a detachment of sappers sent up with explosives to blow some proper holes for us. He chatted for a few moments and then asked my permission – a full general seeking permission from a second-lieutenant, the lowest form of commissioned rank – to talk to my men. He told them they were doing a hell of a job and wished them good luck.

His behaviour was in contrast to that of our own high brass. Lieutenant-General Horrocks, XIII Corps commander, with his silver hair and ascetic features, looked like an unfrocked bishop. None of the forward troops at the sharp end ever saw him in the heat and sweat of the day. But, come the cool late afternoon, once or twice a week, a convoy of jeeps would arrive, sending dust clouds billowing into the calm air. Out would step Horrocks and his entourage, resplendent in newly starched desert service dress, with red tabs, swagger canes, the lot. Horrocks would take the salute from the nearest brigadier or colonel, say, 'Good show. Carry on, chaps', in his melodious tones and climb back into his jeep. The convoy would head back to its safe zone miles behind the lines, sending up the same pillars of dust. The Afrika Korps, a few hundred yards away behind the minefields, would notice all the commotion and would spend the next quarter of an hour bombarding our lines with their heavy mortars. Horrocks & Co would, of course, be miles away out of danger by then.

I had been on an explosives course and knew the drill employed by the Royal Engineers, our own sappers. First of all, a groundsheet would be put down and the sticks of plastic nitroglycerine, the fuses and the percussion caps would be placed in a neat row on it. Then the sergeant in charge would check every item against his written list to ensure nothing was missing and that no extra supplies had wrongly been added. Then, assuming four simultaneous charges were to take place, in turn four men would place the required sticks of TNT each in its designated place – all this under the close scrutiny of the sergeant. Then, either the same men or another four would run out identical lengths of fuse in a fan shape, tied at the near end. Then the sergeant would attach a percussion cap to each of the four fuses and insert it in the plastic explosive. All the men would then retreat a good distance to safe cover, except for the sergeant and a helper. He would light the ends of the four fuses and, as they were spluttering and smoking towards their respective bundles of TNT, he and his helper would stand up and walk quite slowly away to cover. The drill book told you it was essential to walk away, not run. If you got excited and started to run, you might stumble over some object, break your leg and be helplessly immobilised in close range of the about-to-explode charges.

The New Zealand method, we soon learned, was different. The

morning after General Freyberg's visit, two burly men, one a corporal, the other a private, arrived, carrying knapsacks. They looked like prop forwards, broad in the chest and thick in the thighs, the hairs on their arms bleached golden from weeks in the sun. They eyed the scene, did some pacing out, placed the explosives and attached differing lengths of fuses. Then one of them retired while the other lit a cigarette, walked up to each fuse in turn, lit it from the glowing fag-end and walked back to join his comrade on the reverse slope where my platoon and I crouched. With one simultaneous roar, Ruweisat Ridge erupted, flinging rocks, stones and sun-baked slabs of sand up in the air on a soot-black cloud. We would now be down to soft sand and shovelling would be easy. I thanked the New Zealanders for their help, the corporal said, 'No trouble, mate', and, shouldering their knapsacks, they walked back to their own area.

There was a Maori battalion alongside us. In the British Army, there was a strict drill for setting up a night patrol. First the battalion commander would brief the company commander who was going to supply the officer and men for the patrol. Then the company commander would brief the officer. He in turn would brief his sergeant with the numbers required, times out and back, destination and, most important, the password. There was not much point in carrying out a successful patrol and then being shot up by your own sentries for failing to answer the question, 'Halt! Who goes there?'

The Maoris had a different method. The NCO ordered to lead the night patrol would go round his men and ask for volunteers. Once he had the right number, he would gather them in a bunch and tell them in a few sentences the target and its compass bearing. Then with a grin they would slip away silently into the night. They had a neat trick which appealed to their robust sense of humour. Noiselessly, they would infiltrate the enemy lines, edging under his barbed wire or snipping one small corner with wire-cutters. If they found five Germans sound asleep in a scooped out hollow, they would cut the throats of four and leave the fifth man untouched. Back in their own lines, they would roar with laughter, thinking of the look on that man's face when he woke next morning and saw his four friends around him, bloodily dead. It was also a great way to lower enemy morale. Word would slide round the front-line troops about these night visitations and even the bravest would wonder if and where it would be safe to go to sleep.

Digging in was complete and we had erected a strong wire fence with double dannert coils in front of our position. Every day that passed increased the platoon's desert knowhow. We had learned to slice the top off a petrol can, fill it with sand, soak it with petrol and make a desert oven for boiling up tea. Food was plain and unchanging – a tin of bully beef and a packet of dry biscuits (hard tack) for breakfast, lunch and supper.

Occasionally, to make a change, one of the amateur cooks would fry slices of the corned beef in their own fat to be eaten on top of the dry biscuit.

We had learned it was a court-martial offence to get raw shoulders from over-exposure to the fierce sun and so be unable to put on webbing equipment and bandoliers. We had also learned that the temperature, which might be as high as 100° in the shade – if one could find any shade – at mid-day, dropped to the cooling nineties as the sun went down behind the enemy lines. There was no real twilight, just a pink-flushed greyness for a few minutes and then total darkness. And within perhaps forty minutes of the sun's disappearance, the temperature had fallen like a stone to the mid-forties. You could feel the evening growing palpably colder. Flushed and sweating one moment, chilled and shivering the next, there was every risk of catching a heavy cold. So, as the sun went down, out would come khaki sweaters from kitbags. Again, it was a court-martial offence to go sick through failing to stick to the drill.

Our hardest task was to get accustomed to the lack of water in a climate that called out for copious draughts of it. Your waterbottle, holding two pints, was filled in the morning and had to last throughout the day and night until the following morning. Two pints – what a thirsty beer-drinker will knock back in ten minutes. We learned to half-fill a mess tin, dab face and chin, shave and then use the soapy water to wash out a pair of dirty socks. There was more petrol to spare than water and so shirts were often washed in the former and then stretched out to dry on a rock. Smokers, which included most of us, were warned to keep clear. Everyone sweated so much that, when the shirt was taken off at night, it would be stiff and glinting white with salt crystals. A good beating with the flat of a bayonet would dislodge them in a sparkling cloud.

Apart from the washing of faces and clothes, the rationed water allowed for a mug of tea for breakfast, another at mid-day and a third at night. We tried to keep the inside of our mouths moist by sucking pebbles or chewing the bitter leaves of camel thorn, but without great success. Cigarette-smokers fared worst. Not only did the inhaled smoke dry out throat and tongue but lips got dry and cracked in the sun. It was sometimes an effort to pull the end of the cigarette – there were few cork-tipped brands – away from the lower lip and a strip of pink membrane would stick to it and be torn off at the same time, leaving a bloody furrow. Lady Nicotine was a hard mistress but she lost few devotees.

The first night patrol I led was for reconnaissance. 'Killer' Horrocks had been up to his tricks again. He could have learned much from T. S. Eliot – 'Teach me to sit still' – assuming he had ever heard of the poet, but unfortunately he had concocted a suicidal plan; suicidal for others, of course, and not for the General who watched it in safety behind the lines. Squadrons of Sherman and other modern tanks were on their way by sea to replace the battered and outdated remnants in XXX Armoured Corps. Horrocks had to get his blow in first; when the tanks did arrive, they would not come under his command at XIII Corps. So he brigaded the Bren carriers of 44th Division.

A Bren carrier was an open-topped vehicle with small tank tracks and half-inch armour that would stop ordinary small arms fire but hardly a burst from a heavy machine gun and certainly not the wicked impact of an 88mm high velocity gun. Designed as a superior anti-aircraft gun, the 88mm was now universally used in ground warfare and was the most feared weapon on the German side. Four men at the most, including the driver, could squat down in a Bren carrier which, as the name suggests, was designed to carry and fire a Bren gun, a light machine gun.

Horrocks ordered the puny force to attack the Afrika Korps lines under cover of darkness. (Presumably, he failed to realise that their tracks would make considerable noise and that the enemy would at once send up flares to light the whole scene.) What he ever hoped to achieve by the action could now only be deduced by a trained psychiatrist. The Afrika Korps was well dug in behind quite deep minefields with wide fields of fire. It was, of course, a murderous plan, concocted out of who knows what motives. Horrocks was to put forward an even more imbecilic and fatal set of orders when, two years later as commander of XXX Armoured Corps, he sent inexperienced armoured troops charging along a single highway with floodable lower levels on either side in a belated effort to save the gallant Parachute Regiment and other defenders of the Arnhem Bridge. And then he had the nerve, some years after the war, to act as military pundit for a popular BBC television series on the art of warfare. As Goethe put it, 'Against stupidity the gods themselves rail in vain.' He might have added colossal vanity as an additional barrier.

To revert to his earlier bêtise, several of the Buffs' Bren carriers inevitably failed to return from the massed attack. Among them was one commanded by a good friend of mine, Peter Gray. The object of my reconnaissance patrol into no-man's-land was to try to locate the missing carriers. There were three of us, myself, a corporal and a soldier to guard our backs. I took a compass bearing on the area where the carriers had last been seen going in and we crept through the velvety night. The moon was very bright, casting deep shadows alongside higher ground and we tried to keep concealed in the blackness, crouching as we went. We came across one burnt-out carrier but there was no sign of life, although we scoured the ground for fifty yards around for bodies. Please God, we thought, they had managed to be taken prisoner.

Some minutes later, we came across another hulk; facing straight at the enemy lines. The driver, the front passenger – my friend, Peter Gray – and the gunner behind him were sitting in their seats, dead. I crawled around to the front of the vehicle and saw a deep tunnel of light. An 88mm armour-piercing shell had gone straight through the bulkhead, through Peter's chest, through the chest of the man behind him and out through the rear bulkhead. Squatting down, you could see right through from front to back, with the bright moon lighting up the area at the back of the carrier. The driver did not appear to have been wounded; he must have died from the fierce blast of the impact. At least, death for all three would have been instantaneous. They never knew what hit them.

Lieutenant-General Sir Brian Horrocks, KBE, DSO, MC, Gentleman Usher of the Black Rod, House of Lords (1949–63), died in his ninetieth year in 1985. To many of us who served under him, his epitaph should have been: 'He did for them all with his plan of attack.' Obviously lacking all imagination and pleased with his efforts, he probably slept dreamlessly to the very end.

The battalion had suffered fifty or more casualties and, while reinforcements were sent up from base, there were various reshuffles among the officers. I was promoted to Intelligence officer from platoon commander and was sent off on a short course to Sarafand in Palestine. The first leg of the journey was simple. Another officer, who was going on a short leave, would accompany me as far as Cairo: we borrowed a jeep and driver, looked at the map, took a compass bearing on Cairo and then drove there across the desert. We bivouacked for the first night in a small *wadi* and hit the Alexandria–Cairo tarmac road in the early afternoon next day. From there, it was a quick run into the teeming city to leave the jeep safely parked in a Military Police compound. I made a beeline for Shepherds Hotel. My companion knew a young ATS officer stationed in Cairo and had plans of his own.

The memory of those first few hours in the stately old hotel is still vivid. After months of sweaty, sandy, dirty living, the very sight of a big marble bath with a wooden ceiling fan stirring lazily above it and ample hot water and real soap was overwhelming. To lie almost full length and feel the sand washing out of hair and ears and between the toes would have been exhilarating, had I not felt so relaxed. Meanwhile, the *dhobi* had collected my crumpled bush jacket and trousers and shortly returned them, washed and starched. Feeling like a snake that has sloughed its old skin, I dried myself, dressed formally and went down for that well known ceremony – the first drink at the famous Long Bar.

It hardly touched the sides, as they say. To think that water and drink were unlimited when the Eighth Army, hardly fifty miles away to the west, was rationed to two pints a day, all purposes. I was about to order myself a second when my neighbour, a yard or two along the bar, said, 'Here, have this one on me.'

He was about my own age, dressed in smart blue 'patrols' and wearing the insignia of the Blues, banded with the Royals in wartime to form the Household Cavalry. His face looked vaguely familiar. As the barman passed my drink across the marble-topped bar, my host said, 'Didn't you play number one for – what was it? – yeah, I've got it, Downing?'

I nodded and sipped the drink.

'We met in the league. I was playing number one for Magdalene. You won in four games. But it was that lucky nick that did it. Otherwise, I'd've taken the fourth and walked the fifth.'

'Nice try,' I said. 'You wouldn't have beaten me with my legs tied together.'

We both laughed. hen he said, 'You were into books, what? Read quite a bit, I reckon. You ever heard of some scribblin' fella with a funny name – Waugh. Got a girl's Christian name.'

I said, 'Yeah, I know who you mean. Evelyn Waugh.'

'That's the fella. Proper shit he is. He's bin tryin' to get into the

Blues. Sucked up to Boy Laycock, don'tcha know. But Boy wasn't havin' any. He don't want a fella like that in the Blues, scribblin' away. So we blackballed him, what? Fella made a real stink about it but no way was he gettin' in.'

As I bought him a return drink, I thought it ironic that this pipsqueak of a landed gent, who had probably scrambled through Cambridge with a pass degree, should with his equally blockheaded mates, have rejected one of the best living British novelists. Twenty years later, when I had come to know Evelyn Waugh moderately well, I realised that one did not need an excess of brains in order to reach sound decisions.

The intelligence course at Sarafand is a memory blur, except for two things. Our instructor, Major Sandy Thomas, DSO, MC, a New Zealander, had fought with considerable bravery in both the Greece and the Crete campaign. When Crete was evacuated, he had gone into hiding in the mountains, worked his way by night down to the coast, stolen a small boat and sailed single-handed to the north-east shore of Greece. There he had found a friendly abbot, who had taken him into the monastery and hid him from the occupying Germans by allowing him to dress in a monk's robes and cowl. When his wounds had healed, he stealthily crossed the border into neutral Turkey and worked his way eastwards until at last, after much privation and many near misses, he managed o slip across the border into north Lebanon, which just happened to be guarded by the New Zealand Division. Ten months had gone by since the battles in Crete but the soldier on sentry duty was from Thomas's own infantry company.

'G'day, sir,' he said, slapping the butt of his rifle in salute. 'Took your time, didn't you?'

More than the course, I remember a swim in the Dead Sea. Corkscrewing down the twisting mountain road in a truck with dodgy brakes in a heat haze was not perhaps the best preparation for a relaxing swim. But the mood soon changed when I saw a fat woman floating on her back almost out of the water. Near her, an elderly man was sitting up reading a newspaper. He was clearly afloat but making no movement of his legs to support himself. Children were playing with the black, crystal-sparkling mud above the shoreline. The attendant warned me not to swim without first putting on special goggles, which he supplied for a small fee. He also said it was dangerous to come out of the water and sunbathe without first taking a fresh-water shower. I soon learned why. The Dead Sea was so full of salt, the crystals made my mouth and lips feel raw and the normal crawl stroke was almost impossible to perform, as the arms and legs were too high on the surface to achieve proper propulsion.

Back with the battalion 'up the blue' (Eighth Army slang for 'the far distant desert') I found several changes. Lieutenant-Colonel Nicholson, the commanding officer when we landed in Egypt, had been wounded at the Battle of Alam Halfa, shot in the elbow. The bullet, it seemed, had passed from the rear of his arm to the front, the wrong way for an enemy bullet to have travelled. There was at least a reasonable chance it had been fired by a Buff. If so, the culprit never owned up, although he would have been stood many a round of drinks from his comrades. Colonel Nicholson, a sneering, sarcastic man, with an ornate moustache not unlike Kaiser Bill's, had never been popular with his men. He was better suited shuffling documents on the Staff, to which he returned with later distinction. His replacement was Lieutenant Colonel Williams, who had been second-in-command of 1st Battalion The Buffs, the mobile infantry in 7th Armoured Division, the famous Desert Rats. He was a dark, swarthy man who had seen much action in the past two years.

From leading a platoon of thirty men, I was now in charge of the I section, comprising half a dozen or so. There was a sergeant, Chick Henderson, a slight self-possessed man in his twenties, a corporal, a driver for the section jeep, two or three privates and my new batman, Charles Daniels. Daniels was the complete Man of Kent, born and bred in Canterbury, the regimental home of The Buffs. Curly-haired, chubby red face, speaking with the light burr of a countryman, he was the acme of good humour and deep-down resolution. In all the months he looked after me, I never once saw him lose his temper or his nerve. He and I have stayed good friends for well over fifty years now.

But before I finally became IO, the new commanding officer had a job for me. It was to lead a fighting patrol with the aim of snatching a prisoner from the enemy lines a few hundred yards away. The usual drill was for the CO to nominate the company supplying the patrol and the company commander would do the rest. Colonel Williams had other ideas. He sent for me at mid-day and the two of us crouched down in his command-hole with its camouflage netting draped overhead. There was room for the adjutant but I suspected he was a deliberate absentee. The Colonel's thin, clean-shaven but dark-bearded jaw and chin were set and the look in his eyes intense, as he explained (what I already knew) that the night's patrol would be a dangerous manoeuvre. The patrol would need supporting fire from a pair of Bren guns pushed forward on our right flank to get an enfilading angle. The officer in charge of the supporting fire would have a difficult task. If he opened up too soon, all surprise would be lost: too late and he might well riddle the patrol as it tried to cross the enemy barbed wire.

The Colonel went on looking hard at me as he said, 'I've decided, Greenfield, it's up to you. You will choose your own support group leader.'

'But, sir . . .'

'It's an order, Greenfield. You can pick any officer in the battalion below the rank of captain. Think about it, man, take your time. It's your choice.'

I cursed him silently on my way back to my slit trench and again throughout the fierce afternoon. If he had said to me, X or Y will be in support, I might have thought, Oh Christ, that idiot, but I would have accepted it without a second's hesitation. Seniors gave orders, however stupid, and juniors tried to carry them out. But now he had made me judge and jury over my own friends. Men I had gone drinking with in the pubs around Sutton, Surrey, when we were awaiting embarkation orders, men I had accompanied on long route marches, who had played practical jokes on me and I on them. Now I had to ask myself of each one in turn; Do I really trust him? With my life and my patrol's lives? Until then, I had been an overgrown undergraduate. That afternoon, I grew into an adult. Finally, I chose one whom I did not particularly like; he was a stolid fellow and I had never seen him excited. He was not witty like some of the other junior officers, nor did he share a university background. But I reckoned he would be there when we needed him.

Faces blacked, sidearms bound up with cloth strips to stop them rattling and nerves jangling, my eleven men and I fanned out and tiptoed into the dark night. The enemy had only recently moved his lines opposite us and the latest Intelligence briefings indicated that he had not had the time to lay minefields in front of his barbed wire. We had about four hundred yards to cover. A man near me suddenly pounced and began stabbing an object on the ground with his fixed bayonet. It was a dead body, unrecovered from the Alam Halfa battle. I restrained him and we padded on. Crawling the last fifty yards, we could see the enemy's barbed wire, stretched against the night sky. We had rehearsed the drill in daylight and it had all gone slickly – too slickly, perhaps. The man with the wire-cutters crept forward, accompanied by another who would hold the wire tight, to stop it twanging back when cut. I would be alongside them to supervise and, no doubt, get in their way. The idea was to cut the strands of wire to a height of three of four feet and close to an upright stanchion, so that a crouching man could tear through it at speed.

In the event, the gap was too small for more than one man at a time to use it. And, instead of digging their trenches close to their wire, as the Intelligence reports had it, the desert-hardened Afrika Korps veterans had placed them twenty or thirty yards to the rear. Three of us scrambled through the gap, while the other nine queued up behind us. Then the fireworks started. The trio dashed forward, a trench, a blur of awakened faces, flares lit up the scene in a baleful glare, tracer bullets were whipcracking just over our beads. All surprise had been lost. It was time to go – quickly.

One at a time, we scrambled back through the narrow hole in the wire. It seemed to take ages as the firing intensified. I rounded up the rest of the patrol and we ran back into the enveloping darkness. And, as we went, the support fire on our flank opened up, the two Bren guns firing alternate bursts. After several minutes, the enemy tracer fire, directed blindly at the patrol, switched, picking up the muzzle flashes of the Brens. They had found good cover and were not hit. The whole party returned to our lines unharmed. The patrol's objective – to bring back a prisoner – had not been achieved but at least I had made the right choice for support fire leader. Without the immaculate timing of the enfilade fire, the main body could have been shot to pieces under the bright flares in no-man's-land.

The following week I learned another valuable lesson. Because I had done quite a lot of night patrolling, I was ordered to accompany a junior Royal Sussex officer, who was taking a patrol out for the first time. It was a stupid decision. I had no function to perform and the leader, naturally enough, resented my presence. So, with his permission, I placed myself on the extreme left wing of the party and decided to lurch forward and think of England.

I had nothing to do except imagine what a cock-up he must be making. Did he know how to use a compass at night? Why did he keep on stopping? Had he lost his way? Was he taking us round and round in circles? Why didn't the stupid bastard pack it in and take us back to the safety of our own lines? As things turned out, the patrol leader did a first-class job. It was a reconnaissance patrol with the object of discovering the height and depth of the enemy's barbed wire in a certain segment of their defences. The object was well achieved and all members of the patrol, myself included, got back to their own lines in safety. I had done nothing of note but I had learned one valuable lesson. Now I knew just how a private soldier felt when out on patrol. The officer leading had a cushy job. He was so busy taking sights with his luminous-dialled compass and pacing out the distance covered that he had no time to feel anxious or afraid. Others, lacking the luxury of jobs to do, could only traipse along and hope to God the fool knew what he was doing.

Over the next few weeks, Sergeant Chick Henderson and I carried out several two-man patrols. We would slip into no-man's-land, find a small dip about halfway across and spend the next few hours sitting down in it, with a compass, a notebook and a pencil. There was no point in carrying any arms. If a German patrol stumbled across us, we could never fight our way out. Once, indeed, we had to sit tight and hold our breath when a patrol went striding past about thirty yards away. Sounds travel far on the desert air. We used to take a bearing on the point where we first heard the noise of a heavy truck moving behind the lines and again at the point where the noise faded. The two bearings and the timing were then jotted down in the notebook. (There is no great problem about writing in the dark, as long as one leaves wide spaces between entries.) Unexpected lights and noises with their timies and bearings were also noted.

All these entries were marked up next day on the battalion order of battle map. The results of one night's eavesdropping were specially interesting. The comings and goings of heavy trucks appeared to centre on one small area in a wide, fairly shallow *wadi*. The Brigade IO, a jolly major named Dick Fracis, decided the place must be an arms and stores forward depot. The word went back, a detachment of the divisional artillery did its sums and at dusk stand-to that evening it opened up with concentrated salvoes. There was a series of loud explosions and heavy smoke went billowing up. Sergeant Henderson and I, standing side by side in the I section trench, looked at each other and smiled. At least, that was one night's work that was not wasted.

5

❖❖❖

Into Battle

❖❖❖❖❖❖

My main job as Battalion IO was twofold, to gather and distribute as much information as my section and I could discover. Large-scale maps of our desert locale, pinned to mapboards and covered in talc, had to be marked up: in red grease pencil for the enemy and blue for our own side. XIII Corps issued maps of the whole Corps area, which reached us via Divisional and Brigade Headquarters. Each in turn added to or altered the markings so that when the maps finally reached us at the sharp end, they looked like the meanderings of a drunken spider which had dipped alternate feet in red and blue. And the information we gained through our own observations and patrols went back in turn via brigade and division to Corps HQ, where the idiot Horrocks dreamed his Napoleonic dreams.

My worst job, I decided, was to navigate the battalion, eight hundred men, sixty or more trucks, Bren carriers and all the paraphernalia of troops on the move. The only mechanical aid was a sun compass, a kind of mobile sundial perched precariously on the bonnet of my jeep. You took a bearing on the destination point and then set the sun compass so that the shadow fell along that bearing. Then you stood up in the front of the jolting jeep and watched the thin shadow, muttering to the driver, 'Left hand down a bit', or whatever, to keep the vehicle on the right path. The rest of the battalion followed at fifty-yard intervals, so that a dive-bombing Luftwaffe Stuka would not hit more than one target.

It sounds easy if you say it quickly, and it would have been easy if the terrain had been firm and flat. The Western Desert was different. Sometimes, you had to make a wide loop to avoid driving up the steep side of a *wadi*. Sometimes, a broad patch of soft sand would lie across the direct route. That involved another complicated detour with three changes of bearing before, with luck, getting back on to the desired direction. To add to the fun, mirages might develop in the blazing heat of the day. There would be a shimmer of haze and then apparent delectable pools of water rippling from one side of a *wadi* to the other. And all the time the sweat would be running down your forehead, seeping into the tight goggles worn to keep out the sand and the flies, and steaming up the lenses.

To add to the pressure, I knew that Colonel Williams, an impatient man, had spent the last two years up the blue. He had an instinctive sense of direction, taking one glance at the map and scorning the sun compass. He would set off, it seemed haphazardly, darting first in one direction, then in another. And always, after I had laboriously studied the map, drawn lines with protractor and ruler, set the sun compass and slowly crunched forward, I would arrive at the destination to find him there, flicking his leg with his swagger stick in irritation at having been kept waiting five minutes or more.

On one occasion, when no-man's-land had narrowed to a gap of three hundred yards or less, we were dug in on a forward slope. The latrines were sited on the reverse slope. To visit them in daylight, one would have to stand up in full view of the enemy, walk a few yards to the top of the small slope and then disappear on the other side of the hill. It did not pay 15th Panzer Division, opposing us, to have a sniper stay in wait all day long for a possible victim. Instead, they hit on a far more subtle form of torture. A Spandau machine gun with a fixed sight was set up and trained on the hillside where men could be seen coming and going throughout the day. A length of string was attached to the trigger. At any moment during the day, someone on their side might stop and pull the string. A burst of fire would go whipcracking over our heads in the forward trenches and smash into the slope above. An hour or two could elapse and nothing happen. Then there might be two or three bursts at less than a minute's interval. You never knew whether a stranger, a few hundred yards away, might suddenly take it into his head to tug the string just when you had decided that your churning guts could hold off no longer. It was in those fraught weeks that I managed to train my digestive system into operating only at night, when there would be no more sporadic bursts of machine gun fire.

Things were beginning to stir. General Montgomery had arrived to take command of the Eighth Army. To show his broad-mindedness, he took to wearing an Australian slouch hat with the left brim pinned upwards, until a message arrived from the 9th Australian Division HQ, saying they were rather particular over who was entitled to wear their special headgear. Obediently, for once, the vain little man substituted a Royal Tank Regiment beret, which he retained until the end of the desert campaign and beyond.

Brand-new Sherman and Churchill tanks were unloading at Port Tewfik and Port Said to replace the ageing and worn out Valentines. There were extra new heavy guns for the Royal Artillery. The Highland Division arrived, or 'Highway Decorators' as they quickly became known from their habit of painting old petrol cans with the initials 'HD' as route-markers. The rest of us claimed, quite inaccurately, that we knew our way around the desert without the need of reminders. Night patrolling intensified, 'line-straightening' operations took a greater toll of killed and wounded. Deception plans were rife: dummy tanks began to appear in their squadrons close behind our divisional HQ and the recorded sounds of tanks grinding along and changing gear were amplified – to be heard by and confuse the enemy.

At last, it was the night of 23 October, the night of the full moon. On our immediate front a Royal Sussex battalion would launch the assault, leaving the start line and moving through the gaps in the broad minefield that had been cut at night by the sappers and then concealed. 2nd Buffs would follow up and take over the attack after the first wave. We were to press on for several hundred yards, if we could, and establish a bridgehead, so that next day 7th Armoured Division's tanks could burst out into the open spaces behind.

At nine o'clock, the Battalion began to stir. A message arrived for the Colonel to say that the carriers and Scorpions, converted tanks with a device for exploding mines attached to the front of them, were in position a thousand yards back and would be coming forward to clear avenues in the minefield once the bridgehead was established. For some minutes men played quietly with their arms, slowly opening and closing the bolts of their rifles, adjusting the bayonet-frogs on their equipment and feeling their ammunition-pouches to make sure that the rounds were still there. Groundsheets that had kept out the dew and the cold were slowly folded and put back into the small packs. Everyone seemed to be keyed up, waiting.

Behind us the guns along the thirty miles of front were silently pointing upwards. Shells were being slid into the breech and every man in each battery was waiting for the battery commander's signal. Officers looked down at their watches as the minute-hand crawled towards the half-hour. The signal – a quick jerk from each Number One – and the night stillness was smashed by the concerted roar of the guns. The shells whistled over the heads of the infantry, whirring like wild geese in flight, and all along the enemy positions the flashes of their bursts flickered on the skyline. And then more British guns took up the cry and more shells swished through the air until the sounds beat out a wild rhythm, first the sharp crash of the charge as it was fired, the moaning of the shell through the air and the dull reverberation of its landing. And the volume of fire increased until all sounds mingled so that from one point of view could be heard the explosion of one salvo, the airborne rush of another and the firing of a third. The giant drum-notes of noise beat a continual tattoo along the enemy line where men winced and crouched as the shells fell among them with a vicious shriek. And now gunners sweated in the moonlight as they fed the guns, and gun-barrels grew hot and the air smelt bitter with the fumes of the exploded charges. And still they went on firing as battery relieved battery and troop relieved troop all down the British line. And still the barrage went on, thousands of thousands of shells tearing up the ground among the enemy's defences. The sound on the clean night air was like a roll on the drums, beating out the prelude to the attack.

With so many guns and so many men and so many shells, spread over a wide front, there is always a risk of error, just as linking up several orchestras, out of sight of one another, can lead to a cascade of false notes. So it was in our immediate front. The plan was for a creeping barrage that would come down about two hundred yards ahead of the Royal Sussex start-line and move forwards like a protecting curtain as the men on the ground moved forward. So, the plan went, as our leading troops reached the enemy's defensive positions, they would still be crouching and shaken under the impact of the barrage. Alas, human error played its part. The opening salvoes from the gunners well behind us landed right on the start line. Many in the battalion were killed or wounded before they had time to fire a shot in anger at the foe.

There was naturally wild confusion and, worse, a brief delay. Some platoons had lost their officer, others had been decimated. By the time they had formed up again, the tanks had ploughed ahead. Not for the first time, the infantry was going into battle largely unsupported.

Monty had arranged for a printed sheet to be handed out to the assaulting troops. In his schoolboy clichés, he spoke of 'hitting the enemy for six out of Africa' and wished us Godspeed in our efforts. We read it by the bright light of the full moon, crumpled it up and threw it aside in disgust. It might be an interesting game to a general sitting safely in his caravan well behind the lines but it was somewhat more serious to those at the sharp end. Besides, *vide* the casualties from the Royal Sussex and our own D Company being rushed back to the nearest field dressing station, and continuing Monty's own metaphor, the fast bowler had already hit his own wicket.

From then on, the first night of the Battle of Alamein was a blurred kaleidoscope. The barrage at last lifted and, as we trudged forward through the minefield gaps, our deafened ears gradually functioned again and we could pick up the high-pitched rattle of German Spandaus and the lower, slower sound of our Bren guns and medium machine guns. One moment, I was charging towards an Italian *sangar*, the built-up, usually circular defence posts that the Italians preferred to digging trenches. I was waving a Beretta pistol that I had, a week or two earlier, sliced from the belt of a dead officer. A dark shadow ahead fired a burst that whipped wildly overhead. I fired a couple of rounds back. The dark shadow disappeared. Whether I had hit, or even killed, him, I shall never know.

The next moment, it seemed, I was with our MO, Captain Shragovitch. A short, stocky man of great strength, he was a Canadian and had come to Britain with their Forces in 1941. He wanted to get front-line experience and, after months of inactivity, transferred to 2nd Buffs as MO when the battalion was mobilising for the desert. He was squatting alongside one of our corporals, who was lying on his back.

'Hey there, George.'

'What's up, Shrag?'

'This poor guy. Just given him a shot of morphia. The stretcher-bearer got a tourniquet on him. See all that blood?' He indicated an area of black saturated sand with his shaded torch. 'The leg's virtually off. Shell splinter or something. It's only hanging on by this shred of flesh. Here, George, do something useful. Sit down and cradle the lower part on your knees. I'm going to cut it clear and then we can get him back to the FDS. Risk of gangrene if we hang around.'

So I squatted down and grabbed the leg. The thigh bone had been sliced clean through by the shell splinter and the doc only had to make one swift cut to free the upper stump. Then they bundled the now unconscious corporal on to a stretcher and began to move away.

I was left, cradling the unattached leg in my hands. 'What do I do with this, Shrag?' I asked weakly.

'Keep it as a memento.'

I had never realised how heavy a leg is, not least when it is wearing an ammunition boot. Thirty or more pounds in weight, concentrated bone, muscle and flesh packed into a narrow cylinder. With an effort, I shifted it on to the sand, as reverently as I could, and went my way.

Colonel Williams was buzzing around like a blue-arsed fly, sometimes getting ahead of his own men in his brave impatience. I knew he was naturally courageous, but he was also desperate to win a medal. He had been in the desert for over two years and had nothing to show for it. He was a regular soldier, the war would not last for ever and rapid promotion in peacetime tended to follow the man with the decorations. It was a dangerous combination.

The night went on and gradually the forward tempo decreased. The tanks of 7th Armoured Division had ground to a halt, our leading companies had reached a massive minefield and it would be daylight in another two hours. Daniels, ever cheerful, had been darting about like a sparrow at a feeding table and he was now helping to turn a captured *sangar* into a night stop for the Intelligence section. The moon had gone down and the night was at its darkest. I arranged the sentry-go list in case of a surprise return attack, which was most unlikely, pulled my greatcoat collar up and lay back, my head comfortably lodged on what I took to be an old bedroll.

I fell almost at once into a deep, untroubled sleep. Two hours later, waking in a grey dawn in time for stand-to, I discovered my head had been resting on the chest of a dead Italian, lying on his back, legs outstretched. I noticed without really registering the fact that the corpse was wearing thick white woollen socks. Some days later, as I had been wearing the same pair of khaki socks for over a week without once removing them, Daniels suggested I had a change and he produced a pair of white socks. Gratefully, I unwound my short puttees, unlaced and removed my boots, peeled off the dirty socks and pulled on the white ones. They fitted snugly. After a while the penny dropped. I asked Daniels where he had found them. After a little evasion, he confessed to stripping the dead Italian of his boots and socks. Neither fitted him, so I drew the benefit. The socks were a useful addition to my meagre wardrobe.

ABOVE: 2nd Buffs moving up to start-line before the battle of Alam Halfa,
September 1942
BELOW: The Intelligence Section 2nd Buffs in the Western Desert, 1942. Left to
right: Cpl Wilkins, Pte Davies, Lt Greenfield, Ptes Maylum, Daniels and Low

The Battle of El Alamein, October 1942: one of the action shots staged by 'Chet's circus'. Montgomery spoke just before the battle of 'hitting the enemy for six'. Unfortunately, the fast bowler opened by hitting his own wicket

Captain Shragovitch, RCAMC, Battalion MO, 1942–3 who enlisted the author's aid to amputate a leg under fire during the Battle of El Alamein

That dawn, the tanks turned round and began to rumble back towards and beyond the original start line. We did not then know it but Monty, sensing a stalemate in the south of the Alamein line where we were, had decided to group all his armour in the north for a knock-out punch once the infantry had cleared the way. We watched them go, their radio masts whipping to and fro in the grey air, as the massive vehicles lurched to and fro on the twisting path through the mine-fields. The gaps were never cut in a straight line but in zigzags of varying length, so that, once the stanchions and the guiding wires were removed, the enemy could not just hit on the right bearing and then drive straight through. Now we felt isolated, alone.

A day or so later, the CO was getting bored with all the inactivity. Already, he had viewed the battle scene by walking into no-man's-land in sunny daylight, with me keeping a safe distance behind. He called me forward and told me to hand over my mapboard, so that he could study the terrain now occupied by the Folgore Division, one of Mussolini's crack airborne units. He was waving the board to and fro, its talc cover reflecting the sun's rays in all directions, while I cringed behind him. The obvious happened. There was a burst of machine gun fire from in front. I flung myself down and grovelled in the shallowest of sandy depressions. I looked up, to see the colonel staring at me with contempt. Still standing erect, he turned round and walked slowly back to our lines, I followed him, almost crouching on all fours, expecting any minute the fatal burst that would tear my back apart.

That next morning, when I reported to Battalion HQ, Colonel Williams said briskly, 'Right, Greenfield. A spot of reconnaissance, I think.' He pointed a forefinger at the map. 'See this narrow *wadi*, here. Turns out into open ground – there and there. But it's a blind spot. Half the Afrika Korps could be lurking there and we wouldn't have a clue. So you and I'll take a Bren carrier and have a *shufti*, what?'

The man's an idiot, I thought. If a reconnaissance had to be made and I felt that the idea was due more to his inner urge to be up and doing than to military need – it should be carried out by the Battalion Intelligence officer, not by the officer commanding the whole unit. Besides, I had studied the map traces carefully that morning and recalled a symbol in red, the enemy colour, denoting an 88mm gun dug in opposite the exit to the *wadi*. I certainly was not looking for a medal for gallantry, posthumously awarded. So reluctantly I climbed into the front of the Bren carrier, alongside the driver, while the CO occupied the space behind him.

We reached the *wadi* and began threading a path towards the area where it opened out. Fifty yards short, I muttered to the driver under the crunching noise of the tracks, 'Take it easy, slow down.' Our progress dwindled to a crawl.

'Come on,' Colonel Williams shouted, impatiently. 'We'll be all day.'

The pace quickened slightly but when we were about twenty yards from the opening, I kept muttering to the driver, 'Slower, slower.'

The CO could take it no longer. 'Halt!' he shouted. 'For God's sake, Greenfield! You keep farting around like this, it'll be dark before we finish. Here, you take my place. I'll do the navigating.'

We changed places and set off again at a brisk pace. We had hardly travelled ten yards when there was a rending, ear-splitting crash. The left side of the carrier dropped and a pillar of smoke and sand dust rose on that side. Automatically, I vaulted over the other side and lay flat on the sand. The Afrika Korps always set one or more machine guns beside an 88mm, so that troops bailing out of a wounded tank could be shot down as they ran. But nothing happened for a few moments and I cautiously stood up, crouching.

Peering around, I saw the left front of the carrier had slipped into a sizeable hole. The blast had flung a section of the heavy track, over six feet in length, several yards away. Christ, I thought, we ran over a Teller mine, the deadliest kind of mine in the desert war. The CO was huddled up on the floor of the front compartment, moaning softly. There was a green sheen on his face. (We learned later that one leg had been broken a dozen times between ankle and thigh. It had to be amputated.) The driver was shaken and the stout gear lever had wrapped itself around his ankle so that he could not move. The ankle was later found to be broken but he was a stolid countryman and in good spirits.

But I had to do something about the Colonel. He was obviously suffering great pain and he might have serious internal injuries. Looking to my left, I saw a tank hull down about a hundred yards away. Its side was daubed with the Kent Yeomanry insignia. Tanks, I knew, always carried morphine phials. Besides, with its powerful radio transmitter, this one could radio a message back for medical help. The only snag, as I discovered as I trotted towards the tank, was having to cross a minefield to reach it.

In theory, the weight of a man was insufficient to set off an anti-tank mine. On the two other occasions I had to cross an uncharted minefield, the theory proved itself, as fortunately it did this time. Panting, I leaned against the tank, hull down behind a small bump in the desert. The turret opened and a youngish officer with long fair hair popped his head out. He had seen us go up on the minefield and had indeed waved us away; but the CO was too intent on a blinkered forward progress and his back blocked my forward vision. Yes, they had morphine to spare, he said. Give the wounded man this much and try to get him to keep it under his tongue as it dissolves. And, yes, they would radio back at once to their HQ, who would pass the message by RT to ours.

Then he said, 'Aren't you George Greenfield?'

I nodded. 'Yes.'

'Remember me? My name's Allfrey. I played cricket against you at Linton Park in '38 or was it '39?'

It all came back. Country-house cricket at Linton Park, the home of Lord Cornwallis, who himself had played cricket for Kent; in those palmy peaceful days when the sun shone all day long and you could buy a pint of beer, a packet of cigarettes and still have change for a shilling (5p), I had played cricket during the long vacations on private grounds belonging to the rich and the noble. Great fun they were, too, apart from the game itself. In one match at Tovil, when play was halted for drinks, the butler came on to the field with two magnums of champagne in their coolers and an underling bearing a silver tray carrying fifteen glasses.

I recalled this man Allfrey now, a tearaway fast bowler who had frightened the life out of me on a bone-hard pitch. 'Yes,' I said, 'I remember you. Still got the bruises to prove it.'

He grinned as he handed over the precious morphine. 'Changed times.'

'You said it.'

Back at the smashed carrier, I managed to get the CO, half-conscious from the shock, to take the drug. He was still huddled in the bottom of the vehicle with his knees drawn up under his chin. His left leg looked like an unset jelly, as if only the ankle puttees and the long stocking were holding it in place. I did not risk moving him, with the chance of aggravating his injuries and causing him more pain. The driver was sitting there stoically. His broken ankle was clearly hurting him but he smoked a cigarette and made a joke or two as we waited for help to arrive.

Half an hour later, it came, in the shape of Captain Shragovitch, driving his jeep, and a fifteen-hundredweight medical truck. Shrag had a stretcher assembled and the medical orderlies expertly lifted the CO out of the broken carrier and into the truck. The two orderlies and the immensely strong Shrag managed to tug the twisted gear lever clear of the driver's ankle and so release him from his seat. He hopped into the back of the truck, which was ready to drive away.

As Captain Shragovitch was organising the removal of the wounded, I noticed that the backs of his chunky calves were almost brushing a black threadlike wire running parallel to the ground at about six inches' height. I went rigid. It was part of the nastiest kind of anti-personnel mine. If the wire was pushed forwards or backwards, it would tug against the safety catch on top of the covered mine. Once released, the percussion cap would spring the mine about a foot upwards, when it would burst, scattering a curtain of flying steel splinters. Half a step back from Shrag and we would both lose feet, legs, hands and arms – if we were lucky. More likely, we would both be killed and the occupants of the truck severely wounded.

I took a pace nearer him and, as casually as I could, said, 'Shrag, for Chrissake don't move backwards. Take half a pace forward, in fact.'

He began, 'What the hell . . .'

I went on, 'You're almost standing on an AP mine, you clown.'

The good doctor leaped ahead like a startled hare. When he turned round, I explained the significance of the thin black wire. By now the truck was ready to move off, we waved it away and Shrag carefully placed one foot after the other over the wire and returned to the safety of the track. He proposed, and I seconded with alacrity, we should each have a snort from the brandy he always carried in his jeep for emergencies. For 'medicinal purposes', of course. We were both, no doubt, suffering from recent shocks to our respective constitutions. We each downed a large tot and then it occurred to Shrag that I might have undergone two shocks, once with the CO and now with the AP mine. I accepted without too much demur but pointed out that my father had told me the perils of drinking alone. So I insisted he joined me. Which he did.

Then he decided we ought to get back to battalion HQ. He soon had the jeep careering along the narrow zigzag path through the minefield. Two hundred yards from home, he swung a little wide on one bend, there was an enormous thump and a crash – and the front wheel next to where I was sitting shot straight up into the air about eight feet. We had gone over another mine. Luckily, we always followed regulations by covering the floors of jeeps with heavy sandbags. Doc and I both felt the shock but the sandbags absorbed most of it. The fact that the part of the vehicle to run over the mine was an extension to the main body was also fortunate. But it was a sobered up couple who trudged the last part of the journey on foot.

'Never go back' is often a good motto, if one does not wish to lose illusions. In 1967, my friend John Johnson and I drove to a twenty-fifth anniversary party for the 2nd Battalion at Cranbrook in the Weald of Kent. It was fascinating, if somewhat saddening, to meet again middle-aged men who were fixed in the memory as young and vigorous. Colonel Williams came limping in to the buffet supper on his crutches. It was difficult to spot which was the artificial leg.

I went over to him and said, 'Do you remember me, sir? Greenfield.'
'No, should I?'
'I was with you in the carrier – the one that blew up.'
'Really?' We had a minute or two of polite waffle and then I moved away. Here was a man who had lost his mobility and a promising Army career all in one thunderous crash. You would have thought the event would be etched in his memory for ever. But perhaps Nature is kinder than we think and wipes out the memories that are too hard to bear.

Perhaps a couple of days after being blown up twice, there was a battalion move, and the I section was completing its new 'office', which consisted of a pit alongside the fifteen-hundredweight truck. Daniels was helping to pull the truck's cover – 'tilt', as we called it – over the hole to provide shade. I was squatting on the step of the truck, studying the map on its board, and Sergeant Henderson was standing up, peering over my shoulder. There was a sudden scream and an immediate ear-splitting crash. A jagged hole appeared in the mapboard; the sergeant jerked like a hooked fish. He clapped his hand to his thigh, blood welled through his fingers. An enemy shell had landed out of the blue. Its blast knocked Daniels back into the pit he had dug. We patched Sergeant Henderson up with his field dressing and he was quickly evacuated to the nearest ADS (advance dressing station).

When the hubbub died down, I felt a slight itching on my left elbow. There was a two-inch rip in the roll-up of my shirt sleeve which, as I pulled the sleeve down, was repeated every few inches. The shell splinter had sliced through the map board, through the bulk of my rolled up sleeve to strike the sergeant's thigh. If I had been squatting five or six inches to my left, it would have struck me in the heart.

Most men in action secretly think they are invulnerable. Otherwise, the strain of battle would be insupportable. Indeed, experienced observers know that the first look that crosses a man's face when he is wounded is one of surprise that he, of all people, should stop a bullet or a shell splinter. But, having survived unscathed two blowings-up and one freak shell burst, I was beginning to suffer the dangerous delusion that God was not only an Englishman but that the initials G.G. did not merely stand for 'Good God'.

Lieutenant-Colonel Williams was soon replaced by Lieutenant-Colonel Percival, seconded from the Highland Light Infantry. Sandy-haired with an almost ginger moustache, he was a man at ease with himself, dry, laconic and not liable to flap like his predecessor. He had been awarded the DSO in a previous action and so had nothing to prove. He quickly won the confidence of his officers and men. For the first time since leaving England, our leader was a real man.

The measure of the man was evident early on. The battle in the south of the Alamein Line, from being static for its first nine days, was beginning to move forward. The main forces in the north were pounding their way through Afrika Korps defences and minefields, while our diversionary attacks were keeping one Panzer division away from the major action. On this occasion, two or three days after Colonel Percival's arrival, I had been on the go for over twenty-four hours, moving around no-man's-land, mainly on foot, to check enemy sites and pick up immediate information from returning night patrols. I was so tired on return to HQ that I unrolled my sleeping bag, climbed in without even taking my boots off and fell asleep at once. I must not have moved during the night for, when I rolled out of the blankets and stood up, a big black scorpion came prancing out behind me, tail cocked, pincers aggressively thrust out. Just then, the Colonel emerged from his trench.

'Sir, sir,' I shrilled, 'there's been a scorpion in my bedroll all night!'
'Well, if it's female,' he said, 'you'd better marry it.'
Whenever he and I went on a reconnaissance together, he would give me general directions in a casual voice and then let me get on with it, a refreshing change from his predecessor. Our only problem was that he disliked smoking and I was hooked on the weed. On one occasion, where we were away from battalion HQ for most of the day, picking our way between soft sand patches in a jeep, I found that the packet of Victory V, which I would have sworn was on a shelf in the

jeep, was not there. We drove cautiously along and stopped to use binoculars. I was gasping for a cigarette and told the CO. I should have been suspicious when he nonchalantly produced a packet of Victory V and offered to sell me one for a shilling. I jumped at the offer. At the next halt, the price had doubled, and each time it doubled again. By the time we got back to HQ, I owed the CO £12 16s – over two weeks' pay for a subaltern. Being the man he was, the CO handed me back the half-empty packet of cigarettes, which he had indeed swiped from the jeep, and let me off the debt. I should have forsworn smoking at that moment but, alas for these leathery lungs, the filthy habit was to persist for the next fifty years.

At stand-to one morning, after a welcome lull, the enemy launched a vicious and well-aimed mortar attack. In war, they say you never hear the one that hits you because sound travels slower than the speed of a bullet or a shell. But your ears are assaulted by the screaming rush and the brutal explosion of the one that nearly gets you. And there were such shells, dropping from a great height, that thudded and blasted around us. We cowered at the foot of our trenches, often being shaken by the impact and indeed shaking from the terror that can come when there is nothing positive one can do but merely take the bombardment and pray it will soon stop. I was lying at the bottom of my slit trench with my arms bent and my head resting on my interlaced fingers. The constant din was crushing all thoughts except those of survival. Suddenly I felt a trickle of something on the back of my neck. I half-rolled over and saw that a very near-miss had set off a small avalanche of sand.

After ten minutes that seemed an eternity, the mortar attack ended. We stood up in our various slit trenches, shook ourselves down and started looking for casualties, who were fortunately few. Then the postal clerk arrived from HQ. No letters from home had reached the battalion since the battle began well over a week earlier. Finally, a batch had reached brigade HQ, where 'postie' had collected them. On his way up to the front line he had been caught in the mortar attack but he had managed to find some cover in the open ground and had come through safely.

There was just one airmail letter for me – from my mother. It was short and to the point. I had now become a Master of Arts of the University of Cambridge. In peacetime, the Cambridge graduate has to wait three years before he can step up from Bachelor of Arts to

Master of Arts. He has to dress in subfusc (a dark suit), wear his hood, kneel before and clasp hands with the Vice-Chancellor and pay a fee. In wartime, MAs could be awarded by proxy after waiting the due period paying a fee of £3. My parents, thinking it would be a pleasant surprise, had applied secretly on my behalf.

And it was at least an ironic surprise. I could now walk straight across the broad lawns at Downing College, instead of having to go the long way by keeping to the paths. I was eligible to dine at the high table and cast a vote in College affairs. I was now entitled to have the word 'Esquire' put after my name when an envelope was addressed. And here I was, filthy, with grains of sand in every orifice, my shirt stiff with sweat, lucky to be alive after the vicious bombardment. A Master of Arts, indeed. Somehow, F. R. Leavis and 'the line of wit' and *Scrutiny* seemed very far away.

Many of us who had grown up with General Montgomery, first in XII Corps and then South-Eastern Command, thought he was out of his depth against a battle-hardened opponent with panache like Rommel. As the stalemate persisted into the eighth and ninth day, our private doubts were growing. But then luck or force of arms or military skills or a combination of them began to prevail. The little man, of whom Churchill was later to say, 'Unbeatable in battle and unbearable in victory', was on his way. Under cover of darkness. Rommel began to withdraw his troops in an orderly fashion from the north end of the battle line. In the south, where 44th Division remained, the enemy opposite, mainly the Italian Ariete Division with a few units from the tougher Folgore Division, fled in disorder. Operation Supercharge had begun.

It was a hectic period; unconnected episodes as bright as lantern slides remain in the memory. A squadron of the Free French Brigade was lined up in its Bren carriers at the near edge of a broad minefield. They were too impatient to queue up and move in single file along the path cut through the minefield. So, with the trumpet blast of 'La Marseillaise', they drove in a line straight forward. The explosions were like the bass notes of a giant organ. Some of the carriers drove five yards into the minefield before blowing up, some managed ten, a few fifteen yards. It was a combination of idiocy and bravery to match the charge of the Six Hundred but, as the French general drily remarked then, '*C'est magnifique mais ce n'est pas la guerre.*' In less than a minute the carriers, intended to be a mobile screen for our soft-skinned vehicles, were left lurching and smoking in ruins dotted inside the minefield. The unnecessary casualties had to be evacuated at a risk to the medical staff's lives.

We reached a kind of crossroads where a track running north and south bisected one running east and west. Alongside it was a dump of brown cardboard boxes. And the boxes were crammed with contraceptives, each in its little brown paper packet. What on earth were they doing there? In my own experience and from observation, men in action tens of miles from civilisation, where the nearest female would be a dead she-camel caught in a minefield, find that the urge to survive subsumes the sexual drive. As battalion IO, I had a duty to keep in close touch with all the companies but I never came across or even heard a vague rumour of any homosexual relationships developing up the blue. When the troops saw the heaped up boxes, they laughed, muttered something about 'half his luck' and promptly rolled the french letters over the muzzles of their rifles to keep out the sand.

Later the same day, we suddenly came to understand the purpose of all those contraceptives. Making a sweep northward, I spotted a crashed aircraft in a dip not far from the track. I told my driver to approach it in the jeep – but cautiously. It might be a decoy, with a desperate squad from the Folgore Parachute Division dug in close by, prepared to fight it out on a last-man-last-round basis. But as we approached, it was evident that there was no one outside the aircraft. We could see it had been shot down by the RAF from the row of bullet holes across the front screen and the strips of waxed cloth hanging off the wings. They were marked with the sign of the Red Cross, as was the fuselage on both sides.

'Bit saucy, that blue job pilot,' the driver remarked.

'Take a look inside,' I said.

The stench of death encircled the plane. It must have been there for three or four days and the hot sun beating down on two dozen dead bodies still sitting in their seats, slowly going black in the face as putrefaction set in, had accelerated the process. Apart from the pilot and co-pilot, there were only women on board, young women, several of them with long blonde hair. I saw some strange sights in my six years of military service but this was the most macabre of them all.

It confirmed rumours that had circulated round the Eighth Army for many weeks. This was – or had been – a brothel plane. Under the guise of a Red Cross hospital aircraft, its task was to take prostitutes from Europe, some of them no doubt from the Fatherland itself, to an administrative area behind the front line. A row of tents would be set up and men from the Afrika Korps fighting units would be brought back for a few moments of satisfied desire. And, to guard against venereal diseases, the boxes of contraceptives would be required.

By now, prisoners were becoming a problem. In the north, Rommel withdrew his mainly German troops in good order, always keeping slightly ahead of the pursuing armour. But in the south it was a shambles. As far as we could see, the Italian officers had abandoned their men. Hungry, thirsty, many of them barefoot, they lined the tracks, pleading with us to to take them prisoner and set them up in a nice camp with regular meals and plenty of water. But our orders were to keep pressing north-westwards, gradually moving towards the coastal road. We could not even commandeer their rifles and other weapons, as the jeep and the fifteen-hundredweight truck would bog down under the great weight. All we could do was detach one capable private soldier to lead them back towards divisional rear echelon. One wag lined them up like a drill sergeant, made them march in step and taught them the words and melody of a popular jingoistic song, 'There'll Always Be an England.' The splendid Italian baritones, few of whom had even a smattering of English, lustily sang, each man, no doubt, hoping to create a good impression with his captors.

On the whole, our men behaved well towards them, but there were exceptions. Once, I had halted the column and was busy trying to work out back-bearings on prominent features to discover our exact position on the map. Trying to do too many things at once, I did not concentrate properly on a couple of questions asked by a member of the I section.

'Do you know the Italian for water, sir?'

'*Agua*, I think.'

'And for "watch"?'

'God knows. The French for "clock" is *horloge*. Try *orlogio*.'

I went on with my map calculations and then the penny dropped. I jumped out of the jeep and walked some way down the track. There was my man standing by the trackside as the prisoners shambled by, holding up a *chagul* in one hand. A *chagul* was a bag in shape like a hot water bottle but made of thick calico or webbing. It was filled with water, now more plentiful after the break-out, and hung on the outside of trucks and jeeps. The water very slowly seeped through to the outside and the desert breeze kept the contents cool. He was shouting, 'Agua?' and then, pointing to his wrist with the other hand, 'Orlogio.' He was already doing well from the bartering. Four or five handsome wristwatches were strapped above his left wrist. A watch for a mouthful of cold water – it must have seemed a worthwhile exchange to the thirsty prisoners.

I ordered him to hand them back to their owners, an impossible task, but at least he would not score from the deal. And then I told our new Intelligence sergeant to put him on extra duties for the next week. For years afterwards in peacetime, I would look closely at the pictures of property dealers and asset-strippers in the newspapers, to see if the market enterprise shown by a Buff on that occasion had reaped its due reward.

Our biggest problem was with senior Italian officers, and in particular their generals. We overran one headquarters to find silk-lined tents and the staff from the commander downwards dressed in their best silk uniforms, ablaze with a liquorice allsorts of medals, each with a leather case packed, awaiting capture. One tall imposing general refused to surrender to me, a mere subaltern. He would only hand himself over to an officer of equivalent rank. As he spoke fairly fluent English, I explained that our generals were rather too busy fighting a war to attend to the niceties of military etiquette, so he could either surrender to me and get transport back to civilisation or stay on indefinitely in the desert without food and water. He said he would report me to the Geneva Convention, but I did not stay awake at night worrying. Indeed, where I had been thinking of sending him back in a comparatively comfortable spare jeep, I arranged for the tail gate of a bumpy truck to be lowered and for the bemedalled captive to be shoved without ceremony up into the vehicle, where he had to stand, swaying precariously as it lurched along the ruts of the track.

And so it went on until the CO, who had attended early morning orders at Brigade HQ, returned and took me on one side. He quickly explained that the coastal road, which we were due to reach later that day, was already clogged with too many tanks and trucks. If units bunched up too much on the one narrow road, it could make a field day for the Luftwaffe and its dive-bombing Stukas. So the orders were that the Brigade, which had suffered severe casualties on the opening night of the battle, would be withheld. It would withdraw into reserve outside Alexandria and eventually be broken up. Whatever position we had reached at twelve noon that day would be our furthest move westward. The battalion would then halt, regroup and withdraw into safety. But I was not to pass the information on to anyone at all. The enemy sent over reconnaissance aircraft every day and we must give the impression of a normal advance.

I was more frightened in the next three hours than I had been throughout the war up till then and, looking back, than I was to be ever again. To have come so far without a scratch, to have been blown up twice in one morning, to have had several near misses, it would be just my luck, I felt, if a 'stay behind' desperate group of the enemy were to come bursting out of cover and gun down my jeep. It was, after all, the lead vehicle of the whole battalion. Or maybe they would be crafty and let me through unharmed before tackling the trucks of the main body, knowing they could always pick me off afterwards at their leisure. It would have been more comforting to confide in Daniels or one of the other members of the I section but I had to maintain secrecy.

The minute hand of my watch crept round the circle. Ironically, the expanse of soft sand that had held up our progress on previous days had given way to a flat hard area and the jeep could bowl along at twenty miles an hour and more, pressing further on its journey into fear. The last quarter of an hour was almost unbearable. We had seen nothing untoward all morning, no crashed aircraft or burnt out tanks. And that made the arid landscape all the more sinister. Five minutes to the hour, then two minutes to the hour and at last both hands on my watch stood vertically to attention. I told the driver to halt and turn the jeep round. Surprised, he did so. I stood up and, waving both arms, gave the signal to about turn.

For us, the battle was over.

6

❖❖❖

Strange Episodes

❖◆◆◆❖

There are wars and rumours of wars. And wars beget rumours, ranging from the improbable to the impossible.

In the Great War, there was the Angel of Mons, a vision that supposedly inspired the troops, retreating in a rabble, to turn and fight and eventually win the First Battle of Mons. There was also the repeated rumour that Russian forces had landed in Scotland. Everyone knew that Tsarist Russia in winter was covered in deep snow, especially Siberia, and the soldiers, who were always spotted by someone in the next street, never seen by the teller of the tale, were bound to be Russian because – they had snow on their boots. No matter that it might be high summer in Scotland under a hot sun, there was always the snow on their boots, which proved they must be from Russia.

World War Two had its juicy rumours, particularly in the year following Dunkirk. In the Spring of 1941 I had a short home leave. My father and I had gone to a local pub for a quiet drink and, as it was a relief to get out of battledress, I had changed into civilian clothes. We fell into conversation with a middle-aged stranger, who appeared to be a man of some authority. Glancing round the bar to make sure there were no German spies at the next table or casually polishing glasses behind the counter, he lowered his voice and in a husky whisper told us that Hitler had ordered an exploratory invasion. The plan had been for small fast ships to tow first-line troops in open barges across the Channel to land on the Kent coast and form a bridgehead. Then the German tanks and heavy artillery would be shipped over the narrow strip of sea and landed on the beaches. But, fortunately, Royal Navy destroyers patrolling the English Channel chanced on the slow-moving barges and shot them to ribbons. Our new friend had it from a high placed source – naturally, he could not give away details – that hundreds of German dead had been washed up on the beaches between Margate and Hythe. Hitler had accordingly called off the invasion.

I was then stationed at Manston, two or three miles from Margate. One of our tasks was to patrol those very beaches as far south as Sandwich. The Buffs detachment would have been almost the first to know if any such event had happened. We would have to provide guards over the German dead until Military Intelligence had arranged to collect and search them. I could have told the man he was talking absolute rubbish but said nothing until we got home and I could tell my father the facts.

One or two wartime rumours were started for a reason other than showing off. The story went that a girl rushed into the casualty department of a Scottish hospital, screaming and sobbing. In the act of making love, a man had bitten off one of her nipples. The same thing happened again with another young woman, and yet again. The local police made enquiries and, it emerged, as the rumour went, that a squadron of Free Polish airmen was stationed at a nearby airfield. The police discovered that it was apparently a common practice for the young Poles, when fully aroused, to bite their partners quite savagely.

The story was, of course, complete nonsense. But it had been started for a purpose. When Poland had been defeated by the joint forces of Germany and Soviet Russia, several dozen young airmen, instead of surrendering their aircraft, had flown and fought their way westwards until reaching Scotland. Once there, they were a magnet for the local girls. Young, dashing, with that attractiveness of a broken accent, men who had risked everything in their break for freedom, they were soon assailed by hordes of eager young women. One of the local rejected men must have started the rumour which, like the others, was baseless.

Another yarn, probably started for a similar reason, dealt with the Canadian soldier – it was always a Canadian – who was making love to his English girl friend in a promenade shelter on the Brighton sea-front late at night. Immersed in more senses than one in his pleasurable task, he was quite unaware that a U-boat had surfaced two or three hundred yards offshore and had despatched a rubber dinghy, paddled by two German soldiers with blacked up faces. Carefully avoiding the underwater obstacles and the mines and barbed wire liberally strewn across the shingled beach, they tiptoed up to the shelter, thrust a Luger into the back of the heaving Canadian and escorted him down to the dinghy and back to the U-boat, which returned with its prisoner to Occupied France.

The moral of the story needs no underlining. If you are a nice English girl in the Brighton area – or anywhere else along the South Coast, for that matter, since U-boats could travel quite a distance – don't let a Canadian soldier lure you to a shelter on the promenade late at night. If you are silly enough to do so, you may well discover a new meaning of the adjective '*interruptus*'.

The one I liked best was that of the German paratrooper dressed up as a nun. He had been spotted at various localities along the East Coast from Lincolnshire as far south as Sandwich Bay. His disguise was almost perfect, his face largely hidden under the cowl but there was always one big give-away. He wore heavy ammunition boots with hobnails on the soles. For several months, the story was rife. No one of my acquaintance actually saw the paratrooper but many knew someone who knew someone else who had been in the area when the nun with the heavy boots had been stopped, arrested and literally unfrocked to be revealed as the suspected German spy.

There was a neat variation on this rumour which I almost wish could have proved true. A farmer in Thanet whose fields ran close to the south-eastern shoreline was driving his lorry along the coastal road late one afternoon. Ahead, he saw a nun huddled by the roadside, obviously in real pain. He drew up and offered her a lift. In broken English and in a rather guttural accent, she told him that she had been out for a constitutional with other nuns from the local convent but had been taken ill with severe stomach pains. The others walked on, promising to telephone for a doctor when they got home. They had gone perhaps five minutes earlier.

He said he would give her a lift to catch up with her companions or even to run her right back to the convent if she would give him directions. She thanked him and he helped her into the passenger seat at the front of the lorry. They had only driven a short distance when he happened to look down to his left. There were the dreaded ammunition boots with their thick soles and hobnails. And was that an inch or two of hairy leg between the top of the boot and the nun's habit? Oh Lord, he thought, this man is armed and dangerous. It was growing dusk and they were on a lonely road.

Thinking furiously, he switched off the ignition when the 'nun' was not looking. The lorry coasted to a stop at the side of the road. He asked his passenger to get out and hold up the bonnet while he investigated. As soon as 'she' was out and standing by the roadside, he slammed the bonnet down, leaped back into the driver's seat, switched on the engine and roared off with a clashing of gears.

The next corner was some two hundred yards away. As he drove, he expected to hear the crack-crack of a Luger pistol and a fusillade of bullets whipping past his head. If he was lucky. He drove with his shoulders hunched and his heart pounding. Round the next corner, he came upon a crocodile of nuns, marching briskly and singing a Gregorian chant as they went. Each one of them wore heavy ammunition boots with thick hobnailed soles.

Whether each such rumour was created in the first place by an individual, to be picked up and spread by one gossiper to another, or whether they were a form of collective consciousness that occurred simultaneously must be left to the experts to decide. I can only say that the next two events I describe were actually witnessed by me. They have remained in mind for more than fifty years and, no matter how often I reflect on them, I still cannot present anything approaching a rational explanation.

The first happened in the summer of 1942, when 2nd Battalion the Buffs, having finished its acclimatisation, was, along with the rest of 44th Division, rushed forward to help construct and man the Alamein defensive position. In June Rommel had delivered a crushing blow to the Eighth Army's armoured divisions at the Battle of Knightsbridge and the whole force had come reeling back, hotly pursued by the Afrika Korps. The Alamein line was the narrowest stretch of the desert between the Mediterranean and the impassable Qattara Depression, where tanks would bog down to their axles in the treacherous black ooze. If the Eighth Army failed to hold out at Alamein, the Afrika Korps would come rampaging through the short flattish distance from the defenceless cities of Alexandria and Cairo. If the Suez Canal fell to the enemy, the whole Middle East with its invaluable oil wells in Iraq and Persia would be doomed.

Detachments of Royal Engineers, the sappers, were ordered to lay down the widest possible minefields on the far side of the rudimentary defences. Some of these minefields were three hundred, even four hundred, yards wide. It was necessary to leave the obligatory zigzag paths through them, both as a safe passage for some of the belated units still trickling back from the Knightsbridge defeat and, perhaps optimistically, for the Eighth Army to use when it had regrouped, held off the Afrika Korps, and launched its own attack. When the path was open – it would be wide enough to take a tank with a few feet to spare on either side – stakes would be driven in at intervals, coupled with long tapes to form a kind of avenue. Closing off the minefield took little time. The mother stakes and tapes would be removed and barbed wire spread across the gap at both ends, to link up with the wire already lining the extremities.

There was gunfire in the distance as we reached our designated stretch of front-line desert. The Afrika Korps was closing in fast. I was ordered to take a fifteen-hundredweight truck, two Bren guns and a section from my platoon to drive to the nearside of the minefield and, if necessary, give supporting fire to the sappers who were completing the task of closing off the path in front. Stragglers were still pouring back but several determined troops, mainly from the Afrika Korps's crack 90th Light Infantry Brigade, were known to have commandeered abandoned British trucks and under cover of their markings had infiltrated genuine Eighth Army units.

We were a hundred yards or so short of our objective when we heard the crump-thump of a high-explosive shell landing not far ahead. When we arrived, there was a young bare-headed and fair-haired sapper officer lying dead. He was the only one caught out in the open. His men had been on the far side of their truck, which had taken most of the blast and the shell splinters. It was a write-off but at least it had saved their lives. They were naturally very shaken. I told them they could come back on our truck when the job was done and meanwhile I told my driver to park our truck under cover in a small *wadi* close by.

The orders were to hold the position until twelve noon, even though the sappers had already finished closing off the minefield. Noon arrived and we were on the point of packing up when one of the Bren gunners gave a shout. There on the far side of the minefield was a truck with British markings. Was it a late straggler or were there 90th Light desperadoes lurking in the back? I told the men to be extra alert and watched through my field glasses.

To our growing amazement, the front passenger – in British khaki – jumped out, went over to the barbed wire and removed the strip securing the path through the minefield. Then very slowly, at no more than walking pace, the truck drove in. It followed exactly the meandering path, zigging when it zigged and zagging when it zagged. Always at the same slow pace. Finally, after perhaps five minutes, which seemed like an age, it arrived. On its approach and seeing it was a friendly vehicle, I had instructed a couple of my fellows to remove the barbed wire that closed off the minefield at our end.

'How the hell did you get through there?' I asked the driver, a sergeant. 'You could have been blown up any minute.'

'It was that young officer, sir,' he said. 'That young one with the fair hair. He showed us where the track had been closed off and then walked ahead of us. Every time we came to an angle, he showed us which way it went. He was the one.'

He glanced around and saw the body of the dead officer on the ground. We had not had time to put him in the back of our truck, covered by a groundsheet.

'Christ!' said the sergeant. 'That's him. But what's he doing, dead over there?'

'He was killed about twenty minutes ago,' I said. 'Long before you reached the far side of the minefield.'

Payne , a dark-haired, sallow young man in his early twenties, had been my batman ever since I joined 2nd Battalion the Buffs. He was quiet, self-possessed, seemingly older than his years.

A few weeks after the previous episode at the minefield's edge, we had finished our frantic digging of defences among the rocky outcrops that became the Alamein line with its slit trenches and gun emplacements. It was an irregular line that followed the ins and out of the ridges with their supposed commanding heights, forty or fifty feet, perhaps, above sea level. Rommel made one abortive attempt to break through the southern, our, sector of the line in September but then for the next five or six weeks a stalemate arrived. The enemy front might be only a few hundred yards away. On a still night, you could hear a chorus of 'Lili Marlene' or the grinding of a panzer tank's bogeys.

But the brass hated the front line troops to be inactive. 'Bad for morale, what?' a general might mutter, as he sat in his shady caravan a few miles back from the sharp end, sipping his pink gin. 'How about a bit of straightening the line? That'll keep 'em on their toes.'

In practice, straightening the line meant that if the Alamein front caved inwards by perhaps quarter of a mile and the enemy occupied a stretch of high ground opposite, the British infantry were to attack and in their turn occupy that high ground. The Western Desert is, generally speaking, flattish and over the centuries the wind will have heaped up sandbanks and carved out *wadis*, long, usually narrow, valleys. One hundred feet would be quite a commanding height. On this occasion, the 2nd Royal Sussex was to make the initial attack, supported by artillery and mortars. 2nd Buffs would be in close support and would attack in a second wave if the opening assault failed. In any case, at dusk, the Royal Sussex would be withdrawn and the Buffs take over, to be relieved in turn at last light the following evening.

The fighting was fierce; the Royal Sussex received many casualties but they drove the Folgore Division, the Italian airborne division sent forward as reinforcements, off the small ridge. As it grew dark, we shuffled up the reverse slope and relieved our weary comrades, who had fought a good fight. There was nothing now for us to do in the next twenty-four hours but keep an eye out for counter-attacks – unlikely – and keep our heads well down in case of enemy shelling and mortaring. Many of us infantrymen felt we were more likely to be hit by inaccurate shelling from our own gunners.

At dawn stand-to next morning, as Intelligence officer, I walked or crawled round the leading companies to check things for myself before reporting back to my colonel. Company-Sergeant-Major Ben Hogben popped his head up from his slit trench and beckoned to me. Red-faced, cross-eyed, he never missed a point; a regular soldier with the best part of twenty years' service behind him and a Dunkirk veteran, he was the kind of calm, tough individual on which every army relies. Looking back, I would like to think we were mates.

'I'm worried about that batman of yours,' he said. 'He's telling all the lads he's going to be killed today. We've got enough problems, I reckon, without him blowing off that way?'

'You had a word with him, sar'nt-major?'

'Yessir. I took him away from the others and had a quiet chat. But all he said was, 'I'm gonna be killed today.' Nothing dramatic, you know. Just matter of fact – like he was saying it's gonna be a fine day.'

'Do you think it might help if I tried to talk him out of it?'

'Would you, sir? It might work.'

There was a conveniently abandoned Italian sangar nearby and in the dawn light I sat there with Payne for a quiet chat among the sand bags.

'What is all this?' I asked.

'I'm going to be killed today, sir,' he replied. It was a matter of fact statement, no melodramatics. As Ben Hogben had said, he might have been commenting on the weather. His face was composed into its usual polite but reserved mask.

'That's rubbish,' I said. 'Sorry, I'm not trying to hurt your feelings.

But, one time or another, we all get gloomy thoughts. And it never happens.'

I went on in that vein for a few minutes, pointing out that he and his mates were well dug in. As long as they kept their heads down, the chances of a direct hit were one in a thousand. Less than that, in fact. I would be up there with him and any shell that got him would get me, too. And I wasn't reckoning on being killed today, no way.

But all he would say was, 'I know you're trying to help me, sir – and I appreciate it. But I can't make you understand. I'm going to be killed today.'

By now I could well see what CSM Hogben had been hinting. If Private Payne kept on like that, he would soon get on the nerves of his friends and make them a bit shaky. He was so courteously adamant over his fate. I conferred again with the sergeant-major. A runner was due to report back to Battalion HQ at B Echelon and I decided to send Payne back with him. B Echelon was the military name for the soft-skinned transport and the quartermaster's stores of ammunition, petrol, spare equipment and pairs of boots. It was sited the best part of a mile to the rear, as safe an area as I could think of.

That problem solved, I completed my tour of the companies and reported to the colonel, who insisted on remaining forward with his troops. There was nothing for him or anyone else, for that matter, to do. We just had to stay put. The enemy pounded our positions with artillery and mortars off and on during the day but we kept well down in our slit trenches – 'cowered' might be an apt description – while the screaming of shells and the earth-shaking blast of their landing continued. But gradually the day passed and late in the afternoon we were relieved by another battalion of the Royal Sussex. I did a hasty check. There had been no casualties, apart from one soldier with a scalded wrist. Against orders, he had been brewing up in his trench. A mortar bomb had landed a few feet away; the blast so shook him that he spilled the boiling water over his other hand.

It was dark when I got back to B Echelon. As Battalion IO, I was part of the CO's forward HQ and he, like the admiral on board a sinking ship, wanted to be the last to leave the battleground. The first man I bumped into back in the rear area was Captain Ransley, the quartermaster.

'Pity about your batman, he said.

'What the hell do you mean?'

'Oh, didn't anyone tell you? Happened this morning. He was

coming back from the latrines over there and a single shell landed about fifty yards away. It was an Eye-tie overshoot, the only shell we had all day. A splinter hit young Payne clean in the heart. He wouldn't have known a thing. You'll need a drink and some grub but later on this evening I'll let you have his things. You'll want to write to his mother.'

'Anyone else hurt, Q?'

'Not a scratch. Apart from that one incident, it was peace and quiet all day.'

Which had left me wondering. Had I inadvertently ordered Private Payne to his death by sending him back to B Echelon? Or, if he had stayed forward with the rest of the troops, would a splinter from a solitary shell have got him all the same? The question still haunts me over fifty years later.

7

✦✦✦

Arabian Days

✦✦✦✦✦✦✦

In reserve, several miles west of Alexandria on the coast, the battalion spent a few weeks refitting and absorbing an intake of fresh reinforcements. D Company had suffered worst in the fighting and in the previous Alam Halfa battle. Over a hundred men had been killed or severely wounded – one in eight of the battalion strength. And the rest of us could do with a break, a rest from dawn stand-to, being shelled and mortared, fighting back to gain a few yards here and there, night patrols, uneasy sleep.

There was little to occupy the Intelligence section. When the MO, Captain Shragovitch, had finished his morning surgery, he and I would stroll through the sand dunes to the beach and swim out five or six hundred yards in the calm Mediterranean, still warm in early December. Then, with his odd sense of medical humour, he would roll over and float on his back, reminding me that the sinking of HMS *Barham*, a year earlier, had for the first time brought sharks into the inland sea. And they were supposed to be working their way eastwards in the direction of Alex and the Nile delta. Was that a black fin cruising over there or just a trick of the light? My return to the shore was quicker than the outward swim.

I had been about fourteen stone when disembarking from the troopship almost half a year before. The physical activity, the continual high daytime temperatures, with too low an intake of liquids to replace the unceasing sweating, the nervous energy needed to keep alert and alive, all these had reduced me to a spare and hard twelve stone when we came out of action. But a daily intake of cream cakes from Pastroudi's, the best confectionery shop in the city, plenty of beer and scotch quickly replaced the all too solid flesh. Never again was I to approach the fitness I briefly knew at the age of twenty-five.

The Army high command seemed to have a knack of waiting till a unit was nicely dug in at one location and then moving it abruptly elsewhere. We were suddenly informed that 44th Division was to be broken up and that 2nd Buffs as an individual battalion was to travel to Aleppo in Syria, spend a few weeks there and then move a thousand miles east to become the British battalion in one of the brigades of 6th Indian Infantry Division. Thus began a slow railway journey with stops and starts and hours spent shunted into a siding while other traffic took precedence. Four times we had to change our money – from Egyptian piastres into Palestine pounds into Lebanese francs and finally into Syrian dinars. And every time astute money-changers took their cut: and more.

Aleppo was a bustling city, largely untouched by the war, with a vast *soukh* through whose alleyways you could come across nimble-fingered merchants heating silver wire over a small furnace and beating and bending it into intricate filigree patterns. Everywhere, there were carpet sellers displaying rolls of Persian and Damascus carpets. The bargaining was slow motion, quite unsuited to Western impatience. You had to squat down while the vendor poured you a small cup of black, overly sweet and grainy coffee and then undergo the drawn out haggling. Most of the merchants spoke French as well as their native Arabic and my schoolboy French soon became fairly fluent. The weather was raw and cold; many of us bought *poshtins*, sheepskin coats where the fleece was on the inside. They looked quite dashing but none of us realised that the skins had not been properly cured. Within weeks, they began to smell of old socks and the fleeces fell out in large tufts. By then, we were many hundreds of miles away from Aleppo without chance of redress.

We were not told before the move from Egypt but apparently the Buffs were to act as a reconnaissance battalion not far from the Turco–Syrian border. Although Rommel had by now withdrawn the Afrika Korps into Tunisia and the immediate danger to the Middle East was halted, Hitler's armies north of the Mediterranean were pressing close to Turkey. That country had remained strictly neutral to date but if it were by internal wish or external pressure come to in on the German side, there could be a sudden invasion of Syria. The oilfields of Kirkuk in northern Iraq were temptingly close.

So one morning Colonel Percival and I began a swan round our territory. We drove north in a jeep and then struck east, then south, in a circular swing. On the eastward leg, one village along the route straddled the frontier. Everything north of a broad white line that bisected the macadam road was Turkish; everything to the south Syrian. The villagers who lived on the north were just as Arab as their brethren who lived across the road. I was driving and the Colonel and I were wondering to each other what would happen in a Romeo and Juliet situation, where a young man from north of the street fell in love with a girl from the other side. My attention must have wandered and the offside wheels of the jeep strayed across the broad white line at one corner. At once, between our heads, there was that whipcracking report of a bullet's trajectory and, a split second later, the sound of a rifle firing. On the parapet of one of the larger houses, a Turkish sentry in a drab uniform was lowering his rifle. He had fired at us for infringing sovereign territory. Whether it was a warning shot or aimed to kill we did not hang around to discover.

Hours later, as dusk was falling, we stopped at a small Syrian village to seek permission to spend the night. We knew about their code of hospitality and, in the role of honoured guests, we would be immune from harm or theft. Camping for the night outside the village could have been a very different option. The sheikh greeted us in French almost as rusty as my own but he gravely invited us to dine with him and showed us to a barn with straw in one corner where we could sleep in our valises.

He was a dignified old man with a thin face, grooved from years of struggle, and a straggly white beard. In our honour he said, there would be a special delicacy for supper, something they had saved up for years until sufficiently worthy guests arrived. *Corné de boeuf.* And, sure enough, with great reverence, he produced two rusty old tins of corned beef. Considering that for many months, apart from the brief stops in Alexandria and Aleppo, the Colonel and I had lived on bully beef and biscuits exclusively, the gratitude we showed for this rare treat would have qualified for an Oscar.

After the meal, the sheikh lit up his hookah, his hubble-bubble pipe. Luckily, he did not follow the usual custom of passing the stained mouthpiece around for his guests to have a suck. He had a bubbling cough, which to my non-medical mind could have spelled tuberculosis. But slowly and with increasing passion he told us about the greatest event in his life. It was in 1917, when his father had been sheikh of the village and he, the eldest son, a young man in his twenties. 'El Aurens' had come to the village and spent the night there on his way to the final victory at Damascus. He had gathered the elders – and the present sheikh as his father's potential successor – around the campfire and had talked to them for hours in Arabic that was not only fluent but *au fait* with the local dialect. He had told them the enemy would be crushed and the great Ottoman empire, which had oppressed them for centuries, would dissolve and disappear. From now on, they would have justice and fair dealing under the British. Alas for T. E. Lawrence. He was right about the forthcoming victory at Damascus but he sadly underestimated, even though he was to be a participant, the results of the Treaty of Versailles, brought about by greedy and conniving politicians.

Lawrence's personality, his deep understanding of and love for the Arab peoples, were not to be forgotten in that small remote village. Early in 1941, when fighting against the British was imminent, the Vichy French, who still controlled Syria and the Lebanon, issued an edict. All firearms were to be surrendered at once to the authorities. Anyone found hiding a firearm would be summarily executed. The villagers collected together their ancient muskets and one or two shotguns, tied them in a bundle and lowered them to the bottom of a dry well. They knew that the British would come one day. After all, 'El Aurens' was British. The Colonel and I were the first representatives from the British Army to visit them since the Vichy French were sent packing, the sheikh said gravely. He had the old guns and rifles pulled up from the well and offered them to us as a token of friendship. They were useless and probably more dangerous to the one firing than the one aimed at. Colonel Percival made a speech in his fractured French, accepting them '*avec tous les mercis de l'armée de Grande Bretagne*' and then handing them back again as a further token of His Majesty's faith in and gratitude for the support of the Syrian villagers. The honours were equal.

Before we left that morning, the sheikh had one more surprise to spring. 'El Aurens' had spent one night in the dilapidated two-bedroom house belonging to the present sheikh's father. We were shown up the rickety staircase and into the bedroom itself. Nothing had been moved or changed in the twenty-five or so years since then. The bedclothes were flung back, just as Lawrence had left them. You could see the crease in the rather greyish undersheet where his body had lain and even the dent in the pillow his head had made. An ordinary, rather seedy little room: but it was a shrine to a great man they had loved.

That afternoon we crossed into the northern corner of Trans-Jordan. We knew from the marked up map that there was an outpost of the Trans-Jordan Frontier Force, later made internationally known by Glubb Pasha, in the area and that several British officers were stationed there. It seemed like a good place for a wash and brush up. We were on the third day of living rough and Colonel Percival, that battle-hardened veteran decorated for bravery, had as his motto, 'Any damn fool can be uncomfortable.' So we made tracks for the outpost.

It was as if we had stepped back ten years into the stables of the Belvoir or Beaufort Hunts. There was a yard with a dozen or more fine Arab horses tethered. The officers' mess was a long low bungalow with broad plate glass windows. Inside young men in jodhpurs lounged in deep armchairs. A whippet or two, the mess pets, gambolled around. A major arrived as we did. Our scruffy battledress made a sad contrast to his shining top-boots, jingling bright spurs and his smart cutaway cavalry jacket. He unbuckled his Sam Browne belt – it was strictly against the code of conduct to wear a Sam Browne in the mess – and, after hanging it, along with his equally shiny leather pistol holster on a convenient hanger, greeted us quite cordially. I say 'quite' because, even in wartime, there was always a feeling that the cavalry – *la chevallerie* – looked down on the poor bloody foot-sloggers.

After a shower, we enjoyed a glass of malt – none of your blended whisky – with them, amid the copies of *Country Life* and *The Field*, with the whippets nuzzling our fingers for titbits. We heard a strange tale. Around 1936, there was a substantial part of the regular British Army stationed in Palestine. Mussolini had invaded Libya and the Italian Air Force had bombed Ethiopia. The situation had been tense. Up to that time, cavalry regiments were still horsed but, fifteen years too late, the War Office decided that modern warfare would be mechanised. It would require tanks, not horses. So the Hussars and the Lancers and the Dragoons would exchange the scent of new mown hay for the smell of an oily rag. It was too much for several of the more orthodox young officers. *En bloc*, they resigned their commissions and joined the Trans-Jordan Frontier Force, which was still wedded to four-legged warfare. In 1939 and 1940, particularly when the Western Desert fighting began, some of them changed their minds again, resigned from the TJFF and joined the Eighth Army. But the diehards, a few still in their twenties, remained faithful to their chargers. Apparently, they spent a strange and somewhat uneventful life, an occasional patrol along the frontier – on horseback, of course –

hunting the gazelle across the broad plains, pig-sticking, the occasional gymkhana; a sterile existence.

The Buffs had had their traditional Christmas in Aleppo, when the officers served the men their Christmas dinner amid much joshing. That evening, again by tradition, the officers were invited to the sergeants' mess. On arrival, each one removed his service dress jacket and added it to the heap on a nearby table. He then went to another table, where the RSM, the various company-sergeant-majors and the plain sergeants had left their battledress tops. Shutting his eyes, he would grab one and put it on. The CO might end up as an ordinary sergeant and the sergeant find himself a major for the night. The beer flowed like Niagara and soon we would all be singing lustily,

> I don't want to join the Army
> I don't want to go to war,
> I'd rather hang around Piccadilly underground,
> Living on the earnings of a high-born lady . . .

or

> My love has for a soldier gone
> Away across the deep blue sea.
> I often thinks and writes to 'im,
> 'E never thinks nor writes to me . . .

or one of my favourites,

> Oh, the eagles they fly high in Mobile,
> Oh, the eagles they fly high in Mobile,
> Oh, the eagles they fly high
> And they shit right in your eye,
> I'm so glad the cows can't fly
> In Mobile.

After the sergeants' mess party, a few of us, hardy enough to have retrieved our own jackets, went for a nightcap at a club on the hill overlooking Aleppo. In the dim light we could see it was almost empty. The sole occupant of the bar was a much decorated and very drunk RAF officer. He was drinking *arak,* that potent drink that looks like plain water but which turns milky if a few drops of water are added. The RAF man put back his head, to drain the last drop, then bit a large chunk from the rim of the glass, chewed it thoroughly and swallowed it with the help of a gulp from the water jug. Then he bit out another

The Battalion HQ Section, Aleppo. Christmas Day 1942. I am seated second from left. Pte Daniels is on the left of the four seated on the ground

Brewing up on the way to Rowanduz

chunk and chewed it in turn; and so on until he had reached the solid base.

I was horrified and suddenly sober, expecting any minute to see a thin trickle of blood coursing down from the side of his mouth. He must have seen the look of horror on my face; he paused and, gazing at us, bleary-eyed, said, 'You shee, it'sh all in the chewing. You gotta chew it very small. Then it goesh through your gut like shit off a shovel.'

It was a dramatic end to what was to be my first and last Christmas with 2nd Battalion the Buffs.

In mid-January 1943, we were on the move again, a drive of nearly one thousand miles, first to Damascus, then across Iraq to Baghdad, to end up in the Zagros Mountains on the borders of Iraq and Persia. We were to drive Eighth Army-style, twenty miles per hour, fifty yards between vehicles, a ten-minute halt every two hours. There was only one snag. Our vehicles were still in their desert trim. The first thing the fitters did when a brand new truck was handed over would be to remove the windscreen. The reflection made by glaring sunlight on clean glass would produce an excellent target for the Afrika Korps. In winter, the weather is very cold in the high plains of Syria and Iraq and a biting east wind blowing straight, hour after hour, into faces unprotected by a windscreen and moving at some speed into the wind, makes faces numb and eyes water. Add in the effect of starting early in the morning and driving for hour after hour into the glare of a low hanging sun and the torment is almost complete. 'Almost' because the monotony was the final factor. The tarmac road from Rutbah Wells to Baghdad ran straight as a ruler for six hundred miles. Driving at a speed that does not occupy the full attention, eyes screwed up against the wind and the glare of the sun, merely keeping the truck or the jeep dead straight for mile after mile after mile – even the toughest will doze off sooner or later and will only be jerked awake when the nearside wheels slide off the smooth tarmac and judder against the bumpy sand alongside.

We were to be the British battalion in a brigade of 6th Indian Division. 4th Indian Division had fought with great distinction in the Desert and, particularly, on Ruweisat Ridge when the Eighth Army at last checked Rommel's advance. 5th Indian Division had been training in Iraq and was on the point of leaving for eventual action in Italy, along with 56th (London) Division. 6th Indian had seen no action thus far. Brigaded with 1st/1st Gurkhas and a battalion of the Punjab

Rifles, we were supposed to pass on our experience of warfare.

The division was stationed a few miles inside Iran, east of the border town of Khanaqin, on the edge of the saw-toothed Zagros Mountains. There was a foot of snow on the ground when we arrived and we were largely confined to our tents but, when we were not carrying out some futile military exercise, spring found us scrambling up one ridge, then down into the dead ground behind it, then upwards again to the next higher ridge. Gazelles leapt delicately from rock to rock and the troops often carried a ·303 rifle to pot at – and always miss – the elusive prey. Once Shrag and I had trekked to the top of one ridge with much puffing and blowing; we sat astride the ridge, trying to get our breath back. We were chatting and our faces were perhaps three feet apart. Suddenly, there was that well known whipcracking sound as the passage of a bullet split the air. Automatically, we rolled over the ridge into the dead ground behind.

'That was a near one,' Shrag said. 'Right past my nose.'

'Correction,' I said. 'Right past *my* nose.'

'They must've thought I was a gazelle,' he said.

'Anyone mistaking you for a gazelle would have grounds for discharge – lack of vision in both eyes. More like a comment on your medical skills, doctor.'

We never discovered the culprit and indeed made no effort to find out. Captain Shragovitch was popular with all ranks and a first-rate MO. That someone might possibly have a score to settle with me has only now crossed my mind.

During the early training months, there was little call for the Intelligence section to use its supposed expertise. We were sent to check the security arrangements of a large ordnance depot south of Baghdad. It was close to Habbaniyah, the RAF base, but contained only Army stores; small arms ammunition, shells, rifles and Bren guns and a large pile of motorcar tyres. It was clearly important that rifles and ammunition should not fall into the hands of Rashid Ali's supporters or other pro-German Iraqis. But the main target were the civilian-type car tyres. The Baghdad taxi drivers had worn the original tyres on their cabs down to the canvas and had had to 're-sole' them with strips of rubber sliced from the sidewalls of other tyres. We were told that on the black market in Baghdad, a new tyre would fetch £75 (over £1,500 in today's terms). A new carburettor would fetch £100.

On the whole, the security arrangements were pretty effective. The depot formed a rough square with a wire fence running round it and double dannert coils of wire alongside. Sentries were posted high up on look-outs at each corner. A growth of thick scrub, which might provide good cover, lay all too close to the perimeter fence on one side and I suggested it should be cleared back for at least fifty yards. After walking round the outside of the depot a few times, I discovered a potential blind spot in the sentry layout and suggested a new guard site at night.

I reported to the Royal Army Ordnance Corps captain in charge of the depot. He was in his early thirties, glib and a little too accommodating – 'Yes, of course, whatever you say.' In my experience of the Army up till then, any stranger of junior rank coming into your well-ordered life and telling you to change this and alter that should expect a cool, if not antagonistic, reception. Naturally, I was pleased he seemed to accept all my recommendations – but it made me feel slightly uneasy.

Two nights later I was woken by the shouting of many voices and the flashing of lights. I tugged my clothes on and ran to the scene. A neat but narrow gap had been cut in the perimeter fence. Several of the RAOC staff were milling around and the depot commander was shouting orders. As I came running up, he said, 'Christ, there's been a break-in. A squad of my chaps are after them but it's hopeless in the dark. Hell's teeth, they've stolen seventy-eight tyres, twenty-one boxes of ·303 ammo and a dozen carburettors.'

Funny, I thought. Surely, it would take hours, particularly at night, to check the exact number of items stolen? But this break-in had happened ten minutes before. And it would take at least an hour for thieves to shift so many bulky objects through the narrow gap without rousing the camp.

A major loss of this nature swiftly brought the SIB (Special Investigation Branch) of the Military Police on to the scene. I was one of the first to be interviewed by a broad-shouldered man with a cropped head of ginger hair and small, suspicious eyes. I had to state my unease which was endorsed when the SIB carried out a thorough inventory check and found that, yes, exactly seventy-eight tyres, twenty-one boxes of ammunition and twelve carburettors were missing. They subjected the depot commander to intensive questioning. He stuck to his fanciful story for a while but at last broke down and confessed. For weeks and months, he had quietly been flogging a few tyres here, a few boxes of ammo there, to local black marketeers. Only cursory checks on the depot stocks were made by his seniors, brief visits to the desert from their Baghdad comfort. After paying off his sergeant-major, who was his accomplice, he had a pleasant addition to his Army pay and even better prospects ahead.

Then, out of the blue, his HQ ordered an external review of all stocks held by the depot, to be carried out a week later. He knew all too well that the stocks held could not match the inventory. So he had to fix a bogus break-in by nomadic tribesmen. Even then, he might have got away with it, had he not blurted out the exact figures of missing items. He was court-martialled and given three years' hard labour in an Army prison camp outside Basra.

About a year later, I became a temporary MA (military assistant) to Lieutenant-General Baillon, who was about to carry out an inspection tour of Southern Iraq and Persia. One of our stops was at the prison camp. I spotted the ex-RAOC officer, who had wangled himself a soft job in the kitchens, and while my general was talking to the senior prison officials, I had a chat with the man. After a few passing-the-time remarks, I said, 'Look, there's one thing I've never understood. You strike me as pretty bright and quick on the draw. Why for God's sake try such an obvious bit of theft? You were bound to be caught once there was an official stocktaking. A smart fellow like you could be strolling around, free as a bell, right now.'

He grinned. 'You never understand, you public school types. The war's gonna last another couple of years – who knows? You're just as much in jail as I am. You're stuck here, until they send you back into action and get your balls shot off. You can't even leave the command without official permission. That's not prison? Difference is. I made £45,000, a fortune, out of flogging that gear. And it's all safely tucked away in different bank accounts in my wife's name. My sentence over, they'll give me a dishonourable discharge and I shan't have to wait until my demob number comes up. After the war, there'll be big pickings on the black market, property deals, the lot. You'll be looking for an honest job, *I'll* be handing 'em out!'

As I walked back to rejoin my general, I thought what I did not have the nerve to say to him. Let's hope, with all that money in her name, your wife is still waiting for you when you get out.

A story of grim endeavour, extreme privation, irresistible pride and patriotism and unbreakable determination that has never been fully told is the foundation of the Polish Corps. Stalin effectively demobilised the Polish forces that had fought against him until squeezed by the advancing Germans from the west by the Katyn Forest massacres. Virtually every fit officer of fighting years was lined up on the edge of the vast open graves and shot in the back of the head. But that still left the NCOs and other ranks, their womenfolk and children, and old men and women who had been taken prisoner in the early days. Even a sadist of Stain's dimensions could hardly kill all those thousands. He knew they hated Russians even more than the German enemy; they would be a festering sore as long as they were cooped up on Soviet soil. Besides, even on starvation rations, they would be reducing vital foodstocks. So he set up his own version of the Long March. All the Polish captives, the old folk and babies in arms amongst them, were rounded up and set marching. Over many months, through the driving rain, blizzards in winter, the scorching sun in summer, they walked perhaps three thousand miles, across mountain passes and open desert, all down the length of the Caucasus, into Iran and along the edge of the Zagros Mountains, through Hamadan, Kermanshah, the Pai-tak Pass, Khanaqin, coming to rest at last on the plains south of Kirkuk. There, the British and Indian Armies rallied round, treating the sick, feeding the emaciated survivors and fitting them out with new uniforms. The re-formed Polish Corps eventually performed with great gallantry in the Italian campaign, notably at the Battle of Monte Cassino. Battle-hardened troops of the New Zealand Division lined the tracks and wept openly as truck after truck, loaded high with the Polish dead, drove slowly back from the battlefield. Before it is too late and the last of them have gone, someone with greater eloquence than mine should research and write the full story.

By the summer of 1943, the Poles had been trained in the British Army's way and were ready to carry out a full-scale military exercise. Colonel Percival sent me along as a junior umpire, with the special task of looking into their Intelligence methods under active service conditions. An exercise can never properly simulate the conditions of real war. In those days, the firing of live ammunition was strictly banned; faked bangs were never the same thing.

At a suitable point in the 'battle', an umpire was supposed to ask the local commander, 'What is your object?'

The correct answer was, 'My object is to capture that hill with the bushy-top tree alongside' or 'My object is to provide a diversion, so C Company can do a flanking movement.' I asked one Polish captain,

'What is your object?' He looked me in the eye and said coldly, 'Kill Germans.' I thought, I'm glad we're on the same side.

Before the exercise started, I did a reconnaissance trip by jeep across the rolling plains north of Kirkuk to Erbil and back again. Erbil then was – it probably still is – the oldest permanently inhabited town in the world. For many thousands of years, as the buildings of one civilisation crumbled and fell, the newcomers built their homes on the ruins of their predecessors, creating an artificial hill rising from the plain. It looked like a muddy brown, misshapen wedding cake, with bits plastered on at all angles.

Private Hoskins was driving the jeep as we worked our way south again. Cresting a small slope, we saw a darkish lake about a hundred yards wide rippling in the light breeze. I told him tó pull up and I took a close look at the map. 'This is weird,' I said. 'Not supposed to be a lake there. And no sign of a river that might have flooded. Drive on slowly, will you.'

As the jeep drew close, we saw it was not a lake but a swarm of locusts. They were on the ground astride the track and, as we approached, they took off. The air did literally go dark as several million locusts in close proximity took off over our heads. They were smashing themselves to death on the jeep's windscreen and the wheels slipped and skidded on the juices they were crushing from hundreds and thousands still on the ground. Half a dozen flew in and landed on my battledress jacket – twice the size of grasshoppers, horny and thicker in legs and body. A hundred yards on, we were clear and the sky had lightened again. But there were still two or three locusts in the footwell of the jeep to be crushed by the boot. In peacetime, I had glibly used phrases like 'the forces of nature'. Now I had encountered that force and disturbing it was.

Even with your eyes shut, you always knew when you were approaching Kirkuk. There was that all-pervasive stench of oil. Apart from the deep set wells, there was a surface area a mile or more wide which was almost marshy, although surrounded by desert. Oil deposits leaked up to the surface and were deliberately set fire to. At night, you could sit in the oil company's club, sipping a good whisky and watching the bluish flames, a foot or more high, dancing across the immediate horizon. I was told that it was the origin of the 'burning fiery furnace' and the way Shadrach, Meshach and Abednego proved their faith in their God. At one stage earlier in the war, when the

Germans might possibly invade and the Luftwaffe send long-range bombers against the oil installations, the KPC (Kirkuk Petroleum Company) was ordered to dowse the flames. The story went that they then indented for thousands of aspirins to cure the headaches arising from the permanent oil fumes.

A month later, in high summer, I was back again north of Kirkuk, this time accompanied by the I section in a fifteen-hundredweight truck. There had been rumours of unrest among the Kurdish tribes north and east of Rowanduz, a deep gorge leading into the mountains. Like most hilltribes, the Kurds seemed a short-tempered lot. If they weren't raiding the plainsmen's property, they were knocking hell out of one another. Back in the 'thirties, the RAF used to make bombing raids to quell their ardour. On one occasion, it was said, an aircraft got hit by small arms fire – the Kurds were crack shots – and the pilot had to bail out. He happened to have flaming red hair which, in Kurdish beliefs, meant that he was either a god or descended from the gods. So his captivity consisted of servicing every woman of child-bearing age in the tribe. What must have seemed a splendid bonus to start with soon became a dreaded chore and, they say, it was sad to behold the quivering pilot, shielding his eyes whenever a woman hove into sight, when he was finally released.

The I section was ordered to reconnoitre ground leading up to Rowanduz, check for concealed approaches, obstacles, lines of fire – the usual drill before a battalion or a brigade advances. The local Kurds were reported to be withdrawn far into their mountain retreat; we could approach to the edge of the gorge but not enter it. The track was narrow and bumpy with loose stones and boulders to negotiate and the sun blazed down out of a hard sky. To our right, a steep slope led to the mountain and away to our left a precipice of rock stretched up to the distant skyline. In between was a tributary of the River Euphrates, about thirty yards wide. In spring, it would have been a rushing torrent as the melted snows from the mountains added to its tumbling waters. Now it was a dried-out river bed, with mounds of shingle and small bushes springing up from the alluvial earth. Alongside the banks in permanent shadow there were narrow pools, a few feet wide and twenty or thirty feet long. We were all sweating and uncomfortable, cramped from hours of sitting in the swaying, bumpy truck. I proposed a halt and a bathe.

The men piled arms, then tore off their clothes and climbed down the bank into the ice-cold refreshing water. We each had a small Army-issue towel but, of course, no costumes. Towels were almost unnecessary because five minutes' exposure to the sunlit air would easily dry our bodies.

We were splashing about, laughing and joking, when there was a loud rumbling noise from the top of the slope. Then half a dozen or so fierce looking men in caftans and turbans came sliding and clattering down, their ponies almost back on their haunches from the angle of descent. They slid to a halt on the track and their leader sprang down from his pony. They were a villainous-looking bunch, with swarthy faces, long moustaches and luxuriant beards. Huge curved knives in their scabbards were stuck in the sashes around their waists and several had ornately chased muskets slung on their backs. And they had stopped between us and our piled rifles.

To be defenceless in the face of the enemy is bad enough. To be naked and defenceless is terrible. I scrambled out of the pool, dripping on the dusty track, and tried to wrap myself into decency with the meagre towel. All the while, I was recalling what Arab womenfolk were thought to do to prisoners. In fact, a pre-war schoolfriend of mine, who joined the Palestine Police on leaving school, was captured in an ambush by the Mufti of Jerusalem's followers. Their women cut off his penis and testicles while he was still alive, stuffed them in his mouth and then sewed his lips together. I have never felt more frightened.

Their leading Kurd, a youngish man, gave me a wolfish grin. He was wearing leather boots and with one pointed toe he marked a strange kind of cross in the dust of the track. Then he spat on the sign and said, 'Fokkitler.' This must be some kind of invocation, I thought, before they kill us. A quick death was preferable to captivity and torture. He redrew the cross with bits hanging off it, spat again, looked at me and said, 'Fokkitler.' The penny suddenly dropped. I grinned back at him, spat on the symbol and shouted 'Fuck Hitler!' He grinned yet again, came close and held my upper arm for a moment, then sprang back on his pony and led his men up the slope and out of sight. We had met a friend in the wilds of Rowanduz.

It was even hotter when we reached the plains on our way back. Finding a large pool beside a bridge, we undressed again and had another bathe, watched by a morose-looking Arab leaning against the bridge. I had clean forgotten that exposing the body is a sin for strict Muslims. If one of them wanted to wash in the Sea of Galilee or the Mediterranean coast, he would stand in shallow water in his top robe and baggy under breeches, soaping himself secretly.

A few weeks later, GHQ PAIFORCE issued a directive, ordering that the officer who had been reported bathing in the nude with his men at such-and-such a map reference on that particular day was to see his commanding officer without delay and confess. It was an easily ignored invitation. If GHQ couldn't find out from their own resources, why enlighten their ignorance? One evening Colonel Percival came over to me in the mess and bought me a drink.

He asked casually, 'You were in that part of the world right then, weren't you, George? See any keen swimmers around?'

'Not me, sir.'

'Funny. There can't be all that number of white officers with just a small detachment knocking around there. Anyway, George, you wouldn't be such a fool as to swim naked and upset our local friends – I hope.'

'Absolutely not, sir.'

'Damned idiots, these GHQ types. They put out a directive and expect the culprit to own up. Just like that. No imagination, that's the problem. Why, it'd be a case of double-exposure, what?'

8

◆◆◆

Capital Punishment

◆◆◆◆◆◆

When the Ottoman Empire collapsed at the end of the Great War, two of the three victors rubbed their hands and seized on the pickings. Woodrow Wilson, the American President, wanted no part in empire-building but Clemenceau and Lloyd George had no such qualms. Besides, they argued, without a firm ruling hand, the individual parts of the ramshackle rule would fall prey to internal strife and further aggression. So Great Britain took under its mandate what were to become Jordan and Iraq – Palestine was already a mandated territory – while France confined its influence to Syria and the Lebanon.

By the late spring of 1941, no sane person would have laid a bet on Germany's losing the war. My mother may have announced with glee, 'We're in the final now!' (after being machine gunned on her allotment). But it seemed to have become a one-sided game the following year. The Afrika Korps was advancing in the Western Desert, Greece had fallen and after a stout defence led by General Freyberg of New Zealand, Crete too had fallen to superior numbers and the first ever use of paratroops in a military action.

To add to the major problems crowding in on General Wavell, Commander in Chief of Middle East Forces, on 2nd April 1941, there was a *coup d'état* in Iraq and Rashid Ali became prime minister. He was known to be a supporter of Hitler. The British-run Kirkuk Petroleum Company (KPC) had a pipeline leading through to the Palestine coast, which had to be kept open to fuel the Royal Navy. German forces controlled the north-eastern Mediterranean and Turkey was a wobbly neutral. If the Turks, who had fought against the Allies in the Great War, threw their lot in with the apparent conqueror, and with a favourable government in Iraq, Hitler's forces could walk into Iraq, take over the oilfields and threaten India from the Persian Gulf.

Thus, with only few spare troops under command, Wavell was forced to move swiftly and decisively. A column of mechanised cavalry, infantry and mobile gunners raced across the six hundred miles of desert, relieved Habbaniyah, the headquarters of the RAF, and restored the British Ambassador to his pre-eminent role. Rashid Ali and his supporters were arrested, Nuri Pasha, known to favour Britain, became Prime Minister and the revolt ended on 30th May. Somerset de Chair, who took part in the daring raid, summed it up vividly and stylishly in his book, *The Golden Carpet.*

Iran presented similar problems to those of its neighbour. Reza Shah, an officer in the Turkish cavalry, had seized power a decade earlier, and had gripped the country in a regime of ruthless despotism. His dealings with the nomadic Bakhtiari and Quashgai tribes from the south of Iran were typical. Their chiefs were restless and rebellious; he ordered them to attend meetings in Tehran. They refused to walk into the lion's den until he swore a holy oath on the Koran that he would not hurt a hair of their heads. Reassured, they went to Tehran. Reza Shah had them all hanged without trial. When taxed with the barbaric breaking of his oath, he laughed and pointed out that indeed hanging had not hurt the hairs on their heads.

But this time he tangled with a more powerful foe when he declared himself and his country in favour of Hitler. The danger to Britain and the Commonwealth was even greater than the Rashid Ali revolt in Iraq. The oil wells of Ibadan in southern Iran produced far more oil than those of Kirkuk; whoever controlled Iran controlled the Persian Gulf and the Indian Ocean. On 25th May 1941, British troops entered Iran via the Pai-tak Pass and Kermanshah, where other fertile oil wells abounded, and drove on to Tehran. The Russians, not yet forced into becoming allies through the Wehrmacht's invasion, marched into Iran from the north. Four months later, Reza Shah abdicated and spent the rest of his days as an exile in Madagascar. His young son, the last of the Shahs, took his place, firmly under the tutelage of the British military and diplomats. He was a proud and sensitive young man. Being treated as a lesser breed by a series of sometimes well-meaning British tutors and being confined to a regal palace and a thin show of authority, but knowing all the time that he was a virtual prisoner in command of nothing except a few obsequious courtiers, later made him virulently anti-British and pro-American, encouraging Mossadeq, his post-war prime minister, to nationalise the Iranian oil industry, a bad financial and industrial blow to the United Kingdom. But that, as they say, is another story.

With two febrile oil-producing nations now under command, it was essential to establish a separate independent GHQ as the control centre, with a sufficiency of front-line troops to offset any threats to the overall security. Although still preoccupied with the Afrika Korps' advances in the Western Desert and salvaging what men and equipment could be brought away from Crete by the Royal Navy and all the time sensing Churchill's growing and impatient dislike of his efforts, General Wavell dropped everything else and flew from Cairo to Baghdad. He was driven to the major centres, including the oilfields, and then on the eve of his hurried return to Cairo, sat down and wrote out his operational instructions. Over three years later, when research-ing the history of the Command, I came across Wavell's original orders, written in his neat, small handwriting, in an old file. They were a model of accurate forecasting and crisp, clear proposals, with not a wasted word. From then until the end of hostilities, the Persia and Iraq Command (PAIC or PAIFORCE) was run according to the great man's guidelines.

For he was a great man. A general with a taste for literature – his poetry anthology, *Other Men's Flowers,* had a deserved and enduring success – and with a keen sense of humour to keep him modest, he fought a skilful but necessarily defensive series of actions against an enemy with far superior tanks, artillery and numbers of troops. Later, as Viceroy of India, he once remarked, 'When I give a command, one hundred thousand men spring to attention. But do you think I can get my daughters down to breakfast on time?' He resigned as Viceroy when he realised the new post-war Labour government was rushing to abdicate its authority over the Indian sub-continent, realising all too correctly the bloodshed, pillage and murder that would result. The way was left clear for the bombastic Mountbatten to preside over the carnage.

The summer of 1943 saw 2nd Battalion the Buffs camped on the side of a Persian mountain, a mile or two north of the oil-town, Kermanshah. We were brigaded with the Gurkhas and our supposed task was to defend the oil installations against enemy attack. Kermanshah was just about in range of a Luftwaffe bomber squadron operating out of Greece but it would have to be a one-way only flight. Air to air refuelling had not yet become feasible and no long-range

German bomber could manage an unaided return flight. So the chances of an air attack were virtually nil. By the same token, land-based forces would either have to invade neutral Turkey and advance nearly a thousand miles across largely barren territory or drive down through the Caucasus, bypass or capture Tehran and cross the sawtooth mountain ranges to reach their target. There could have been few safer zones in the now global war.

And we were bored. After a few weeks, I was beginning to understand that strange complaint, *le cafard*, that attacked Foreign Legionnaires in remote desert camps. To give us a change from the monotony of physical training, the brigade thought up unit challenges. A company from the Buffs would challenge a company of the Gurkhas to see which would be the first to rush up to the top of a nearby peak and then get back to base. Naturally, the Gurkhas, most of whom came from mountain villages like Khumjung and Namche Bazar, always won. We could ascend as quickly as them but in the descent they leaped from crag to crag, like the mountain gazelles that frequented the Zagros range.

The town of Kermanshah was out of bounds to the troops and socialising with the 'oily boys' as we arrogantly called them, the senior staff at the oil installations, was often tedious. We had so little in common. They were adept at pumping oil from the depths of the earth, we were supposedly adept at fighting and killing the enemy. The outlooks and attitudes were miles apart. So the whole battalion spent several nights a week playing 'House' – or 'Housey-Housey' as we called it. The old Army game, rechristened 'Bingo', has become a commercial success.

It was quite a sight. Eight hundred men sitting out on the lower slopes of the mountain, clutching paper and pencil and marking off the numbers as they were called out. The CO reckoned I had the loudest voice in the battalion and so I was usually nominated as caller. We had no microphones or electrical boosters. Even in the clear, high air, you had to have a good pair of lungs and a tough hard palate to make yourself understood at perhaps a hundred yards' range. I can still remember most of the jargon: 'Nelson's eye – number 1!'; 'a pair of ducks – 22!'; 'never been kissed – sweet 17!'; 'legs eleven' and so forth. Every few minutes, there would be a roar from eight hundred excited throats – 'And shake that bag!'

The only other excitement in our first two months there was when a mini-tornado, what we called a sand devil from desert days, came swirling through the camp like a moving twisted pillar of dust and dirt. It wrenched a couple of tents out of their taut ropes, like a dentist pulling a tooth, and hit the corner of the cook hut, sending a sheet of corrugated iron some six feet long spinning through the murky air. Unfortunately, one of the troops happened to be walking past the cook hut when the typhoon tore through the camp. The edge of the corrugated iron slashed his head and he died instantly: a tragic and ironic end for a young man who had gone through months of desert warfare without a scratch.

Major Derek Norris, who had left the battalion when we first arrived in Iraq and had joined GHQ staff, happened to be passing through Kermanshah on duty and paid us a visit. He and I had been good friends and he singled me out for a stroll up the mountain side in the cool, thin air. He said that the SD (staff duties) department at GHQ was looking out for junior officers to make up numbers. If I was interested, he would gladly put my name forward, subject to the CO's approval. I did not hesitate for long. As battalion Intelligence officer, I had little to do, as we were now well out of action. My only chance of promotion to captain would be as adjutant and that post was firmly occupied by Ian Percival (later to become Sir Ian Percival, QC, MP, Solicitor-General in Margaret Thatcher's government). He was was no relation of the CO but was a couple of years younger than me and all too fit and healthy. So I took a deep breath, thanked Derek warmly and agreed to apply.

I remembered a short conversation with the Regimental Sergeant-Major a few days earlier. To help the troops pass the time, a brigade tug-of-war competition had been arranged and every unit entered a team. As one of the heaviest Buffs, I found myself in the battalion eight. The RSM was our coach. With sore hands and stomach muscles as rigid as tramlines, we hauled on the rope while the RSM, crouching like a sumo wrestler, grunted ''Eave, 'eave!'

He was built like a sumo wrestler as well and would have been a prime asset to us tuggers. Once, after a bout when I had got my breath back, I asked him, 'Mr. Martin, why don't you join the team? We could use a strong man like you.'

'No, sir,' he said promptly. 'I know my place, sir. *I* grunt, *you* 'eave.'

As my days with the battalion were running out after more than two years service, I felt there had been enough heaving. Now it would be my turn to grunt.

The commanding officer backed my application, a signal came

through from GHQ about a week later calling me forward to become General Staff Officer Grade III (GSO 3 for short) with the rank of acting captain. There was a riotous farewell party in the mess and, nursing my aching head as I was driven with all my belongings in the back of a fifteen-hundredweight truck down through the tortuous Pai-tak Pass to a transit camp in the border town of Khanaqin, I left 2nd Battalion the Buffs for ever. Two months later, they would be shipped from Basra to India to fight with some distinction in the Burma campaign.

As with so many Middle Eastern cities, Beirut, Cairo, Alexandria and Tehran, Baghdad was a mixture of great opulence and abysmal poverty. The Semiramis Hotel with its marble floors and pillars and its well-stocked bar presided over by an adept barman named Jesus, ('Hey, Jesus, another pink gin over here!') was the acme of luxury. From the wide windows of the bar, looking out over the oily brown Tigris, several hundred yards wide, you could quite often see a dead donkey floating downstream, its stiff legs sticking up like small periscopes. At night, crossing the broad sweep of King Faisal Bridge, you might pass at intervals half a dozen bundles of rags that turned out to be destitute beggars snatching what sleep they could on the granite pavements. There were areas of great squalor, stinking alleys down which no individual Briton would dare wander, and areas of great luxury. There were few motor taxis, their tyres patched and re-patched, but everywhere the clatter and rattle of horse-drawn carriages or *gharris*. The average British soldier learned only two words of Arabic: *iggurri-iggurri* (Go on, faster) and *asti* (enough, stop) but most of the cab-drivers had picked up a few words of English. (*Shufti* and *bint* had long been absorbed into the language spoken by the military.)

Alec Waugh, Evelyn's elder brother and himself a notable novelist, was an Army major attached to the RAF in a supposedly hush-hush top secret operation. He had a small villa on the east bank of the Tigris and was a generous host. You only had to climb into a *gharri*, say to the driver in a loud voice 'Waugh – very secret' and the driver would give a wide grin, shake the reins and go clip-clopping straight off to the forbidden rendezvous.

There was a commercial cinema in Al Rashid Street, the main thoroughfare, if that is the correct description for a smelly, noisy, teeming street with *gharris* contending with vegetable stalls, beggars thrusting out wizened or often mutilated hands for *bakshish* and veiled women, only their dark eyes glowing above the *chador*. The Army roared with laughter throughout the week when MGM's *The Thief of Baghdad* was showing. To see the cloud-capped towers, the gorgeous palaces, and the air of sanitised fantasy in glorious Technicolour and then to emerge in daylight to see and smell the reality was indeed worth a detour.

But a feeling of the British Raj was not far away. In the wooded north-west suburbs of the city was the Alwiyah Club with its swimming pool, its tennis courts, its squash courts and its terrace where immaculate white-clad waiters would bring another drink at the snap of the colonial fingers. There were, as I recall, just a few polyglot Baghdadi men who were members of the Club and one brave Armenian girl, Sharqi Topalian, who even swam in the pool in a fairly modest costume. The ascetic male Shia Muslims – and even the more broad-church Sunnis – would never have dreamed of revealing their bodies in public and, as for their womenfolk, to do so would be a capital offence.

I had not played squash since my Cambridge days, three of four years earlier, when at various times I was number five in the university team, and I now seized the opportunity with alacrity. A hard game in the coldest Cambridge winter, when the biting east wind blew straight from the Urals, would work up a real sweat. Even ambling around the Alwiyah Club lawns on a summer afternoon when the temperature was over 100° could make the sweat stand out on cheeks and chin and trickle down between the shoulder blades; charging to and fro in a closed court brought out a formidable lather. Only a cold shower afterwards, followed by a succession of iced drinks, could bring the body heat back towards normal.

One of my regular opponents was the Second Secretary at the British Embassy, Hubert Freese-Pennefather. An amiable Old Etonian, he used to converse with his servant through hand-gestures and pidgin English. This struck me as odd and I said, 'Here you are, in an important diplomatic position in a major Arab country. Surely, you ought to speak Arabic?'

'Good God, no!' he replied. 'Get fluent in Arabic and you're stuck in these dreary hell-holes for the rest of your career. Lebanon's none too bad but this place or Oman and the Trucial Coast states, Kuwait – Christ! – or, for God's sake, Saudi Arabia – it'd be a lifetime of misery. All right for these old Persian Gulfers like Sir Percy Cox or my chief, who knew Allenby and Lawrence in the old days. No, when I get to be a first secretary, I want Paris or Rome. Washington would be acceptable, what? Places where there's a bit of life and civilised people speak the old Anglo-Saxon tongue, don't you know.'

I often wondered in after-years whether British diplomats' failure to learn Arabic or Farsi when *en poste* in Tehran contributed to the insurrection in the 'fifties by Saddam Hussein's Ba'ath party and the brutal murder of the young King Feisal and the Prince Regent or to Iran's nationalisation of the British-run and mainly financed oil installations in the same era. Or is it finicky to expect diplomats to learn something of a nation's traditions and expectations by also learning its language?

There were two halves to Baghdad, divided by the broad Tigris. On the west bank, the teeming city with its hotels, its cinemas and its brothels, dirt and overcrowding but always a pulsating energy: on the east bank a few rows of small villas and beyond them the fairly tranquil suburbs. Palm trees lined the streets. In late September and October, you could reach up and pick a few sticky ripe dates from a low branch and eat them as you strolled. The roads were wide, there were lawns and many of the big houses had been requisitioned as military offices and messes. The GHQ Operations building was typical. It had three stories with stone staircases and iron banisters. (Wood rots quickly in tropical conditions.) On the ground floor, half a dozen sergeant clerks hammered away on military typewriters or filed the never-ending sheets of paper that moved slowly round the building. There were, of course, no photocopying machines in those days but there was an ancient contraption by which an order could be typed without using a ribbon on to a kind of waxed sheet. If you put a blank piece of paper underneath, when the typing was completed, and applied a roller smeared with a black pitch-like sticky liquid, the words came out on the blank paper. At least, that was the theory.

There were three captains, the lowest of the low, tucked into spare corners on the ground floor. Next floor up, there were two majors, each in his separate room. Major Hope, a regular officer in the Royal Artillery, was naturally known as Bob. A sandy-haired, foxy creature, he was always sneering at the 'temporary officers and gentlemen' who lacked the good fortune to belong to the regular Army. He also had an Ancient Briton sense of humour. The father of one captain had been involved in a notorious City trial pre-war and had been sentenced to a long term of imprisonment. Bob Hope's idea of a joke was to bellow, 'Hands on your pockets, chaps – here comes Cecil', every time the young captain entered a room. It was about as funny as malaria the first time round and only grew more rancid with repetition.

The other major was a complete contrast. William Fox of the Royal Irish Fusiliers had been a rising actor when the war broke out. He had played the juvenile lead, as it was then called, in several West End and Old Vic productions and he was married to Patricia Hilliard, herself a promising young actress. Many British actors either skulked in Hollywood like James Mason or went into roving troupes entertaining the Forces or, like Laurence Olivier, accepted a nominal commission in the Royal Navy but spent the war acting on stage or screen. Bill Fox did it the hard way. He had seen action in North Africa and had had a strenuous war. Handsome, usually with a twinkle in his eye, he possessed a wit and easy humour that made him an ideal companion for the lonely and the miserable – which all of us, with too much time on our hands, all too often became. There were rare occasions when Bill himself was gloomy, knowing that many of his contemporaries were using the war to better their acting careers and reputations and wondering whether, when peace finally broke out, he would ever get back into competition with them. Alas, the six years he spent in 'hot stations' did jeopardise his prospects. Apart from one or two short runs on the stage and some television appearances in secondary roles, he never achieved the status as an actor that his talents and his patriotism deserved.

And finally, on the second floor of our building in solitary eminence Lieutenant-Colonel Woodhouse had his office. He was a runt of a man, white-haired though only in his early fifties, with a querulous voice. A regular officer who must have been at least a major when war broke out, he should almost four years later have been a brigadier or a major-general. Perhaps his mean-minded negative attitude had been to blame or that splendid Army phrase to explain why someone had been passed over for promotion – 'His face didn't fit.' Being under five and a half feet in height, he was known all round GHQ as Colonel Shorthouse – a military bowdlerising for 'short arse'. There was a dance step at the time which Danny Kaye had popularised known as the Shorty George and Bill Fox re-christened him accordingly. 'Shorty wants you urgently' – the word would go round the ground floor and one of us captains knew he was in for an oral death of a thousand cuts.

Professor Parkinson was right. Work *does* expand to fill the time available for its completion. GHQ PAIFORCE would have made an apt study for him. If you set up perhaps a dozen departments and sub-divide them as necessary, Operations, Intelligence, Staff Duties, Signals, Legal, Transport, Ordnance, Supplies, Welfare and so forth, then staff them with several hundred officers and clerks, provide stacks of paper, typewriters and telephones, they will be so busy communi-cating with one another and sending copies of letters to perhaps half a dozen other departments that may be vaguely concerned that they soon forget there is a war on and its object is to defeat the enemy. PAIFORCE was at that time a quiet haven for training troops or for divisions in transit to or from India and there might be as many as fifty thousand men spread around the vast territory, apart from those doing guard duty at oil installations. Their presence required a controlling headquarters – but the headquarters could have gone on existing happily without the presence of troops outside.

On one occasion, the War Cabinet in Whitehall decided that too many fit young officers were tucked away in sedentary staff jobs when they should have been on really active service. Churchill's son-in-law, Duncan Sandys, was selected to visit Cairo and Baghdad to flush out the malingerers. His good looks were matched by his lack of brains and his sole claim to one form of fame is that he was the 'headless man' in that notorious photograph of the then Duchess of Argyll heading for disaster, one might say, in her divorce case.

He was no match for the crafty Colonel Ryan, commanding GHQ Intelligence, who had an inventive mind and an Irish gift of the gab. Ryan installed an enormous map of Iraq and Persia on one wall of his room and had it covered with red and blue arrows. The Kurds were fighting amongst themselves in the remote mountain range north of Rowanduz but that was the Kurdish equivalent to running a football league. Otherwise, tranquillity reigned. But Colonel Ryan's map resembled the savage hand-to-hand fighting between the German and Russian forces in and around Stalingrad. The red arrows denoting the enemy swooped towards the heart of the command. Hostile Kurds, it seemed, were massing on the borders, poised to rip through the placid countryside and seize Baghdad. In the Zagros Mountains menacing Qum and even Tehran itself lurked hordes of German agents, inciting the local tribes to rise and advance on the cities. Only the gallant Colonel Ryan and his loyal subordinates apparently stood between the command and total disaster.

While Sandys was asking him inept questions, which the Colonel smothered in a flow of Irish broguery, junior officers would come panting into the room, excuse their presence and then erase one or two arrows from the map, substituting for them even redder and more threatening symbols. When one of them saluted smartly and then ran from the room on his next urgent quest, another would steal in brandishing a TOP SECRET MOST URGENT signal. The Colonel apologised to his august guest, explained that the matter could not wait and then gave crisp orders to his junior. When they were alone again, he would turn to the inquisitor, give a deprecating smile and say 'Forgive me, sir.' And then with a shrug, 'Just a typical day, I'm afraid. But I suppose duty takes precedence over good manners, sir.'

It was a clever manoeuvre, impeccably carried out. And it worked. Instead of recommending that G Intelligence should be reduced to a man and a boy, which would have been ample to carry out its almost non-existent duties, Sandys proposed that the staff should be substantially increased, as the present incumbents were clearly under severe pressure of work; and that the commanding officer of the department should be promoted from full colonel to brigadier. Churchill's loyalty to his son and to one of his son-in-laws (Vic Oliver, the comedian, was not a popular member of the family) was a real detriment to the war effort.

'Know anything about law, George?' Bill Fox asked me one morning.

'Not much, thanks.'

'Well, now's your chance. We have to supply the junior officer for a court-martial – and you're it. You've got to be at the JAG (Judge Advocate General's) department at eleven hundred hours. In service dress. You'd better double back and get changed now.'

'Oh Christ, do I have to?' I asked. 'How about Bruce or Cecil?'

'You disobey an order, young man, and you could find yourself on the wrong side of that court-martial table.' His amused tone belied the threat. I stopped shuffling papers and walked to my room in the nearby mess, where I changed into service dress and Sam Browne leather belt.

I was a strict believer in the Army code – 'Never volunteer' – but secretly I was quite interested to discover how a court-martial functioned from the justice-dispensing side. During my months with the 70th (Young Soldiers) Battalion, I had on a couple of occasions acted as 'prisoner's friend', a non-lawyer junior officer trying to defend the accused. Indeed, once when appearing for Private Pang, a ruffian

123

of Chinese descent who had drawn a knife in a brawl with a comrade, I managed to get him off by arguing that (a) for a Chinaman a knife was just as natural a means of defence as a pair of fists would be for a true-blue Englishman and that (b) it was only a kitchen knife. In the Army, bullshit does occasionally baffle brains. I did not draw to the court's attention the fact that Pang had taken a harmless kitchen knife, had ground the blunt end into a needle-sharp point and had honed one side into a razor edge.

At the JAG's department, I was shown into a large room with a raised platform, a long bare table and three chairs behind it. There was a row of seats in the body of the hall, about five yards back from the edge of the platform and in the vacant space two desks set perhaps ten feet apart with chairs behind them. I was invited to have a cup of coffee in the anteroom where I met my fellow judges, a brigadier from one of the infantry divisions; resplendent with his red tabs and highly polished sword, and a major from one of the GHQ departments. Also present was a senior member of the JAG's office, who had been a barrister in private life. He was there to advise us on the finer points of military law and to ensure that justice was seen to be done.

Because it was, I learned, a serious charge. Murder. As Iraq was then mandated territory, anyone in the Forces who committed a civil crime was not handed over to the civil authority but tried by a military court. We assembled in the hall, the Brigadier unstrapped his sheathed sword and placed it on the table as symbol of our power to act as judges, the accused was smartly marched in and stood to attention facing us as the charge was read out.

He was a havildar (sergeant) in the Sikh battalion that was part of 6th Indian Division. A fine-looking man, he stood there in his neatly furled turban and his starched lightweight uniform, his face composed and almost serene. The facts were straightforward and indeed he had wanted to plead Guilty until being advised not to do so by the JAG's representative. Sikhs are splendid fighters and their battalions in 4th Indian Division had covered themselves with glory in the Western Desert campaigns. But when their soldiers had no battles to concentrate their minds, they tended to indulge in intrigues, we learned, and even eternal triangles could develop among otherwise heterosexual troops.

Our havildar was alleged to have had a boy friend in his battalion, an attractive young fellow. All went well with their love affair until the havildar-major spotted the youth and pulled rank to seduce him away from his first lover. Our man's jealous rage seethed until he could hold back no longer. One night he stole to the havildar-major's tent and caught him in the act of love with the boy. Sikhs, it seems, always carry a knife as one of the five items that make up their religion. The havildar whipped out his knife, pulled the couple apart, sliced off the havildar-major's still erect penis and then plunged the blade into his heart. He died almost at once. The young soldier was saved, perhaps because his one-time partner still loved him. (The brown member, no longer proudly upright but reclining in a jar of spirits, was Exhibit A and remained on a side table before our mesmerised gaze throughout the sultry summer day.)

An interpreter, a British officer with long service in the Sikh Regiment, had to be used, as the defendant's knowledge of English was confined to the usual words of command. The proceedings were fairly straightforward. There were two main witnesses from the regiment, one another havildar and the other a private soldier, who had been roused by the commotion and who saw the defendant leaving the havildar-major's tent, still clutching the blood-stained knife and with blood stains on his shirt sleeve. Entering the tent, they had found the havildar-major lying in a heap, dying, and the young soldier huddled in a corner, screaming with terror. The defending officer tried hard in cross-examination but he could not whittle away such concrete evidence.

In these supposedly more enlightened times, a skilful barrister can sometimes get a sentence of murder reduced to one of manslaughter, if he can prove to the satisfaction of the court that the perpetrator was driven by spontaneous rage, derived from intense provocation, to carry out the act. But to the Manual of Military Law fifty years ago, things were far simpler, more cut and dried. If you killed someone who was not an enemy in battle, the only possible verdict was 'Guilty of murder'. All three of us were loath to pronounce it and we tried to argue with the Judge Advocate General's representative, but he was courteously adamant. The law was the law: the fact that the accused had broken it had been proved to our satisfaction. There was regrettably only one course open to us. Even then, the Brigadier, as the most senior officer of the court, insisted that the three of us should without further discussion or argument write our separate verdicts down on a piece of paper. The verdict had to be unanimous and I think he secretly hoped to find an odd ball among the remaining two of us.

But it was not to be. When the slips of paper were unfolded, each of us had written down the one word 'Guilty'. We replaced our caps and the Sikh havildar was marched back in for sentencing. He stood there, his shoulders square and his features as serene and composed as ever. The brigadier read out the verdict in short phrases, allowing time for the interpreter to translate as he went along. The verdict of the court was 'Guilty of murder' and the sentence – death by firing squad. I noticed that the brigadier's face had gone red as he pronounced the verdict and sentence; I could feel my own cheeks flushing with the gravity of the moment. The havildar bowed gravely and then gave a smart salute. There was not a flicker of emotion on that handsome face. His handcuffs were put on again and he was marched out to await his fate for the next few days.

A small problem arose. By military law and tradition soldiers cannot be ordered to make up numbers for a firing squad. It would be slightly awkward if a press-ganged squad deliberately aimed off in their volley and left the target unharmed. Thus, only volunteers could take part, but no British soldier in the GHQ general area would step forward. I learned that the old myth whereby one rifle in the firing squad is loaded with a blank round but none of the squad knows the exact rifle and so can afterwards console himself that he might not have fired a killing round is just a complete myth with no substance whatsoever. As anyone experienced enough in rifle shooting to take part in a firing squad would realise, if he stopped to think. There is a great difference between the force of recoil of a live round and that of a blank. Each of the squad members would know at once whether he had fired a live round or a blank.

The 1st/1st Gurkhas were offered an extra day's pay to volunteer and apparently every private in the battalion stepped forward. The havildar had been granted the opportunity of appealing against the sentence but declined to do so. The execution was set for a week hence at the GHQ 25-yard firing range. Before then, I was told that, as junior officer in the court-martial, it was my duty to attend on the grounds, presumably, of ensuring that justice was seen to be done.

Under British Army firing squad regulations, which of course no longer apply, an officer from the battalion supplying the firing squad has to be present to get his troops in position, see that each is supplied with one round of ammunition to be inserted straight into the breech of the rifle and then give the orders, 'Take aim. Fire!' And, if the target is wounded but not killed outright by the volley, it is that officer's gruesome duty to deliver the *coup de grace* by going forward and firing his revolver at close range into the guilty man's head until he can safely be declared dead. That was not my function at the execution, fortunately. I was only there on a watching brief.

But the memory of that spectacle will never leave me: the rickety wooden chair placed in front of the earthworks at the end of the firing range; the way two military policemen hustled the havildar forward and strapped him into the chair; he was in a prison suit but still wearing a neatly coiled saffron-coloured Sikh turban; how he shook his head impatiently when they tried to fit a sack-like hood over it; he wanted to look death in the eye like a proper soldier; and the cold-blooded way they pinned an ordinary range target to his chest.

The Gurkha officer gave the words of command in a slightly quavering falsetto. The volley rang out, the havildar's body, still bound to the chair, crashed over and down with the force of the impact and, as the wisps of smoke and smell of cordite hung on the stale air inside the range, I realised that the young officer would not have to perform the *coup de grace*. The Sikh was dead before his body hit the ground. The squad had done their stuff with zeal.

Up till then, I had been vaguely in favour of capital punishment, I suppose. An eye for an eye and all that. On the whole, pre-war, Britons had not been a very murderous bunch. Indeed, many such crimes resulted from maintaining public moral standards. Doctor Crippen would never have murdered his wife had he lived at this end of the century. He would have moved out, waited the due time and sought a divorce on the grounds of irretrievable breakdown. And society would not have blamed him. I had never really thought through the awfulness of having to put someone to death at a pre-determined time as society's revenge. Attending that firing squad in Baghdad certainly concentrated the mind, if in an opposite way to Doctor Johnson's declaration.

When 'Lord Haw-Haw' was hanged shortly after the war, I felt it was done through a technical legal fudge. The man was an Irish republican, strongly opposed to Britain and its way of life, who had never made use of his British passport. Again, the famous – or infamous – case of Derek Bentley, presided over by that notorious hanging judge, Lord Chief Justice Goddard, made me feel sick. Because the main culprit, who actually fired the shot that killed the policeman could not be tried on grounds of age, his accomplice, Bentley, weak-willed and weak-witted, became the focus for legal revenge and was duly hanged. There were also several cases of wrongful conviction occurring in the years before capital punishment was erased from the statute book in 1965. When the true facts were known, it was too late to bring them back from the quicklime in which their executed bodies had rotted.

Some five years after the end of the war, I was a guest at a public dinner when Lord Chief Justice Goddard was the main speaker. A tiny little man with poached egg eyes and a parrot's beak of a nose, he was then about seventy-three but he continued his hanging and flogging attitudes in office until his eighties. The climax of his speech was thus. As a young judge in the inter-war years, his first ever murder trial was held at Winchester Assizes. Three men who had burgled a house – one of whom had killed the householder when he tried to resist – were jointly and severally charged with murder. The Winchester court apparently is close to a main thoroughfare and the court usher had to go outside and stop an organ-grinder from playing his instrument too loudly. The jury found the three defendants guilty at the end of the proceedings and there came the ominous hushed moment when the (then) Mr Justice Goddard had to don the black cap and pronounce the awful words, 'You will be taken from here to a place of execution and there be hanged by the neck until you are dead. And may God have mercy on your souls.'

Just then, our speaker said with relish, the organ-grinder started up again outside the court, playing the Eton Boating Song, 'We'll all swing together'. There were a few nervous titters but the body of the audience sat there in appalled silence. The most senior judge in the land, we felt, ought to respect life and treat the taking away of life with some dignity, not make a cheap joke of it

'That'll teach the old bastard a lesson,' I said to my host as we came away from the dinner. 'That finale went down like a lead balloon. He'll never use it again.'

But I seriously underestimated Lord Goddard's thickness of hide. About a month later, I happened to be at a literary dinner where again he was the guest of – if one may use the word in this context – honour. And again he ended his after-dinner speech with the same anecdote about the organ-grinder. And again it was received, although by a quite different audience, in appalled silence.

But who judges the judges, especially when at the top of the legal tree?

In 1965 the Murder (Abolition of the Death Penalty) Act was

passed by Parliament. It stated that 'No person shall suffer death for murder' and substituted life imprisonment. As there had been much controversy and heated argument leading up to the passing of the Act, it was set to expire in 1970, unless prolonged by both Houses of Parliament. The death penalty was finally abolished in 1969 by assent of both Houses.

The ex-Lord Chief Justice had a timely death in May 1971 in his ninety-fourth year. A long-term sadist like him, knowing that the black cap and sick jokes about the Eton Boating Song were now part of history, must have died of a broken heart.

9

◆◆◆

A Glimpse of the Great

◆◆◆◆◆◆

The Tehran Conference began with a fiasco and ended with a birthday fiesta. Of the horse-trading or, rather, trading in men's lives, that was conducted between times, statesmen and generals better qualified than I am have written at length. These are just the personal observations of one who chanced to be there on the fringe of the proceedings.

The fiasco occurred at GHQ, Baghdad. The duty officer in the Ops Branch on that particular night was Major Bob Hope, he who was always lecturing the temporary officers and gentlemen on their shortcomings. He was woken in the middle of the night by a dispatch rider from the Royal Signals who bore a sealed envelope. Bob scribbled his name on the receipt slip and, still half-asleep, shoved the envelope, unopened, on to the desk at his bedside. By accident, he pushed it under a blotting pad and promptly fell asleep again, forgetting the whole incident. Two days later, a junior officer happened to move the blotter and there to his horror saw the sealed envelope – marked MOST IMMEDIATE, TOP SECRET, PERSONAL TO SMITH FROM FORMER NAVAL PERSON. ('Smith' was Lieutenant-General Sir Arthur Smith, GOC Persia and Iraq. 'Former Naval Person' was, of course, Winston Churchill himself.) The message was a warning order, so we learned later, that for the first time in the war, the three Allied leaders were to meet in person at Tehran. Destiny had to wait on a sleepy duty officer.

But all of us at GHQ Baghdad knew by then that something was up. Odd things were happening in and over that quiet backwater of the war. A squadron of Spitfires had flown from Cairo, refuelled at Habbaniya in Iraq, and flown on in a north-easterly direction. (We heard afterwards that Stalin had refused to go to Tehran unless the British could guarantee air cover against a marauding German bomber force on a suicide mission.) One of the prominent chefs attached to GHQ Middle East and his retinue of junior cooks had flown from Cairo to 'somewhere north-east'. (Memo to spies: don't worry about the movements of a VIP. Wherever his chef, his valet or his chauffeur go, the great man will not be far behind.)

But a careful cover plan had been evolved for the rank and file. Early one morning, two other junior staff officers and I were ordered to pack our camp kit, draw field rations and report to the airfield within two hours. Destination unknown. We were issued with Palestinian pounds, Syrian dinars, Egyptian piastres and Persian rials, in dirty little bundles of used notes. The sceptical theory was that Turkey had suddenly entered the war – this on the grounds that the all-seeing General Staff would be sure to hand out all the local currencies except the one essential kind. But the Dakota we boarded flew north-east across the alluvial plains and along that bumpy, wingtip-scraping route through the Persian mountain passes. The target could only be Tehran.

It was the most exotic of Middle East capitals. Set 6,000 feet above sea level, with the conical snow-capped Mount Demavend soaring to nearly three times that height as a permanent backdrop, the very air of Tehran has the thin, sharp taste of old wine. Reza Shah, once a cavalryman in the Turkish Army and then the despot who snatched the Peacock Throne of Persia for himself, had ruthlessly carved out a miniature Manhattan from the old city by tearing down blocks of houses to drive straight boulevards, with avenues intersecting at right angles, through the tangle of alleys that had made up the mediaeval town. Tehran clings to a hillside and instead of gutters the main streets have shallow conduits where sparkling mountain water gushes – at least in the smart residential centre high on the hill. The conduits were used to dispose of slops and bulkier refuse. The sparkle and the gush disappeared as the water flowed downhill; by the time it reached the *soukh* and the poorer quarters, the limpid torrent had become a sluggish, muddy trickle, slowly pushing filthy rags, crumpled cartons and even the bodies of dead cats down the hill.

In the cafés and bars of Tehran, pots of caviare and dry biscuits were put on the tables for guests to help themselves freely, much as an English bar might put out plates of crisps or peanuts. And, in wartime, every café had its quota of spies. There were always sad-looking men who never removed their overcoats, hunched over empty coffee cups or fondling a glass of arak by the hour. They might be paid by CICI (Combined Intelligence Centre, Iraq) to spy on the Russian and the German agents, or paid by the Germans to spy on the Allies – or paid by the American OSS to spy on everybody. Nor was this comic opera atmosphere entirely unserious. Not long after the Tehran Conference, the Germans managed to land professional agents among the nomadic tribes near the Persian oilfields with the aim of inciting them to sabotage the installations.

The British Embassy was quite an imposing building with a flight of steps leading up to the main doorway and a verandah running along its front. It stood at the lower end of a rectangle of gardens and was enclosed by a high wall on all sides. Halfway up the east side and fronting on a main street was an iron gate with a gatehouse alongside. On the opposite wall was a small wicket gate. At the top of the rectangle were stables and outhouses, in one of which my companions and I had our sleeping quarters. The grounds were dotted with trees and bushes; a thick shrubbery grew at the back of the Embassy. It was a pleasant area for the Ambassador and his guests to stroll around in the cool of the evening after a good dinner, but it was a security officer's nightmare. Determined assassins – and the original Castle of the Assassins, named after the hashish-smokers who drugged themselves into frenzy before committing their murders, is not two days' drive from Tehran – could have scaled the wall anywhere and would then have found ample cover right up to the Embassy itself. We had hardly unpacked our camp beds before demonstrators began to march up and down the main street outside with placards inscribed in Russian and English demanding self-determination for Persia and the immediate exit of the Allies who were defending her in spite of herself. During the war there must have been better kept secrets than the whereabouts of the big conference.

Luckily, I found that I had fallen among friends. My own regiment, 2nd Buffs, had been assigned for guard duties at the conference. After months of living under canvas in active service conditions, they were now scurrying around and applying the bull, polishing long-tarnished brasses and trying to get a sheen on scuffed boots. But soldiers, to whom the occasional sight of a major-general had been a matter of awe, swiftly grew blasé when they were daily in the company of multitudes of the mighty. On one occasion, walking from my out-house to the main building, seventy yards perhaps, I passed – and saluted – Admiral Sir Dudley Pound, the First Sea Lord, Field-Marshal

Lord Alanbrooke, Chief of the Imperial General Staff, Mr Anthony Eden, Foreign Secretary, General Marshall, head of the American Forces, Harry Hopkins, the President's adviser, General Ismay and various other lesser fry such as lieutenant-generals and mere admirals.

Four events in those crowded few days stand out in the memory and all of them are connected with celebrations: the night of the big party at the Russian Embassy; the night of Churchill's birthday party at the British Embassy; the presentation of the Sword of Stalingrad; and the end of term celebration when the Buffs gave their own birthday present to Churchill.

On the night of the Russian Embassy party, a parallel junior Party was thrown by the Russian liaison staff for their British counterparts. We soon learned the tenor of their attitude towards us, and indeed towards the outside world in general. We were standing round drinking pre-dinner vodka when a young Soviet officer, who spoke good English, arrived in their equivalent to our battledress; the rest of us had changed into service dress for the occasion. He came round each of us in turn, explaining that he had not one but two parade uniforms, one of them lined in red silk. The only reason he had not changed was because he had been on duty up to the last minute. One might expect such a scene in Tsarist days but coming from 'a man of the people' it sounded odd.

The Colonel in charge of the British liaison team did not fare so well. He too was held up on duty and arrived at the party just as we were going in to dinner. Our Russian host, a junior general, announced that it would be a blot on his reputation for hospitality if our leader went sober in to dine when the rest of us had imbibed at least eight vodkas each (a gross exaggeration). He called for eight glasses of vodka to be brought in on a salver and presented to our Colonel, who took up the challenge and downed each glass in turn in one swallow. Then he walked, rather haltingly, into the next room where dinner was to be served. The first course was borscht soup. When he saw the red shreds of cabbage swimming in a greasy pool, his face turned green. Holding a napkin up to his mouth, he dashed out of the room. We never saw him again during that dinner.

At the end of it, there was a series of toasts. A Soviet officer would stand up, holding his glass aloft, and shout 'The Battle for Kiev!' or 'To Stalingrad!' or one of their other famous victories. All the diners would stand, repeat the toast and down their drinks. Somewhat drunk myself, I felt we should try to redress the balance and so, when there was a pause, I stood up and shouted 'To Alamein!' The Britons present leapt up with alacrity; looking puzzled, the Russians followed suit. The officer with the two ceremonial parade uniforms happened to be opposite me. When we sat down, he asked, 'What is this Alamein?'

'A big battle,' I replied. 'We beat the Germans – and the Italians.'

'How many divisions on the British side?'

I did some quick mental arithmetic. 'About ten,' I said.

'And on the enemy side?'

To make the Eighth Army look good, I told a lie, or at least a wild exaggeration. 'About fifteen.'

He thought for a moment, then he pronounced. 'In the Soviet Army, we do not call that a battle. To us, that is a skirmish.'

By late 1943, over four years into the war, the Russians were bearing the brunt of the fighting. Stalin had only come to Tehran to press the Allies into starting the Second Front and alleviating the pressure and the sacrifices his countrymen were making. Slightly ashamed of themselves and soft-hearted as ever, the British people, including most of their leaders, had forgotten that the Soviet Union was only an ally *faute de mieux*. They had been quite happy to set up the Ribbentrop-Molotov Pact and would probably have remained neutral had not Hitler invaded in May 1941. There were songs like 'My Lovely Russian Rose' and continual talk of 'our gallant allies'. The truth was that Stalin and his colleagues cared nothing for the British and Americans, except as democracies to be infiltrated and overcome when peace returned. And yet, eighteen months later when I gave a lecture at the Staff College, Haifa, and mentioned these and the following points, I was gently chided by the commandant for questioning the motives of 'the gallant allies'. For eighteen months after the war, the idealistic and short-sighted Labour government went on kow-towing to Stalin. It was only Churchill's Fulton speech in 1947 that brought down the Iron Curtain.

Hundreds, even thousands, of open trucks were manufactured in the United States and shipped round the Cape of Good Hope, into the Indian Ocean and up the Persian Gulf to Basra. There they were unloaded and handed over to a Russian contingent for transport via Tehran, alongside the Caspian Sea and into the Soviet Union. Naturally, the Soviet representative checked each vehicle carefully to make sure it was effectively in running order.

On one occasion, I had to call at Basra. It was the early autumn but the sun still shone ferociously down on the docks. 'Bread is the staff of life but the life of the Staff is one long loaf'. Derek Norris, who had introduced me to staff work as the motto had it, was now running the Q side at Basra. I saw dozens upon dozens of trucks, neatly drawn up and blocking one whole area and asked him what the hell was going on. He told me. Apparently, in all the previous consignments, the spare wheel had been secured to the side of the truck by four nuts and bolts, forming a square. A time-and-motion expert had obviously been let loose on the American factory turning out the trucks. He had proclaimed that, if the spare wheel were attached by three nuts and bolts in an equilateral triangle, that would save (a) drilling an extra hole in the side of the vehicle, (b) one nut and (c) one bolt. Multiplied by hundreds and thousands, it was apparently a worthwhile saving.

But to the Russian assignee, it was a devilish, pluto-democratic, anti-bolshevik plot. However much Derek and his staff tried to explain and even point out for Christ's sake that every single bloody truck was buckshee, free, gratis, thanks to the generosity of the Yanks. The Russian officer was having none of it. The consignment was not exactly as he had been led to believe it would be, even though, as he admitted, every other single detail was exactly similar to previous consignments. He had to refer the matter back through 'channels' as far as some high-ranking officer in the Kremlin who would decide whether or not the trucks should be accepted.

When I looked incredulous, Derek explained another point I had not known. In the Russian Army, if an officer or another rank made a mistake, no matter how trivial, his punishment was to be removed from his position and sent at once to that part of the front where the fighting was most fierce. There were no excuses, no defence permitted. You killed a fellow soldier in a brawl or you got one unit wrong when adding up a column of figures – bingo! You packed your kit, cleaned your no doubt rusting rifle and were off next morning to the battle front, where too often the bloodshed was reminiscent of the Somme in World War One. The system led to efficiency among the rank and file but it was a nightmare for more senior officers, who had to take decisions based not only on their military correctness but how they would 'play' in the Kremlin's paranoid atmosphere. Which was why their man in Basra was playing it safe and letting someone else take the decision, even though the front-line troops were being denied essential transport.

Another incident, some months earlier, had given an insight into the Russian mentality and methods of summary justice. Many of these

convoys of American-built trucks drove up past the Caspian into
Soviet Russia, loaded with cases of corned beef, to be shared among
the forces and worst hit civilians. The officer in charge of one such
convoy, a young lieutenant, suspected that at halts in Persian villages
one of his men was trading tins of bully beef for fresh eggs. Carrying
his Kalashnikov, he tiptoed down the side of the drawn up trucks and
caught the man in the very act of handing a tin across the tailboard to
a villager who had a clutch of pullets' eggs in his hand. The officer
waved the soldier down off the truck and made him stand up against
a wall, holding the tin above his head. Then the officer fired a burst
and his victim crashed to the dusty earth. The convoy drove on,
leaving the corpse of the soldier *'pour encourager les autres'*.

   The incident was reported by GHQ Intelligence to the Operations
and Judge Advocate General's departments, as the murder – which the
so-called summary justice amounted to – technically speaking took
place in territory controlled by the (British) Persia and Iraq
Command. But it was quickly judged a case of 'file and forget'. No one
in authority wanted to get more on the wrong side of 'our gallant
allies' than was strictly necessary.

   But back to Tehran. On the night of the Russian party, we all had
to be on the alert until the Prime Minister and the Foreign Secretary
were safely back inside the cordon of guards on duty at the Embassy.
The streets of Tehran were never safe and least of all in the dark. It was
also a matter of pride for the Buffs that the guard could turn out in
time to give the Prime Ministerial car a general salute as it swept
through the Embassy gate. An elaborate system of watchers and
signals had been arranged, so that the guard on the main gate would
be alerted the moment the car was spotted at the top of the street.
After hours of hanging around in the cold night air, at last the warning
was given. The guard tumbled out of the gatehouse, fell in and were
presenting arms when the big car, flying the proud badge of Warden
of the Cinque Ports, shot past. Yawning and stretching for it was well
past midnight, the guards and we liaison officers decided to call it a
day.

   As already mentioned, there was a small wicket gate in the opposite
wall. A single sentry, who had orders to let no one in at night, stood
inside the locked gate. Outside there were mean streets and alleyways
and beyond them the grounds of the Russian Embassy. The Buffs
sentry was relaxing at his post (for the main event was over) when he
heard sounds of merriment in the street outside, a snatch of song and

an oath when one of the mysterious passers-by – there seemed to be two of them – stumbled. Obviously a couple of drunks, he thought, and wondered vaguely where they were heading at this time of night. He was not long in doubt. The couple lurched up to the gate and one of them banged on it. The sentry's reflexes were working: he pointed his rifle and bayonet in the general direction of the noise on the other side of the wall and shouted, 'Halt! Who goes there?'

A thick voice replied, 'It's the Prime Minister and Mr Eden. Let us in!'

It was quite a passable imitation of that famous guttural voice with its slight lisp, the sentry thought. But what the hell. He'd already been tipped the wink that the PM had safely returned through the main gate.

'Go on,' he said irritably. 'Fuck off.'

But the banging continued and the voice demanding entry grew more peremptory. The Buffs sentry began to lose his temper. Sentry-go from midnight till two a.m. on a cold, frosty night was no time for practical jokes. 'Fuck off,' he shouted. 'Who the fuckin' hell d'you think you're fooling? You heard me – fuck off!'

Now the voice on the other side of the wall became magisterial. And something in the tone made the sentry do what he might well have done sooner. He lowered his rifle and bayonet, slid open the spyhole at the top of the gate and peered through. In the lamplight he saw the two figures supporting each other: one was short and broad, the other tall and willowy. One looked like a pugnacious and very bad-tempered cherub: the other was handsome and moustached. It must have been a nightmare moment for the private.

We discovered afterwards that at the end of a copious dinner with the Russians, Mr Churchill decided that he needed a breath of fresh air and some gentle exercise before turning in. So he had ordered his car and his guards to go back to the Embassy, while he and the Foreign Secretary strolled the short distance through the alleyways of old Tehran. They could easily have been knocked on the head and robbed by common footpads or abducted or assassinated by a group of enemy agents. But the Churchillian luck had held – to the eventual discomfiture of the sentry. It is pleasant to relate that no disciplinary action was taken against him for doing his duty. He must have been the only soldier of any rank who swore at Winston Churchill to his face during the war and got away with it. Would Adolf Hitler or Marshal Stalin, one wonders, have behaved as well in the same situation?

Churchill's sixty-ninth birthday occurred during the conference. It was only fitting that a big party should be held at the British Embassy to celebrate it. The preparations were hectic. The heads of the three Great Powers would all be present, along with their senior advisers. As the only way of entering the Embassy itself was up one or other steep flight of steps, a wooden ramp had to be built over one of the flights so that Mr Roosevelt's wheelchair could be pushed into the building. I was not on duty that night but I found a pretext for being there and, early on, discovered a niche at the top of the main stairs leading on to the verandah.

Half an hour before the distinguished guests were due, there was a great bustle of activity along the verandah. Several big men with crew cuts and ominous bulges under their armpits – members of Roosevelt's FBI guard – scoured every nook and cranny with a single-minded rudeness. Mr Churchill, dressed in a dinner jacket and smoking an enormous cigar, wandered around as a good host might, making sure that everything was in order. On a couple of occasions, at least, the FBI team shouldered him unceremoniously out of their way.

Roosevelt arrived quite early and was pushed along the verandah in his wheelchair. He was instantly recognisable – the pince-nez, the straight patrician nose, firm chin and the jaunty cigarette-holder clenched in one corner of his mouth. He had a shawl round his shoulders for the night was crisp. He exchanged cordial greetings with his host but I noticed that when the light was reflected off his rimless pince-nez, you could not see the expression in the eyes behind them. A supreme politician's – a poker player's – face.

Stalin never went anywhere without his picked bodyguard of four-teen burly Georgians to protect him. Nearly thirty minutes before he was due, they arrived and without a by-your-leave stationed them-selves on each side of the main steps leading to the lobby. They stood shoulder to shoulder in their yellowish blouse-like uniforms and baggy trousers. Most of them had their right hands tucked under the waist of their blouses, quite obviously gripping an automatic or machine-pistol. Once a Persian servant tried to slip through the cordon but he was shoved aside contemptuously by the impassive bodyguard.

What with the Georgians lining the entrance and the FBI men lurking behind every pillar, it was a pleasant relief to watch Mr Churchill wandering freely among his guests with only a bored-looking Military Police corporal posted unobtrusively in a nearby corner.

A picked guard of honour from the Buffs had been standing rigidly on the driveway outside the main steps for over quarter of an hour. They were without greatcoats, even though the night was frosty, and I knew how they must feel, with fingers and feet growing more numb by the minute and with the weight of the rifle boring into the left shoulder. They were awaiting the entry of the most powerful man in the world, and with typical, deliberate discourtesy, he was already ten minutes late.

At last the long black limousine – bullet-proof, it was said – crunched to a stop on the gravelled drive. Out stepped Molotov, Marshal Voroshilov and, on his own, Stalin. They completely ignored the guard of honour, now presenting arms like statues. The two subordinates walked side by side up the steps, Voroshilov with his pale Slav face looking like a retired boxer and Molotov, plump, pink-cheeked, toothbrush moustache and gold-rimmed glasses, for all the world like a reasonably successful tradesman who might take the collection plate around the congregation at morning service.

I could only spare them a passing glance. Something compelled me to focus my whole attention on Stalin, who had paused near the top of the stairs. I was close enough to have leaned forward and touched him by stretching past the broad shoulders of the Georgian bodyguard.

One always expects world leaders to be larger than life size but Stalin was short, almost tiny – no more than five feet four inches I would have guessed. He wore a gorgeous saffron-coloured uniform of some silky material with red piping down the seams of the trousers. Square on his head was a peaked cap, a cross between a *képi* and a postman's cap, and round his shoulders a saffron cape with a brilliant scarlet lining. In his photographs, his hair and walrus moustache always appeared dark, almost black, and I was surprised to notice it was very grey, verging on white. There were harsh, diagonal creases running down his face from his nostrils to his chin.

But it is his eyes that I remember most vividly after more than fifty years. They were small, dark brown, unswerving. It would be impossible to read this man's thoughts from his eyes. He stood rigidly on the steps, staring straight ahead, his features an impassive mask. It is easy now in retrospect to think of him as a tyrannical despot, a mass murderer who would make Genghis Khan or Tamerlane look like innocent schoolboys, but in 1943 we knew so much less about him. He was honoured as the resolute leader of a great people who were playing the major role in the defeat of Hitler – and, indeed, he was just that. But, seeing him in the flesh an arm's length away, I could sense something of that strange, bleak personality, foxy, sardonic, suspicious and, more than anything, possessing the stubborn, patient endurance of a peasant.

The pause began to grow embarrassing. A Persian servant from the British Embassy staff slipped through the cordon of guards and came up behind Marshal Stalin to remove his cloak. At once the Georgians broke ranks. One grabbed the servant and another had his automatic out in a flash, shoved at the man's ribs. It was an awkward moment: the servant had unwittingly broken a sovereign rule. No one – no one at all – was ever to approach Stalin from the rear. But the Marshal stood stock still during the momentary hubbub, never deigning to glance round to see what was happening. He certainly had courage and dignity.

To cover up the awkwardness, Mr Churchill came bustling forward to the top of the steps and said in a cheery voice, 'Good evening, Marshal. Welcome to my party.' His right hand was thrust out in greeting.

Stalin just stood there, unsmiling, poker-faced, his arms firmly to his sides. He stared at Churchill for several seconds and then walked stiffly up the few remaining stairs. He did not offer to shake hands nor, as far as I could see, to return the Prime Minister's welcome in any way. Those of us who were mere hangers-on at the fringes of the conference grasped some inkling in those few minutes of the problems of bargaining around the table with this formidable figure.

Several hours later that night – it must have been about two in the morning when the birthday party was breaking up – we had further confirmation of our suspicions. A couple of other liaison officers and I bumped into the senior British official who had been interpreting for Churchill and Stalin during the dinner. The drink must have flowed like Niagara and the interpreter was in a mellow, unusually confiding, mood. He told us of one brush between the two leaders. The conversation had turned to the treatment of the German leaders after the Allies had won the war. Stalin had said, 'The answer is simple. The ones that fall into your hands will be put on trial, found guilty and then executed. We Russians are not hypocrites like the English. The ones we capture will just be shot – like that!' And he snapped his fingers contemptuously. 'With us there will be no need for the farce and the expense of a trial. The German criminals will get what they deserve – at once.'

Churchill apparently made a non-committal noise in his throat but Stalin was determined to pursue the point. 'I am sure we are agreed on one thing,' he said. 'Whatever their eventual fate, the German criminals must be brought to justice the moment they are captured. Will you not agree with that, Mr Prime Minister?'

Churchill agreed that Hitler and his minions, if taken alive, were to be brought swiftly to justice. But he added the rider that the whole world must see that the trials adhered to international law and were not just a form of revenge by the victors.

'But you do agree that some decisive action, legal or otherwise, must be taken as soon as these guilty men fall into our hands?' Stalin pressed him.

Churchill agreed.

'Then tell me, Mr Prime Minister, why is Rudolf Hess, one of the worst criminals, still alive and untried? You English have had him in your power for more than two years. Where is your swift justice?'

According to the interpreter, Churchill, the orator and expert at repartee, was nonplussed.

The birthday party evening held one comic interlude. Harry Hopkins, the presidential adviser, had a son who was a private in the US Army, stationed in Persia. He had been given an invitation to the party and duly presented himself at the Buffs' guardroom. He was not perhaps the most smartly turned out member of the American armed forces and when this scruffy soldier started telling a cock-and-bull story about being invited as a guest with all the great ones from three nations, the guard commander, a man of action, knew just what to do. He arrested Private Hopkins as a suspicious character.

An hour or so later, when his son's absence caused the presidential adviser to make enquiries, Private Hopkins was quietly released and escorted to the Embassy main building. The pre-dinner anteroom was already crowded; it was hot and stuffy with smoke. So Private Hopkins, drink in hand, decided to step out on to the verandah at the back of the building for a breath of fresh air. An FBI man, lurking in the shrubbery, saw this suspicious-looking private soldier in a place where he so obviously shouldn't be, grabbed him and at gun-point marched him off to the safest spot in the neighbourhood – which was, of course, the Buffs' guardroom.

Next day, the ceremony of handing over the Sword of Stalingrad also had its odd moments. Originally arranged for two p.m. at the Russian Embassy, it was first postponed till two-thirty and then again till quarter to three. The reason? Churchill had retired to bed in a foul temper in the early hours and no one dared rouse him. I met Anthony Eden on the steps of the villa occupied by the great man. Eden was full of blarney, showing another liaison officer and me the gold sovereign he was to hand over with the Sword as part of the old tradition. Had we seen such a coin before? Yes, we had. And did we know why it was to be handed over along with the Sword? Yes, we did. Mortified, the Foreign Secretary turned his back on us and walked to the top of the steps. But he still lacked the nerve to enter the villa and tell his leader that he was holding up the vital ceremony.

At last, Sarah Churchill, who was a WAAF officer and had accompanied her father to Tehran, risked his wrath. Finally, a very grumpy-looking Mr Churchill in his siren suit put in an appearance and, muttering something about an adjectival farce, climbed into his car.

I was not present at the handing-over ceremony but several of my Buffs friends told me afterwards that disaster was only just averted. The sword-party, a junior officer, two sergeant-majors and three other ranks, all from the Buffs, marched smartly up the large room which had a low dais where Stalin and his senior entourage were waiting. The sword-party crashed to a halt, saluted, and then the officer took the great Sword and, holding it parallel to the ground, bowed and presented it to Stalin. He passed it towards Molotov but unfortunately lowered the hilt towards the ground. The Sword, forged by craftsmen, slid smoothly out of its jewelled scabbard and the weight of the hilt made it accelerate. Luckily, Marshal Voroshilov, who for all his years and portly figure would have made a first-rate slip fielder, stooped and grabbed the hilt when it was only inches away from the floor. He rammed the Sword back into its scabbard and an international incident was averted.

At length the conference ground to its end and the captains and the kings departed. On the last morning, the Buffs had a private, informal ceremony where they handed over their own birthday present to Mr Churchill. It was held by the ornamental pool in front of the main building. The great man arrived in his uniform of Colonel of Hussars. He stood there in the pale November sunshine and shyly accepted the gift. Then he asked the troops to break ranks and he talked to us for a few minutes – about the war and his gratitude for the way the men had carried out their onerous guard duties. One sentry who had been on late night duty might have blushed. The Prime Minister looked tired and wan – within a few days he would be critically ill with pneumonia – but he seemed happy to be with young men who offered him a simple affection, and away from the critical negotiations and international poker of the conference rooms.

Colonel Percival called for three cheers and the noise must have made the demonstrators in the streets outside wonder who their rivals were. Then Winston Churchill puffed at his cigar, gave his cherubic grin, made his famous V-sign, and walked slowly back to the Embassy. The Tehran Conference was over.

10

❖❖❖

'This World Is Yet Wide Enough'

◆◆◆◆◆◆

Private Payne had been dead for more than a year. I had seen a lot of death before and during the battle of Alamein, both in action and in its aftermath. Indeed, like Eliot's Webster, I had been 'much possessed by death'. As battalion Intelligence officer, I had the job of searching the enemy dead for clues to the identity of their units. It was not a pleasant task. With daytime temperatures over a 100°, putrefaction sets in fast, faces go black, retained gases make a body swell so much that the belt and tunic may have to be cut away to get at the inner pockets. Once, with a corpse lying on its back, I thrust my hand under the tunic and then quickly pulled it out, clutching lumps of reddish-black flesh. The dead Italian had stopped the blast of a grenade, which had lacerated his back and chest into a gory pulp.

But one quickly became inured. The only time I was on the verge of retching was when searching a dead officer from the Folgore Division. A grenade had burst a few feet in front of him. The blast had blown his right eye out of its socket, leaving a red pit in which a cluster of flies was guzzling. I could see an identity disc around the man's neck and I had to stoop down with my face a few inches from his smashed features to cut loose the disc. The flies rose and paddled around my sweating face, nuzzling at my lips and mouth. I could feel the bile rising.

On this particular night, I was duty officer in the General Staff (Operations) office at GHQ, PAIFORCE, Baghdad. In that wartime backwater, the orderly officer's duties were not onerous. From eight o'clock at night – twenty-hundred hours, we would have called it – until eight in the morning, he occupied a room on the first floor of the Ops building. There was a reasonably comfortable camp bed and a vacuum flask of hot coffee. For the first hour or so, while he was still fairly awake and alert, there might be the odd Most Secret signal from GHQ, Middle East, or on rare occasions from the War Office in London. But even in the midst of a bitter war, staff officers were not accustomed to work too late; the flow of signals and 'burn-before-reading' cables would stop well before midnight.

The name 'Samarra' was much on my mind that night. It was then more of a village than a town, north of Baghdad and fairly close to the main railway line that ran southwards from Kirkuk to Baghdad and on to Basra. There had been some problems with the line, a near-derailment, a broken-down engine. The cause was more likely to be ancient equipment than sabotage but, anyway, the previous week I had been ordered to accompany a senior British police officer and then report on the sheikh's status as a local ally. He had invited us to lunch with him.

As our jeep approached the courtyard, we could hear the *muezzin*'s cry and glimpsed a scattering of veiled women who sought the sanctuary of the harem. As a sign of ancient Arab hospitality, the sheikh had had an ornate tent erected alongside his house. The dusty surface was covered with layer upon layer of splendid Persian rugs, so that one's feet sank in a few inches with every step. As usual, we sat on cushions, cross-legged in a circle around the communal food, steaming rice, slices of lamb and shreds of bitter lettuce. I knew enough of local customs only to use my right hand – we two Westerners were in fact given forks and spoons – and to keep the soles of my boots pointing away from the host and his staff. It is an unforgivable insult, even if accidental, to show a devout Moslem the soles of one's footwear, as they continually tread in all manner of dirt.

After the meal, when the hookah was being passed round, we heard from one corner of the large tent the wailing of a pipe, accompanied by a drum and a kind of guitar. The remnants of the food had been removed and into the oval space, a fattish woman stepped. With her protruding bare belly and voluminous breasts, she bowed to our host, who waved her to proceed.

The senior policeman sitting next to me whispered, 'My God, this is an honour.' He quickly explained that she was one of the most famous belly dancers in the Middle East, usually working at the exclusive nightclubs in Cairo or at King Farouk's palace. It must have cost the Samarra sheikh a fortune to secure her services, let alone the problems of transport from Cairo and back.

She began to dance. It took an ignoramus like me less than a minute to realise that here indeed was a star. She stood in front of each guest in turn, oscillating to the wailing music, writhing her limbs with an erotic grace that is hard to describe. Herrick called his Julia's silks – 'the liquefaction of her clothes'. Here was a physical liquefaction that was truly an art. Her first turn was in front of the police officer as the most honoured guest. On finishing, she spun round so that her back was in front of him. He stretched up and gave her a hearty smack on her plump bottom. I thought she might rip him with her long fingernails for such an insult but she turned again and smiled graciously at him. Then she performed in front of me. At the end, she followed the same routine. I did not know what to do.

'Go on,' the policeman urged in a whisper. 'Hit her!'

I leaned forward and gave her a gentle tap. She turned round, glanced at me haughtily, and moved on to the man on my right. I learned afterwards from the knowledgeable copper that the belly dancer gauges the audience's appreciation by the strength of the slap.

We had a few paperback books in our mess and, before going off on my duty officer's vigil the following week, I looked through them, spotting John O'Hara's *Appointment in Samarra*. I wondered why he had hit on that particular title and glanced at the preliminary pages. They contained a quotation from Somerset Maugham in which a rich merchant in the market place at Baghdad sees the figure of Death not far away. He tells his servant to saddle his fastest horse, as he intends to avoid Death by rushing to Samarra. Someone in the crowd sees Death give a start when he spots the merchant galloping away and asks him why. Death replies in more or less these words, 'I did not expect to see him here today for tomorrow I have an appointment with him in Samarra.'

And that in turn reminded me of Private Payne.

I settled down in the duty room, made sure the field telephone was working and sat back. All was quiet; there were no incoming messages to cope with. After reading O'Hara for an hour or two until my eyes were getting tired, I had one last swig of coffee, undressed, climbed into the camp bed and was soon fast asleep.

I was woken up about five in the morning by the racket of the field telephone on the desk about two feet from my head. Shaking myself – it had been a deep sleep – I picked up the 'phone and croaked, 'Duty officer, G Ops.'

The voice at the other end was quite breathless, urgent. 'It's HQ

Basra, sir. Duty officer here. That special train of Russians. Seems a guard spotted one of the Russians jumping off the train. It had slowed down on an embankment five or so miles north of Ahwaz. We just heard about the incident and I had to pass the word on right away.'

I was GHQ and he was one of the outposts. It was like a Roman citizen dealing with a woad-painted barbarian. 'Look,' I said imperiously, 'for a start, it doesn't make sense. They're all going back to the motherland, courtesy of British Army transport. Why the hell would one of them jump the train when he'll be seeing his loved ones in a few days? You sure the guard hadn't had a drop or two?'

'Same thought crossed my mind, sir. But I checked with the railway engineer sergeant who reported it and he reckoned the guard was pretty alert.'

'Well, there's nothing we can do until first light. If you haven't already done so, I suggest you alert the nearest infantry battalion to start searching the area once it's daylight. As I recall, the territory's pretty bleak and barren. The fellow – there was only one? – might be glad to be caught.'

That was the end of our conversation, but before settling back to sleep, I felt annoyed with myself. There were other questions I could and should have asked. Could the Russian have fallen out of the train, not jumped? The rolling stock, particularly in Persia, was ancient and rickety. Anyone leaning his bodyweight against a door might get a nasty surprise when the door catch suddenly gave way. And what was the general atmosphere aboard the train? Were there any unruly elements? Could he even have been flung off the train by an enemy or two?

The one thing I found hard to stomach was that a man homeward bound after years of privation and who was now hardly more than a day away from his destination should voluntarily have left the train at the risk of breaking his neck, or at least a leg. When Hitler smashed the Ribbentrop-Molotov Pact and sent his armies rolling across the Soviet frontier in June 1941, some thousands of fit young Russian civilians, when captured, were put to work building defences for the Germans, a flagrant breach of the Geneva Convention. In 1943, when the American Fifth Army and the British Eighth Army, having captured Sicily, landed at Anzio and fought their way northwards, those same civilians were moved to Italy to build fortifications for the German troops. As the Allied advance quickened, many of the Russian labourers were recaptured and put into temporary camps. As a gesture to placate Marshal Stalin after the Tehran Conference, they were shipped from ports like Bari via the Suez Canal and up through the Persian Gulf, where special trains were to run them northwards through Persia and the Caucasus into Soviet Russia, their homeland. Although they had been doing forced labour for the German war effort, at the certain risk of being shot if they refused to take part, they were naturally treated as Allied prisoners of war and the British Army guards aboard the trains were more friendly nannies than jailers. Many of these POWs were suffering from the aftermath of semi-starvation, ulcers, sores and minor injuries. They had been carefully screened for typhus and typhoid fever back at the Italian camps but a medical contingent accompanied them on the trains as a precaution. The episode that had just been reported to me occurred on one of the first, if not the very first, trains bound for home in Soviet Russia.

Perhaps a quarter of an hour before my tour of duty was to end, the field telephone rang again. It was the same Basra duty officer, reporting that the man had been picked up about a couple of miles from the railway line. He had apparently rolled down an embankment and had suffered no injuries. The train, labouring up an incline, was probably travelling at about ten miles an hour when he jumped.

I said, 'You'd better send him up to GHQ here by the next train out of Basra. Treat him well – after all, he's not a *real* prisoner – but, for Christ's sake, make sure the escort stays wide awake! We don't want a repetition.'

Before clocking off, I rang the Military Police HQ nearby to warn them to expect a special prisoner off the Basra–Baghdad train in the afternoon. I explained the situation briefly and added that he must be given VIP treatment until he had been interrogated. Indeed, he was not a prisoner but rather a 'temporary guest'. Before leaving the duty room, I scribbled out a report and left it downstairs for one of the clerks to type while I went off for the Army's proverbial three 'sh's' – which included a shave and a shower. 'Shorty George', my CO, was a stickler for following staff duties to the letter.

When I reported back after breakfast in the mess, he sent for me at once. I had a small cubbyhole on the ground floor, along with the military typists and the clerical staff sergeants. He occupied a large airy room on the third floor. He had a querulous voice and even when he was making a plain statement, it sounded like a complaint. I told him what had happened, although it was there as a neatly typed report on the desk blotter in front of him. But I always suspected that, as a clever barrister in court often tries to poke out discrepancies between a witness's written statement and later oral evidence in the witness box, so my senior officer liked to catch out his juniors.

Finally, he said, 'Well, you started this thing, Greenfield. You'd better finish it off.'

'Sir?'

'Don't be stupid, man. When they've got this – this runaway safely installed in the Provost Marshal's cells, *you* go and interrogate him. Understood?'

'Sir.'

I could not salute as I was not wearing any form of headgear. So I clicked my heels and bowed my head stiffly, like a dashing Viennese officer in one of Ivor Novello's romantic pre-war musical comedies. It was enough to reassure 'Shorty' that he was the chief round here.

Accompanied by a Russian-speaking interpreter, I went round that afternoon to the Military Police HQ. With great slamming of iron gates and the unlocking of vast steel doors, we were finally let into a rather gloomy small cell. It was clean enough but sparsely furnished, even spartan. There was a trestle bed screwed to the floor, so that a prisoner could not smash it up and use it as a weapon against a warder, a latrine bucket with a lid in the far corner and a solitary chair, again screwed tight to the floor. The MP who had conducted us to the cell went off and returned with two wooden chairs. His orders were to lock the cell door during my interrogation but he invited me to bang on the door when I had finished.

My eyes were growing accustomed to the gloom. We were only a few weeks into 1944 and the light failed early. When there were also heavy rain clouds around, as now, it was often dark by mid-afternoon. I motioned to the man who was sitting hunched up on the bed to stand. We shook hands. His was a strong grip, hard and leathery with calluses from years of manual toil. He was shortish but with powerful sloping shoulders and a barrel chest. Dark-haired and dark-eyed, he was staring at me suspiciously.

I waved to him to sit on the chair and the Russian-speaking sergeant interpreter and I sat down side by side on the bed. I said to the sergeant, 'Let's play him in gently. Get his name, age, married or single – that kind of detail – before we get on to why he jumped.'

The only Russian word I knew was '*Nyet*' – 'No.' I had heard it often enough in Basra and Tehran when officers of the Soviet Army refused to accept a friendly gesture. So I had to leave everything to the interpreter. He began to jabber away but I noticed that our prisoner looked blank. Then he shook his head vigorously, pointed a finger at his chest and replied at some length in a tongue that even to my uneducated ear sounded different from the interpreter's intonations.

This went on for a minute or two. Then the sergeant turned to me and said, 'I don't think this lad is Russian, sir. Or else he's a hell of an actor. I was asking simple questions – like you said, sir – and he didn't understand a word.'

'But what was that language he used when he answered?'

'I didn't really get it but it could have been Polish.'

'Do you know any Polish, sergeant?'

'Only the odd word, I'm afraid, sir.'

'Well, try him out with what you do know.'

The result was quite extraordinary. The man's eyes lit up, he nodded briskly and went off into a torrent of unintelligible speech.

'Did you get any of that?' I asked.

'Just a bit here and there. I'd lay odds he's Polish.'

'So what's he doing mixed up in a convoy of Russians? You must have Polish-speaking interpreters in your unit, sergeant? Dammit, we had the whole Polish Corps here until last year.'

He assured me there were several fluent Polish-speakers in the unit and I asked him to arrange for one of them to report to the Military Police HQ at the same time next day. Meanwhile, I shook hands again with the prisoner, pointed to my wristwatch and made two circular clockwise movements with my index finger. He seemed to get the message and for the first time smiled.

Back at G Ops, I typed a two-line report for the CO, just to say that my investigations were continuing. With luck, that would stop him from sniffing around and issuing stupid orders. I considered myself to be at least twice as intelligent as 'Shorty' and, if I was at a total loss to understand the situation, how would he respond? Either the man was a consummate actor and was indeed Russian or else he was, as the interpreter reckoned, Polish. If the latter, his escape from the train was readily understandable. Well back into the days of the Tsars, Russians had treated Poles with great brutality. I had read the Top Secret signals even then, nearly eighteen months before the end of the war, proving it was not Hitler but Stalin who had ordered the massacre of the Polish officers in the Katyn Forest.

But if he really was Russian, why on earth should he jump the train when within a day or two of his homeland? There could to my mind be only one answer. He was wanted for crimes committed during his captivity and the day of reckoning was looming. I did not then know Stalin's way with compatriots who allowed themselves to be captured. The whole of that consignment and all the trainloads that followed were sent at once to undergo even worse privation in the Siberian gulags.

That next afternoon, I met the new interpreter, who happened to be a fluent Russian – as well as Polish – speaker. Again, I briefed him to ask simple factual questions at first. But it soon developed into an oral table tennis match with the pair of them jabbering away and myself as spectator vainly switching my gaze from one to the other in quick succession. At length, the interpreter turned and said, 'I think I've got it straight, sir. He's definitely a Pole. Absolutely no doubt. He's picked up a bit of Russian – the odd phrase – but if you ask him to answer at length in Russian, he's stumped.'

'Could he be from one of the outer republics – like Uzbekhistan – where they might speak a weird dialect?'

The sergeant shook his head. 'Not a chance. He sounds completely Polish. He *looks* Polish. If you'd had anything to do with the Polish Corps, sir, you'd spot it.'

As it happened, I had spent two or three weeks training the Polish Corps in the plains around Kirkuk. Now he mentioned it, I saw what he was saying. I had to agree. The man looked Polish.

'What's his name?'

The interpreter asked the question and the man replied with a consonantal sneeze. I could recognise 'p', 't' and 'r' sounds. 'Okay,' I said, 'let's christen him Petrov. At least, I'll be able to pronounce that. Now find out some of his background, if you please. Leading up to how come he jumped the train.'

There was more quickfire jabbering that went on for five or ten minutes. Then the interpreter patted the prisoner on the arm and turned to tell me the story. Petrov and his family had farmed a smallholding in eastern Poland for many generations. When Hitler's armies invaded western Poland in September 1939, the Soviet forces had marched into the other half. Petrov, an able-bodied man in his early thirties, was captured and removed from his wife and family to undergo forced labour in the Soviet Union. Over eighteen months passed and then in June 1941 Hitler invaded Russia. At first, the Wehrmacht advanced in swift strides, having already occupied the whole of what had been Poland. Petrov was recaptured, along with several thousand other Poles, by the German spearhead and was forcibly enrolled to work on one of Albert von Speer's special fortifications. They were overworked, underfed, living (if that is the right definition) in the most squalid circumstances. Many died of starvation, disease or sheer exhaustion. When, two years later, the Allies invaded Italy at the port of Anzio and began their slow advance northwards, Petrov and the remaining Poles in his contingent were moved to build defences south of Florence.

By now, their diminishing numbers were made up by Russian prisoners of war. To the Wehrmacht, particularly the SS divisions in Italy, a serf was a serf, irrespective of what language he spoke. The forced labourers were lumped together. It so happened that Petrov was the only Pole still alive and working among a gang of Russian workers. When the Allies overran their encampment, he tried to explain to the officer in charge that he was not a Russian and should not be sent back to the Soviet Union. But either the officer could not understand him – apparently, there was no interpreter present – or he thought, What's the difference? Let's get on with it. Whatever the reason, Petrov found himself first on a ship and then on a train, bound for Soviet Russia. He did not have to be told of the age-old enmity between the two nations. He had grown up, nurtured in fear and hatred of the powerful neighbour to the east. He knew little of geography but he guessed that the train was closing in on its destination.

Literally afraid for his life, he stood in the corridor of the lurching train, leaning casually against the door. He tried it with his hand behind his back. The catch gave. The door was not locked. When the engine began to labour up an incline and the train slowed down, he flung the door open and jumped. Landing on the side of a steep embankment, he rolled over and over down the slope until abruptly halted by a clump of camel thorn. The sky was dark with looming clouds and he slipped away, crouching and running in a zigzag line in case the guards on the train shot at him. But nothing happened. Exhausted by the strain, he fell asleep in a hollow protected by bushes. After a few hours, he woke with a start to see the muzzles of two rifles about six inches from his face. It was but a brief spell of liberty.

'Hell,' I said to the sergeant-interpreter as we came away, 'another MFU [military fuck-up]. You'd think they'd screen these fellows properly before sending them off.'

'You going to do anything about it, sir?' he asked.

'If I can.'

Before leaving the Military Police compound, I told the sergeant-major in charge that this was a special case and would almost certainly be taken up 'at a high level'. It looked like a case of mistaken identity. The man was not to be treated, I said once more, as a prisoner but more as a guest until we had established who he really was. He had been a farmer and should be handy with plants and vegetables. Why not let him loose on that bare patch of earth just behind the cell block? I would be back – probably the next day – and I expected to see him fit and well.

The sergeant-major looked hard at me but merely grunted, 'Sir.'

Four years earlier, as a private in the Lincolnshire Regiment, I had been sent as escort to a fellow private. He was a gypsy and communal life, doing everything by numbers, was not for him. He had climbed over the barbed wire surrounding the depot and gone AWOL. He had been picked up in Norwich and put in the detention cells. He was a heavy smoker and the MPs played their usual trick. They allowed him to keep his packet of cigarettes but took away his box of matches. At the next inspection, to their angry surprise, the cell was wreathed in smoke. Somehow, the gypsy had managed to unscrew the protected light bulb from the ceiling, heat a piece of wire across the points and light one cigarette after another. By the time, the corporal in charge of the escort and I reported to the MP barracks to collect the prisoner who would be dealt with back at Lincoln, the two Military Policemen in charge of him were steamed up, ready for action. They quick-marched the prisoner into an anteroom where he would be formally handed over to us. One preceded him, the other was close on his heels. He stumbled over the threshold and lightly bumped into the guard in front.

'Right,' shouted the MP. He turned to us. 'You see that? Striking a senior in the course of his duty and attempting escape. He needs a good lesson.'

'Ah, fuck off,' said the gypsy private.

'And verbal abuse on top! You asked for it, son.'

One of them pinned the prisoner against the wall while the other drew a pair of leather gloves from this hip pocket and slowly put them on. He smoothed them down and wriggled his fingers to make sure the fit was perfect. He then took his place holding down the prisoner while his comrade in turn donned his leather gloves. It was clearly a practised routine. Then coldly and deliberately they beat the gypsy up, punching him hard in the chest and stomach, careful always not to leave any incriminating bruises on his face or neck. I made an involuntary half-move forwards but my corporal put a restraining hand on my arm. 'Hold it,' he muttered out of the side of his mouth, 'unless you want a beating.'

Red in the face and breathing hard from their efforts, the two MPs at length moved back, leaving their man huddled in a corner, head in his arms, knees drawn up. 'All right,' said one of them contemptuously, 'he's all yours. Just sign here' – to my corporal – 'and take the bastard away.'

I wondered for a long time afterwards whether there was all that difference between Hitler's Gestapo and our own Corps of Military Police. Although by now, four years later and several thousand miles further east, I realised there was a real difference, I still thought it worth giving the sergeant-major an implied warning.

Officers in the regular British Army of those days, particularly any who had been slowly promoted or even bypassed, often looked down with contempt and resentment on the 'temporary gentlemen' who had volunteered or been conscripted since war was declared. It was an understandable reaction. They looked on themselves as expert professionals, trained through long and often dull years of peace for one end – to fight and win a war. Promotion in peacetime was slow and mainly depended on length of service. It took at least five years to rise from lieutenant to captain and seven or more from captain to major. And then in September 1939 the gates opened wide and all these 'damned amateurs' came rushing in. After a crash course lasting a few months, they were commissioned as officers and before long some of them were leapfrogging over *real* officers with ten or twenty times their length of service. To 'the scarlet majors at the base', it was an outrage.

We may smile in retrospect, but what would happen if the government were suddenly to pass an Act insisting that every boy and girl in the country, on reaching the age of eighteen, must undergo three years of higher education? New universities would have to be set up to cope with the rush and thousands of unqualified men and women would need to undergo an educational crash course before becoming university teachers. One can almost hear the shrieks of wrath that would float heavenwards from All Souls and Balliol and King's College, Cambridge. Would the dons and professors regard the interlopers at all differently from the way peacetime officers regarded their temporary comrades?

Relaxing on the roof of the GHQ Ops building, Baghdad, 1944.
It takes five staff officers to kill a scorpion
Mission accomplished! Standing left to right: Majors Topalian, Fox and Hope.
Seated next to me is Captain Hatry

I knew I would have to plan the campaign carefully if I was going to save Petrov from an onward journey to the Soviet Union and, I believed, almost certain death. In two days and two short meetings, at which I had hardly understood a word, it had suddenly become important to save him. My immediate superior, Major Bill Fox, ex-actor and easygoing man of the world, unfortunately was away on an inspection of the defences around Kermanshah, the oil centre in northern Persia. Major Bob Hope, his counterpart in the G (Ops) building, a regular officer and once a stickler for staff duties, was happily keeping his head well down after his pre-Tehran conference embarrassing debacle. I drew up my detailed report on Petrov, using all the proper military abbreviations and culminating in three short and crisp sentences proving (I hoped) why Petrov should not be classified as a Russian POW and sent on to the Soviet Union. Bob Hope always called at the Officers' Club a couple of hundred yards away for a glass or two of Scotch before continuing to his mess building for dinner. I waited till he had cleared his desk, locked away his files and handed the key to the security sergeant and then I pounced.

'What is all this, Greenfield?' he asked as I shoved the paper at him.

'I'm so sorry, sir. Terribly sorry. But you know what the CO's like. He's asked to see it first thing in the morning and I've got to get your initials on it. Just in case you're held up in the morning, sir.' (Bob was a notorious late arriver.)

'Don't you children ever learn there's a time and place for everything? What's the Army coming to? Oh well . . .'

He skimmed through the report – 'another of your wild-goose chases, what, Greenfield' – but scribbled his initials at the foot of the page. My muttered words of thanks were genuine. One hurdle jumped, but there were higher ones ahead.

In the Army, especially on the General Staff, you had to go through the channels. In other words, a captain, like myself, had to get a report approved by a major, which I had done, before presenting it to his CO, a lieutenant-colonel. If the CO approved the proposal contained in the report but felt that it was too important for him to wave through on his own, his recourse would be to the Brigadier General Staff, the head officer in the Operations branch. I knew Brigadier Kenny, the BGS, to be a warm and humane man; he would almost certainly understand Petrov's desperate situation and act on it. The big problem was to get my report past my CO, Shorty George, and on to the Brigadier's desk.

Shorty was a disappointed man. He had put in thirty years' service 'in hot stations', as the Army saying has it, and in spite of the opportunity for accelerated promotion which an all-out war provides, he had only risen one rank – to that of lieutenant-colonel. When the war finally ended, he would go into retirement and it was essential for him not to put a foot wrong in the meantime; there was a big difference between a major's Army pension and a lieutenant-colonel's. So here was a man, mutely angry with those who had overtaken him, or seemed likely to do so, and yet fearful of making an error, or what his superiors might deem an error. His was the Yorkshire motto: 'When in doubt, do nowt.'

There was no way I could think of to bypass him. The best plan, I thought, was to talk to him face to face before handing over the report, rather than sending it 'through channels' with a covering note. So, taking a few deep breaths and making sure my tie was neatly in place, I walked up the stone stairway and knocked on his door. As always, he had heaps of files on the big desk and his in-tray was full of papers. He was a slow reader.

'What is it, Greenfield?' He sounded testy.

'I'm sorry to bother you, sir. But this is rather urgent.'

'What is?'

As succinctly as possible, I explained my two visits to Petrov and my certainty, fully backed by the interpreter, that the man was not a Russian but a Pole. It seemed to me, I said, that human justice meant we should not send him on to Russia where he was almost bound to be killed or at the best sent to Siberia for life as a forced labourer.

Shorty looked out of his window at the rows of date palms lining the quiet suburban road. I could guess what he was thinking. How dodgy is this proposal? Will I get a pat on the back if I endorse it – or a metaphorical kick in the balls? Play it safe. Don't forget that pension.

He turned back to me. I was still standing, more or less to attention, in front of his desk. He did not have the grace to wave me to one of the chairs nearby.

'I know you went to Cambridge, Greenfield.' He made it sound as though I had been brought up in a brothel. 'And I know they teach you all those airy-fairy ideas. But this is the real world. You're in the Army. Face the facts. The Russians are our great allies. They took the brunt of the fighting and they've suffered the worst casualties. And they're efficient. The German army is pretty damn' good and you've got to be even better to beat them, the way the Soviets are right now. If this fellow you're so keen on isn't Russian, what's he doing with all the other Russians on a train bound for Russia? With all your degrees, Greenfield, answer me that. Are you saying our people in Italy cocked it up as well? I know we don't all have your education, Greenfield, but most competent British Army officers can tell a Pole from a Russian.'

He tossed the report across his desk towards me. 'Forget it,' he said. 'Get on with some real soldiering.'

The field telephone on his desk rang. It sounded urgent. He picked it up and said, 'Put him on – right away.' A pause and then he said, 'Yes, sir. I see, sir. Yes, of course. He happens to be here in this room. Yes, excellent timing. I'll send him to you this moment, sir.'

He looked up at me and said, 'That was the Brigadier Ops. He wants to see the officer in charge of the escaped prisoner – and that's you. So hurry along. And when you see the Brigadier, Greenfield, don't give him all that guff about human justice. Your job is to just answer his questions – and no sermons. That's an order.'

Brigadier Kenny's office was in a neighbouring but smaller house. His MA (military assistant), an ambitious young gunner who had passed through the Staff College at Haifa, met me and took me straight in to see him. Unlike my own CO, the Brigadier showed me to a chair and left his desk to sit beside me. I told him what had happened from the pre-dawn telephone call from Basra when I was duty officer. He nodded. The BGS, going bald, pink-cheeked, grizzled moustache, spoke little but what he said was usually to the point.

There had been a tough message through, he told me, from the Soviet Military Mission attached to the Soviet Embassy in Tehran. Apparently, the manifest for that particular train journey stated that 322 repatriated compatriots, excluding the train driver and other officials and the British guards, were on board. The numbers had been carefully checked on arrival at Tehran and they amounted to 321 repatriates. One of them must be missing. Did GHQ have any knowledge of the missing man's whereabouts?

'You met a lot of Russians during the Tehran Conference, didn't you, George? You know what they can be like. Anything to show up the Brits or the Yanks as inferior. Or cheats and liars. This fellow you call Petrov – is there any proof he's a Pole?'

'Not proof in the sense we've got his birth certificate, sir. Or the word of his village priest. No chance of that, anyway, with all the chaos in central Europe. The interpreter is positive he's Polish.'

'Could he be acting the part?'

'If he is, then Jean Gabin would have to look out!' The BGS looked a little mystified; I was annoyed with myself. Then, without weighing the situation, I plunged into the same sort of speech I had given Shorty George.

He heard me out in silence and then said, quite gently. 'I accept all you say, George. And privately I agree with most of it. But a lot of my work is a matter of means and ends. What is more important, to keep friendly with the Russians or to consider the future of one – let's face it – unimportant man? Tell me, have you shown this report to Colonel Woodhouse?'

'Yes, sir.'

'And what was his view?'

'He thinks the prisoner should be sent on in the next train. That I'm making a fuss over nothing. Sir.'

The Brigadier looked up at the ceiling and sighed. 'Speaking privately, George, it's a pity you weren't able to come straight to me. Now I'm stuck. I can't go over your CO's head – you must know that? I am truly sorry.'

'Could I ask one favour, sir. Could you stall the Russians in Tehran for another twenty-four hours, say? Forty-eight hours would be even better. If you could just tell 'em enquiries are being pursued, or something like that.'

The BGS stared hard at me. 'You're not thinking of doing anything rash?'

'No, sir. I just want to see if I can drum up some evidence to prove he's a Pole. It's doubtful but I'd like to try.'

'All right. You've got forty-eight hours. And that's it. No supporting evidence by then, off he goes on the next train through. And don't neglect the rest of your duties, George, on a wild-goose chase.'

Back at my desk in the G (Ops) building, I telephoned the interpreter, who was a sergeant in the Intelligence Corps, and arranged to meet him at the detention centre that afternoon. When we got there, Petrov's cell was empty. He was working on the bare patch of earth behind the cell block, watched by a Military Police guard. Shirt open and sleeves rolled up, he was hoeing the weeds and tufts of grass in easy rhythmical strokes. Brought up in the country myself, I could appreciate the practised movements, the economical strokes of the hoe blade. The muscles on his forearms swelled and subsided as he deftly cleared the earth. He broke off on seeing us. His eyes were bright and his body alert, such a contrast with the hunched apathetic figure I had first seen, sitting on the bed with head bowed.

I had already briefed the interpreter to ask if there were any ways of proving his identity. I was not optimistic but everything had to be tried, however unlikely. On being asked, he shrugged his powerful shoulders, shook his head and burst into an impassioned speech.

Sergeant Makepeace, who had a Modern Languages degree from London University, translated for me. 'Not a chance, sir. Before the end of '39, the Russians had carted off all the able-bodied men, including the village priest, and most of the cattle as well. He heard much later from other prisoners that the German army in June '41 pretty well burned down every building in his village, including the communal centre. And they raped and then murdered most of the women. He's heard nothing from or about his wife and kids since the day he was seized. Mid-Europe is a total shambles!'

'Tell him, would you, that I believe his story and am doing all I can to help him. It may take a little while, so he's got to be patient. But make sure he knows I really am trying.'

Makepeace made his speech. When he had finished, Petrov looked at me and impulsively stepped forward and shook my hand. I could feel specks of earth from his encrusted strong hand between my fingers. It was a good feeling.

I had one last throw to try. A regular daily task of mine was to collate the latest information from all the battle fronts throughout the world and then go along to the Commander-in-Chief's villa near the east bank of the Tigris and mark up the huge map that occupied the complete wall behind his desk.

Lieutenant-General Sir Arthur Smith, KCB, KBE, DSO, MC, Croix de Guerre, had been a real fighting general. Thrice wounded, he still dragged his left leg slightly when walking. He was short, sandy-haired with bristling eyebrows and a bristling moustache – a terrifying figure, especially when one realised he was among the six most senior and important generals in the British Army. At first, I used to tiptoe into his vast room with my notes and assorted grease pencils and a duster to wipe yesterday's lines of battle off the talc covering his map and mark in the latest results – blue lines for the Allied troops and red for the enemy. When I reported for duty each day, he would give a dry cough and a brusque nod of the head and I would then detour round him in his big chair at his big desk.

But after a day or two, he started to talk to me. He might ask the state of morale among GHQ personnel or had I qualified for 'Python' home leave. (After two years' continuous overseas service, a soldier was entitled to enter a form of lottery. If his name came up and he could be spared from his unit, he could spend two weeks on leave in the United Kingdom. I underwent four and a quarter years of continuous overseas service but my name never came up.) At first, our conversations were brief and stilted but gradually they warmed up. I had suddenly realised he was lonely. There was no one of his own rank to speak to while conversations with his 'senior' juniors would always be artificial. No regular officer who wanted a good report as a step towards promotion was going to argue with or tease the great man. I have always had respect for fighting seniors, not least those twice my age, but as far as I was concerned, the war was an interlude, not my real career. And he had the wit to sense it.

Once he said to me, when I had finished marking the maps, 'Back home, Greenfield, you ever go to the theatre? The real theatre. I mean. In the West End.'

'Oh yes, sir. Quite a bit, sir.' As a penniless undergraduate pre-war, I regularly spent matinees up in the gods, the gallery, where you got to recognise actors by the tops of their heads. I would never forget Shaw's *The Doctor's Dilemma* and a beautiful dark-haired young actress named Vivien Leigh.

'You heard of this fella Coward?'

'Noel Coward, sir? He's reckoned a great wit.'

'Is he, by God. Anything a bit strange about him?'

'I'm not quite sure I follow you, sir.'

'Well, listen to this, Greenfield. He's come here to entertain the troops, with a pianist – a male pianist – to accompany him. Going to do a tour of the outlying posts.'

I thought, Oh Christ, ENSA (the official body organising shows and entertainments for the Forces), had fucked it up yet again. The troops didn't want Noel Coward's fluting 'Mad Dogs and Englishmen' in an adenoidal tenor. They wanted broad comedians like Max Miller and a chorus line with big teats.

I nodded and waited to hear more.

The General went on, 'The AG tells me they were booked into the Semiramis Hotel – no expense spared – in two single rooms. Seems this Coward fella insists they share a double room. What you make of that, eh?'

'Well, sir, he did once write a song called 'Mad About the Boy.' I should, of course, have added that it was intended to be sung by a woman, but this was getting to be fun.

'Did he, by God! Tell me straight, Greenfield – is this fella Coward a bugger?'

'Well, sir . . .'

'You don't have to make excuses. When I was young, if a fella found he was that way inclined, he did the decent thing and shot himself. Now these pansies prance all round the place, giving themselves airs and graces. He'd better not start mucking around with my men. One whisper of that and he'll be out of this Command next day – under escort!'

Sir Arthur Smith had been born in 1890, growing up in a strict Victorian era. Eton, Sandhurst and the Coldstream Guards had moulded him into the most regular of regular soldiers. Emotional outbursts, even admitting to possessing emotions, had been repressed and stifled by a rigid military code. And yet I sensed a puckishness, a warmth, under the hard carapace. Now I had to put that feeling to the test.

'Could you spare me a moment, sir?'

'What is it, Greenfield? If it's going to take some time, you'd better sit down.'

For the third time in two days, I made my little speech about Petrov and the injustice of sending him on to the Soviet Union. The C-in-C heard me out in silence and then he glared at me.

'Why am I hearing this from you? If it's that important, why hasn't the BGS Ops put me in the picture? Eh?'

'Well, sir . . .'

'Well, sir – what? You chancin' your arm, Greenfield? Been turned down by the BGS, have you?'

'Not exactly, sir.' I thought, the hell with this. I'm going to dump Shorty George right in it, that little shit. 'You see, sir, I think Brigadier Kenny was on my side. But he couldn't really go against the GSO I, my CO, who'd turned it down flat.'

'Did he, indeed? You read your staff duties, Greenfield? In this Army, you go through channels. Ideas are filtered upwards or downwards through the proper channels, brigadier to colonel, colonel to major, major to captain, down to the other ranks. I can't have every Tom, Dick and Harry of a staff captain prancing round my desk with their highfalutin' nonsense about justice and Christ knows what! You – get – the – message, Greenfield.'

'Yes, sir.' So that was it. Beaten by the Army system. Well, at least, I had tried.

'Right,' said the General, 'let's get on with it. Time's running on. There was a signal through this morning from our man in Tehran, Sir Reader Bullard, the Ambassador. The Russians are leaning hard on him. They want their man. "Their man" indeed.'

'You mean, sir . . . you're going to back it?'

'Of course. Now stop flapping about like a dying duck in a thunderstorm! We've got work to do. Your parents ever think of christening you?'

'Yes, sir, my first name's George.'

'All right, George, get some scribbling paper from over there and we'll start.' He buzzed for his MA, a languid Guards major with a bushy moustache, and told him to telephone Lieutenant-Colonel Woodhouse, my CO, to say that the C-in-C was borrowing me for the morning. Then he winked at me. The gesture told me enough. Shorty would be very circumspect while I was under the great man's protection.

Between us, we drafted a signal stating that Petrov was being held in Baghdad, that he was not a Russian but a Pole and that the demands of the Soviet authorities to have him 'repatriated' should be firmly resisted on the grounds that those demands were a breach of the Geneva Convention and of human justice. The signal was marked 'TOP SECRET: FOR THE EYES OF FIELD-MARSHAL ALANBROOKE, CHIEF OF THE IMPERIAL GENERAL STAFF, FROM CINCPAIC.'

The General stood up from his desk and limped to and fro, having first ordered his MA to come and collect the signal and have it sent top priority. 'That's a good job done, George. Let me see now. London's three hours back, what? So it's about nine o'clock in the morning there. That'll hit Brookie's desk at the right time. Fine fella, Brookie – for a gunner!' He grinned at the old joke. 'Mind like a razor and straight as they come. I think this calls for a spot of sherry, eh?'

The La Ina was as dry as its owner, and equally warming.

I floated back to the G Ops building and it was not the effect of one glass of sherry. At last, I had found a regular Army staff officer prepared to break protocol and do the right thing. Petrov had a real supporter now – the head man. It was no longer a one-junior crusade. He would have to stay in Baghdad probably till the war in Europe ended but at least it would be in freedom. I wondered whether I might pass the word round the various messes and the officers' club, which had a sizeable garden stretching under the date palms. They could probably use a jobbing gardener.

Word had already spread round the Ops building. The C-in-C had made a courtesy phone call to Brigadier Kenny who in turn had informed Shorty. I passed him on the stairs as he was going out to lunch. He gave me a withering glance but said nothing. I had a slight sense of sorrow, mingled with guilt; by his rigid code of staff duties, I had behaved badly. Means and ends, I shrugged, and went off for a celebratory lunch myself.

First thing next morning, he sent for me. I stood to attention in front of his desk. 'Greenfield, I've decided to relieve you of your duties marking up the C-in-C's maps. Starting this morning, Bruce will be responsible. That is all.'

'May I say something, sir?'

'What is it? Can't you see I'm busy?'

'I'll try to be brief, sir. Apart from the maps, I'm in the middle of a project with the Commander in Chief . . .'

'A project I expressly forbade you from pursuing! You deliberately go behind my back – and the BGS's back. You realise I could have you court-martialled for that?'

'I'm sorry, sir. All I wanted to say was – I don't think the C-in-C would be terribly happy if I don't turn up at his office this morning.'

There was at least a minute's silence. Then he said grumpily, 'Oh, all right this time. But don't expect any more favours from me.'

When I entered his room, Sir Arthur told me there had been no reply as yet from the War Office in Whitehall. But it was early days. After all it was not seven in the morning yet back home. Things hadn't got moving so far.

About three o'clock that same afternoon, there was a message that the C-in-C wanted me to report to him urgently. Good news travels fast, I thought, as I went at forced march pace the quarter-mile to his villa. I was conducted in almost at once. He sat at his desk, shoulders hunched.

'Read this, George,' he said and tossed a printed signal across the desk. It was marked: TOP SECRET FOR CINCPAIC FROM FOREIGN SECRETARY: COPY TO CIGS WAR OFFICE. It was full of guff about the Russians being our gallant allies and that we must do nothing to hinder their war effort. Their Ambassador in London had sworn that every man on board the trains to be repatriated to the Soviet Union was a true Soviet citizen. It was not for us to question the word of an ally who was bearing the brunt of the fighting against the Nazis. The

Foreign Office understood that another convoy of Russians was due to reach Basra in two to three days. Our man was to be handed over to the Soviet detachment at Basra for onward transmission to Russia with the next train. This order had the complete backing of the War Office. It was signed 'Anthony Eden, Foreign Secretary.'

In that instant, I remembered vividly the thick moustache almost concealing the very red lips, the receding chin, the vibrant baritone voice, the almost obsequious way he had tried to be friendly with me, a junior staff officer, on the steps of Churchill's villa inside the British Embassy compound at Tehran. And his petulance when I said I knew why he was handing over a gold sovereign along with the Sword of Stalingrad that afternoon. 'At all costs, don't let's be beastly to the Russians' was his running motto. He should have learned by now – we hangers-on had sensed it at once on meeting Stalin at Churchill's birthday party and from direct contact with Russian officers there – that the hard man and the hard regime only respected equal toughness from a so-called ally.

Anthony Eden was to make the same mistake again out of weakness over a year later, this time backed up by his ruthless henchman, Harold Macmillan, when he arranged to hand over several thousand Cossacks to the Soviet dictator. Dante would have had a circle prepared for him.

Sir Arthur looked at me and shook his head. 'I'm sorry, George. Truly sorry.'

'You did all you could, sir. It's not your fault.'

'You'll tell the poor fella? Tell him we really tried.'

'I suppose there's no chance, sir? . . .'

'Not an earthly. Read between the lines. Either it was too hot a potato for the CIGS and he passed it across to the FO or, more likely, the FO'd been keeping tabs on it all along and tipped off the Foreign Secretary. But remember, he's next to Winston. What he says goes.'

'It's a shame, sir.'

'It's a bloody shame, George.'

That afternoon, Sergeant Makepeace, the interpreter, and I went once more to the Military Police compound. It was raining lightly but Petrov was still working on his patch of earth. He had hoed it and raked it and now he was sowing lettuce seeds which one of his guards had bought in the market. He came over, smiling, wiping his hands on a piece of cloth. The sergeant broke the news. Petrov turned and looked me straight in the eye. 'I'm sorry,' I said. 'Very sorry. We did try. Tell him that, please. sergeant.'

Makepeace spoke. Petrov's eyes were still locked on mine. Then he nodded his head. 'Sor-ry,' he said, breaking the two syllables of the word. 'Sor-ry.' Then he thrust out his hand and shook mine. He nodded again and gave a half-smile. Without thinking, I snapped out a salute. Then the sergeant and I walked away. It had started to rain harder.

Several years after the war, I was re-reading *Tristram Shandy*. I had reached that passage where My Uncle Toby hears the fly buzzing round the room, irritating him. He stalks it, catches it in his hand, holds it carefully as he opens the window and then he lets it fly away. He says, 'Go thy way, little fly, I'll not hurt a hair of thy head . . . Go thy way. This world is yet wide enough for both thee and me.'

I put the book down and sat back, thinking of Private Payne and Samarra and Petrov in his cell in Baghdad.

The window of the world had stayed firmly shut for him.

11

❖❖❖

'Clean-Living and Under Thirty'

❖❖❖❖❖

After the Petrov affair, I found myself a chunk of grit in GHQ's otherwise smooth machinery. Colonel Woodhouse would cheerfully have ordered me to the local equivalent of the salt-mines but he dared not even glare at me as long as I was under the patronage of the C-in-C. The Brigadier was studiedly neutral and everyone else in the Ops building, apart from Bob Hope, thought it was the funniest thing since that film, *The Thief of Baghdad*.

Then a temporary job cropped up. Certain large American companies never let the Allied pursuit of victory interfere with their post-war plans. They knew that, once peace came, the company that had been smart enough to stake out its claims during the conflict would be the first to cash in in a big way. Thus, during Operation Torch, the Allied invasion of North Africa from the sea in late 1942 – the first time American troops were in action – there was a desperate shortage of tractors and levellers to set up forward bases for fighter aircraft, aircraft needed to provide cover for the advancing ground troops. The reason was quickly discovered. The tractors had been diverted to set up proper airfields for international passenger-carrying firms like Pan-Am and TWA '*après la guerre finit.*'

The 'oily boys' were not far behind in sniffing out potential troughs for their snouts. Substantial deposits of oil had been discovered in Saudi Arabia, which could not be exploited until peace returned. Kuwait was more or less on the same latitude and had similar ground conditions. Indeed, there is almost an 'oil' latitude, running through Texas, the Gulf of Mexico, Saudi Arabia, Kuwait and southern Iran. Any oil discovered inside Kuwait would belong to the sheikh. But the southern borders were not marked by roads or fences or any visible barrier; map bearings, probably determined by Sir Percy Cox, PRPG (Political Resident, Persian Gulf) in the 1920s, were the determining factors. Trial boreholes had announced the presence of oil underground – lots and lots of it. So one or other of the big American prospecting companies (the fact there was a war on did not affect them) might feel that, if the frontier was invisible anyway, why not shift it a few miles northwards? They would lean on the State Department. The powerful lobby was not to be ignored, not if the official concerned wanted to enjoy prosperity as well as peace after the end of hostilities. In turn, the State Department leaned on the Foreign Office, which got on to the War Office, which got on to the C-in-C, PAIFORCE. The buck eventually landed on my desk. Objective: determine the exact southern boundaries of the sheikhdom of Kuwait.

Luckily, I had two good ex-GHQ friends at the Basra HQ, Derek Norris and Bruce Burrage, an Indian Army officer. They insisted on my having a game of squash with each in turn – this with the temperature well over 105° and myself physically unfit through easy living. As Bruce put it with a grin, 'We felt it was our best chance of beating you!' When I had got my breath back and enjoyed an evening's hospitality at their mess, they helped to line up the requirements for my task. The first was a sapper major, the second a theodolite and the rest half a dozen other ranks.

Kuwait in those pre-oil boom days was basically a collection of mud huts with one rather larger building, enclosed by a mud wall, for the sheikh and his entourage. It was a staging post for camel trains travelling on down to Bahrain and the Trucial Coast. Several herds of scrawny goats wandered in and out of the miserable village, gnawing at anything that looked green and edible. Just offshore were oyster beds; you could hire a boat and a diver for a dinar or less and chance your luck that one of the oysters would contain a valuable pearl. The sheikh drew a percentage of the worth from all such 'lucky dips' and thus augmented his meagre income. As a British Army saying put it, 'The Persian Gulf is the arsehole of the world – and Kuwait is four hundred miles up it.' In the course of my travels, I had seen poverty-stricken Persian villages and Egyptian squalor and the filth of Baghdad slums. Kuwait was a cut above those – but only a narrow cut.

Our little convoy drove south to the invisible frontier. Or at least to the point on the map that must be reasonably close. The desert was fairly featureless but the sapper major managed to take bearings on one or other small prominence, the edge of a dry *wadi* or a thirty-foot hill that rose above the plain. By taking a series of back-bearings, he could establish our exact position on the map. After toing and froing on the coastal road, he finally placed the exact degree of latitude about a mile further south. The rest was easy. The southern perimeter of Kuwait ran due west – 270° – and all he now had to do was set up a series of wands at about hundred-yard intervals with the help of the theodolite. The whole operation lasted less than three hours.

Much later, I learned that the American oil company's claims stretched several miles too far north, well inside Kuwaiti territory. They were presumably told – in rather more diplomatic terms – to back off. But already the global war was within a year of its ending; the oil bonanza would only be briefly delayed.

I managed to spin out the project for one more day and decided to try my luck at the pearl diving. Bruce Burrage, who had tried it quite a few times, was sceptical. 'They see a beginner coming along,' he said, 'and they take you to one of the inshore fished-out beds in shallow waters. Less puff required by the bloody diver. There hasn't been a pearl brought up from those beds since Churchill was a boy.'

To me, it was another experience. Finding a pearl would be a nice bonus. So off I went to the stinking docks in the heat of the day. The sun that beat down almost like a weapon and reflected off the still waters would envelop any mad dog or Englishman who ventured out in the middle of the day. At Bruce's suggestion, I carried an old umbrella to provide some shade. The boatman helped me on board the narrow skiff and then the diver joined us. He was a wizened, emaciated creature with his ribs defined every time he drew breath. Dressed in only a loincloth, he had a kind of satchel slung over one shoulder. There was a brief formula in which the boatman frisked the diver to make sure he was not carrying a knife. He must bring up the oysters intact from the seabed, with no chance to open them underwater and secrete any pearls he found.

He went over the side, attached to a long rope and then duck-dived. At school, I had swum two lengths – sixty yards – of the swimming baths under water and could stay down for well over a minute. But this man was extraordinary. When he had disappeared for well over two minutes, I glanced at the boatman, as if to say, 'About time we pulled him up, isn't it?' He gave me an *Insh'allah* look in return. At last there was a plop beside the boat and his head broke the surface. He had half a dozen or so oysters in the bag. The boatman took out a sharp knife, opened each one in turn and showed me the virginal contents. Not a pearl in sight. And so it went on for an hour under the oppressive sun until I had had enough. The following week after I had got back to Baghdad, Bruce telephoned me to say that another absolute beginner like me had hired the same boat and diver, had been taken to exactly the same oyster beds and on his very first plunge the diver had come up with an oyster containing a large black pearl of perfect shape. It was valued at £5,000 (£150,000 or more today) and even after the sheikh had taken his cut, the officer in question would be a wealthy man.

But the temporary assignment had not removed the problems of my position at G Ops. Then, in late July 1944, thanks to Brigadier Kenny, an answer was found. He sent for me and announced that the Command had to put forward the name of a reasonably young officer as a likely student for the next Staff College four-monthly course in Haifa, starting in early September. He had decided, through the Military Secretary, to recommend me. There was no question, of course, of my having the choice to accept or reject the proposal. It was the usual case of 'The following will volunteer . . .' But I was glad to be getting away. A full year in Baghdad was more than enough. It had become a routine, the office, the officers' club, the mess, weekend visits for squash and gossip to the Alwiyah Club on the far side of the river, all amid the sweltering, demoralising heat of the long summer months. Once I had spent an evening chatting with Cecil Hatry under the palm trees in the garden of the officers' club. Between us we demolished a bottle of whisky in the course of an hour or two. In a cold climate, I would have been reeling and slobbering after my half-bottle share but the continual, unnoticed sweating in the high humid temperature of Baghdad dispersed the spirits before they could be absorbed.

In July and August, the mercury rose to 105°, 110°, occasionally higher. Then, at the beginning of September, it began to creep down – to under 100°, 95°, below 90°. To systems attuned to the top temperatures, this was deliciously cool. And then, just as moods rose in line with the drop in temperatures, the *khamsin*, the date-ripening wind, would blow from mid-September to its end. (*Khamsin* means 'fifteen' in Arabic.) The hot wind, blowing in almost suffocating gusts morning and night, swung the mercury back up to 110° and beyond. The suicide rate was said to quadruple during that fortnight; men suddenly broke into insensate rages.

Above all was the feeling of marking time, of seeing one's youth and the glittering rewards youth should bring, slowly drift away in a routine of shifting papers from the 'In' tray into the 'Out' tray. By the summer of 1944, PAIFORCE no longer had a valid role. There was no further risk that the Germans might invade. Their bomber bases were bring driven back into the Fatherland, too far for even a one-way attempt to bomb the oilfields. The command had become a vast staging post, centred on Baghdad. Divisions and brigades might be transported westwards as reinforcements for the Italian campaign or eastwards as reinforcements for General Slim and his 14th Army. But they had no real military purpose inside the command.

Our small coterie all had exciting prospects back in Civvy Street: Bill Fox had his acting career to pick up, Cecil Hatry's father was building a publishing and bookselling empire, based on Hatchards in Piccadilly, Major Topalian had been a successful stockbroker and Captain Howe of GHQ Intelligence a promising barrister. After five years among the brutal and licentious soldiery, I was far too rusty for academe but still had hopes of a career somewhere. We used to sit and drink and moan as the round went on, one day stretched into another and none of us felt we were doing a worthwhile job to help the war effort. For me, a change could only be for the better.

With the prospect of leaving Baghdad for ever, as it then seemed, I was determined to make one journey while the chance still existed. So one Sunday, Derek Norris, another friend and I boarded a southbound train and got off at Ur Junction. There we found a decrepit cab and ancient driver who, after the customary haggle, agreed to drive us the few miles to Babylon. Babylon – the epitome of power, wealth and luxury, a symbol that reached across the centuries into Scott Fitzgerald's day and beyond. On arrival, we saw dusty brown earthworks, with a forlorn breeze blowing eddies of dust into the brown mudbrick walls and open spaces. A shepherd sat huddled in the middle distance with his scrawny sheep grazing on tufts of withered grass. It was a desolate ruin.

Pre-war, Babylon's walls had been covered in bas-reliefs and a special kind of lapis lazuli enamelled surface to the brick-work. It must have glowed and glittered when the sun rose high. But a team of German archaeologists had come along, stripped away the bas-reliefs and the enamelled bricks and re-erected the glory in a special museum in Berlin. And then an RAF bombing mission against Berlin had scored a direct hit on the museum, reducing it and its contents to charred rubble and ashes. Kingdoms and crowns come tumbling down.

A speck of blue in one corner of a muddy wall caught my eye. It was a small chip of the blue enamel the thorough Germans had missed. For many months, I carried it around, to remind me of transience and the feeling that London, Paris, New York – all might follow the same fate one distant day.

On my last night in Baghdad, I took the G Ops senior NCOs out for a meal, followed by a visit to an open-air cinema. We were almost the only Army personnel there and I found myself next to a group of Baghdadi Arabs in their *kefayehs* and robes. It was a pleasant evening and a small token of thanks on my part for the skilful way our sergeant-major and his colleagues had smoothed over and largely concealed my shortcomings.

Next morning, I boarded the Nairn bus for Damascus. The Nairn brothers, two New Zealanders, had invested in express buses plying the five-hundred-mile journey, which was accomplished in about ten hours. As mentioned earlier, the tarmac road ran straight as an arrow alongside the oil pipe line with its pumping stations at intervals and the glaring desert on either side. There was usually one halt, often at Rutbah Wells, for passengers to stretch their legs. In spite of the well-contoured seats and a rudimentary kind of air-conditioning, it was an arduous journey and, for one who throughout his time in the Army had never attended a sick-parade except to have the regulation jabs, I was feeling quite ropey when we disembarked. Even a stroll next morning along the Street Called Strait, to admire the silver filigree workers as they squatted over their charcoal braziers and teased out filaments of silver to twist into arabesques as fine as a spider's web, failed to dispel the mood.

The next stage was in the back of an open Army truck, bumping and swaying through the uplands, past Homs with its giant waterwheel, still working after two thousand years, and across the Cedars of Lebanon, down to the coast and Haifa. A large hotel had been requisitioned to house the Staff College. It stood a little below the summit of the steep hill that overlooks the port and town of Haifa on one side and the open beaches to the west.

The atmosphere was redolent of public school life or, perhaps more accurately, university. Two students shared a bedroom, meals took place in the large hall, we were split up into small groups (syndicates) each with its DS (director of studies). The majority of students were either infantrymen or gunners, with ranks ranging from lieutenant-colonel down to captain. There were written examinations, essays to be composed, TEWTS (tactical exercises without troops), 'operation orders' to be drawn up. I was only five years away from a similar intellectual discipline and found no problem slipping back into the atmosphere. But it was hard on those men, who had perhaps been clerks or commercial travellers in Civvy Street and who had joined the Territorial Army, more often than not gaining promotion through their resourcefulness in action. and who now found themselves having to put ideas and plans on to paper, Haifa was unlike other military staff colleges in one respect: half its students were drawn from the RAF. Although they had their separate tuition in staff duties, in the latter part of the course they were set to undertake joint exercises with the 'brown jobs', each drawing on the other's expertise.

I felt drained of all energy on reaching Haifa and put it down to the arduousness of the journey. I was usually a heavy sleeper but, that first night, I woke up in the small hours, feeling strangely damp. My pyjamas were soaking with sweat and the bottom sheet and mattress were wet through, even though the window was wide open and cooling breezes were blowing off the Mediterranean. I had to change my pyjamas, take off the sopping undersheet and turn the mattress over before I could get back to sleep again. And the following day, I was overcome with lassitude. After walking slowly for fifty yards, I had to pause in the hope that energy would return. For about a week I kept up the routine, sweating profusely at night, getting up and turning over the soaking mattress – even though I had moved my trestle bed on to the verandah outside the bedroom to catch all the cooling breezes – dragging myself around in the daytime, a block on myself and the other members of the syndicate. Something was very wrong. Finally, after about ten days, I reported sick.

The Staff College MO was also a student, who had seen much action in the Italian campaign. He prodded and thumped me, took my temperature, looked at my tongue and then asked me if I had consorted with any women lately. 'Chance would be a fine thing,' was my response. At length, he wrote 'PUO' on the card and assigned me to what was still called the German Hospital, although long taken over by the military. 'Pyrexia (high temperature) of Unknown Origin' – that wonderful catch-all phrase covered a doctor's total ignorance. I was driven by field ambulance and placed in a two-bed ward. The fever specialist examined me, prodding my stomach and defining in a dark plastic pencil line a mound slightly above my left hip. My spleen was swollen. I had caught typhus.

I had been long enough in the Middle East to know that there was then – and still is, I believe – no cure for typhus. The spleen went on swelling until it stood up like a small rugby football and its expansion forced the heart and its supporting muscles across to the right side of the body. (For quite a while I kept an X-ray showing my heart on that less popular side.) Unless, as the saying went, one was 'clean living and under thirty', the chances of recovery were slight indeed. I was aged twenty-seven and reasonably clean-living *faute de mieux*. But the officer in the next bed to mine, who slept under a mosquito net, was fortyish with a blotched drinker's face.

I was exhausted and very weak, spending most of my time dozing, sleeping or in a kind of light coma. But early one morning I was shaken awake by my room-mate, who had struggled out of bed. 'What the bloody hell you done with the imprest account?' he kept shouting. 'It's CO's inspection tomorrow. You know it damn well. He'll find the discrepancy – you bastard?'

He kept on shaking me and raving about the imprest account. He was obviously hallucinating but I was too weak to call for the night sister. Finally, he climbed back into his bed. The room was small and our beds were less than three feet apart. And for the next two hours, he died horribly, snoring and gurgling and racking his lungs with each intake of breath. My face was turned towards his and I was too drained to move. And so I could only watch his slow agonising death.

It was not a cheerful prospect for a fellow-sufferer. A couple of days later, I woke up one morning and lay with my eyes closed in my comatose state. The matron and the specialist were standing at the foot of my bed, talking.

She said, 'I'm rather worried, we're very short of beds. I can't think where to put new admissions.'

He casually kicked the rungs of my bed and said, 'Well, at least this one'll be free by tonight, tomorrow morning perhaps.'

I thought, you arrogant bastard. One day, I'll have the greatest pleasure in spitting on your fucking grave. Something happened; it could be the adrenalin flowing, but from then on, I was on the mend. Slowly, of its own accord, the spleen subsided again, the supporting muscles pulled the heart back into its normal place and my appetite returned. Even my hair, which through the sustained high temperature had been coming out in great tufts every time it was combed, stopped falling out. It was normally thick but by now I had a parting two inches wide with smooth bald skin in the gap. Vain men with little else to occupy them will constantly finger such a blemish. I still recall with exquisite delight fingering the exposed scalp one day and feeling the tiny bristles of new-growing hair breaking through the surface. Eventually, my hair was even thicker than ever.

Recovery led to visitors, one of the first of whom was my DS, Lieutenant-Colonel Edward Ford of the Grenadier Guards, who much later ended his distinguished career in the royal household as Private Secretary to the Queen. He told me I had missed too much of the course to be able to rejoin it on discharge from the hospital but if I were to apply for a place on the next course at the beginning of January, there was every chance of a favourable response. The January course would last six months, half as long again as all previous courses, and the tuition would be that much more detailed. I thanked him, saying I would be delighted to apply, assuming there were no other plans for me back in Baghdad

Now I had beaten the odds in recovering, the fever specialist who had written me off a week or two earlier, began to take an interest. He spent several sessions quizzing me on how I might have contracted the disease. Typhus is a louse-borne plague and usually occurs when conditions are filthy. The medico might have expected me to get infected during my months in the Western Desert, where there were no baths and only rudimentary washing. Or again, during my six months and more under canvas before transferring to Baghdad. But, once there, I was sleeping under a roof in a room cleaned regularly by the staff and with fresh sheets at least once a week and daily showers in the hot season. He was perplexed until I told him about my last-night celebrations and the visit to the open-air cinema, where I sat next to an Arab. He could only conclude that a louse had crawled or jumped off my neighbour and on to me, had bitten me and then gone back to its regular host.

Discharged from hospital, I was sent for two weeks convalescence in Nathaniya, not far from Haifa. The first morning PT class made me realise sharply how weak and out of condition I was. The instructor threw a medicine ball for me to catch. The impact sent me crashing down on my bottom on the hard floor. So enough of PT. In company with a New Zealand flying officer who had broken several bones in a crash landing, I lay on the beach and dozed, then ate a large lunch and returned to the beach for another doze.

It was fascinating and yet saddening to watch the local Jewish kindergarten children being taken for a bathe in the sea. They were, I was told, mainly the children of refugees from Germany. The teacher marched them along the beach in two neat ranks. She blew her whistle – they halted. Another whistle – in unison they turned right, facing the sea. Another whistle – and they put down their wraps and towels, each in a neat bundle. Yet another blast on the whistle – and they marched in step into the shallows, where they splashed sedately for a few moments before there was another blast, at which they immediately walked out and lined up again. And so on in whistle-driven steps until they marched off again back to kindergarten.

'Poor bloody kids,' the New Zealander muttered. I agreed, knowing how English children would have caused chaos and turned the teacher's hair grey with their indisciplined rushing about and shouting. But at least there would have been laughter and yelling and a sense of enjoyment, not the taking exercise by numbers we had witnessed. It was as though the adult immigrants had left their country behind without casting off the desire to be *korrekt*, to pursue orderly drills. The New Zealander told me how he had gone for a stroll along a lane in the hills behind Haifa. In the distance, he had heard the tramp of marching feet in step and the sound of a German marching song bellowed with real lung-power as the marchers approached. He thought, Christ, the Wehrmacht must have landed! Round the bend came a band of Jewish youths, boys and girls, swinging along and belting out what sounded like, but could not possibly have been, the Horst Wessel song. A strange irony, we both agreed.

Back in Baghdad, I reported to Brigadier Kenny. It was now mid-October and I was booked to return to Haifa just after Christmas. My G OPs job had been filled but, rather than have me kicking my heels aimlessly for two months and more, he had found another job for me. The author, R. C. Hutchinson, had been commissioned to write the history of the Persia and Iraq Command. He was to be paid £1,000 (nearly £30,000 in today's terms) and of course have free travel and accommodation. Indeed, a suite at the Semiramis Hotel, one of the two best in the city and overlooking the broad, brown Tigris, was to be put at his disposal. My task, the Brigadier said, was to dig around all the relevant files, some held by PAIFORCE but many still with GHQ in Cairo, flag up the important documents and produce some coherent notes; in other words, save Mr Hutchinson all the weeks of dreary devilling to amass the source material. I could do it in my own time, the only proviso being that the task must be complete when I left for Haifa. The senior officers running various GHQ departments had been warned to give me access to any of their back files I required. I was under his, Brigadier Kenny's, direct command and would report only to him. No one else, apart from the C-in-C, who wished me well by the way, could give me instructions or order me around.

I could have kissed him on each of his pink cheeks. It was a wonderful assignment. In the first place, I admired the author, having read both *The Shining Scabbard* and *Testament*. He clearly understood the military mind. And the task itself was like tackling a PhD thesis, without the chore of having to write reams of turgid prose. I was my own master and I knew the Brigadier would keep me on the lightest of reins. So, for the next two months, I worked eagerly at it. I discovered that the RAF had a daily 'milk-run' flight from Habbaniyah to Cairo and so made several visits, sitting on the floor of a stripped out Dakota with my back propped against the fuselage, all in my quest for the vital files. This was when I discovered in a tatty old box General (as he then was) Wavell's 'appreciation of the situation' and his operational plan for the defence of Persia and Iraq. In the desperate days, when he was already fighting a war on two fronts as C-in-C Middle East, with Crete falling to the Wehrmacht's invasion and the Eighth Army reeling back in defeat by Rommel in the Desert, he had at Churchill's demand flown to Baghdad, carried out a swift survey and then written down his summary and his plans, which held good for the next four years. The papers were in his own handwriting, creased and curling at the edges. The writing was neat, without a blot or a crossing out. The man had a mind big enough and subtle enough to blank off for the moment the pressures of the fighting he had left behind and to assess calmly and concisely the immediate problems of a new situation. To my mind, Wavell was one of the two greatest generals of World War Two and one day perhaps a detailed biography will do him belated justice.

By the end of November, my researches were complete, and I still had a month to go. Then it struck me that R. C. Hutchinson might find it easier and quicker to absorb a running narrative than a bundle of more cryptic notes. Borrowing a spare typewriter from Brigadier Kenny's staff, I set to. Pounding away, by Christmas when I handed over the whole *shabash*, an Urdu word picked up by the troops meaning, in their other phrase, 'the whole shooting match' – I had knocked out around 40,000 words, with all the accompanying files neatly flagged up. The Brigadier thanked me for my efforts, I thanked him warmly for giving me the chance, we wished each other Merry Christmas and parted in almost effusive cordiality.

There was to be a sequel. In the early 1950s, having been a civilian again for well over five years, I was walking down Kingsway in London and happened to glance into the window of His (as it then was) Majesty's Stationery Office. Prominently displayed was a copy of *The History of the Persia and Iraq Command* by R. C. Hutchinson. I went in and started to peruse a copy. Funny, I thought, those first two pages look familiar. I plunged ahead five or six pages and read the *verso* and the *recto* in turn. I recognised each paragraph, even a couple of quotations I had included, which were not part of the notes. Skimming on through the book, I found every page rang a loud bell. I put the copy back on the shelf. An assistant came up and asked me if I wished to purchase Mr Hutchinson's excellent book.

'No, thanks,' I said. 'I know it already.'

He looked surprised as I walked out.

What a fraud! The famous novelist had arrived in Baghdad, read my draft, glanced through the photographs and maps I had selected, written a short introduction and then incorporated the whole thing under his own name. Presumably, he spent the next few weeks drinking pink gins at the bar of the Semiramis Hotel and going on sightseeing trips by staff car around the command. Then back to London, pocketing the £1,000 fee after doing no work at all, and getting on with his own writings.

There was no way I could prove plagiarism, as I had not made a carbon copy of my draft and Hutchinson had no doubt destroyed the incriminating evidence of the original. In any event, my narrative and notes would have been classed as Crown copyright, since they had been part of my military duties. And, five years after the war, I was a young and eager publisher. One does not acquire promising authors by insulting or suing famous heavyweights. Oddly enough, R. C. Hutchinson's post-war career did not flourish and he died in 1975, an embittered man.

In his memoirs, *Take it from Me*, Jimmy Edwards, the comedian, relates the story of sharing a railway compartment with Bud Flanagan and another member of the Crazy Gang. The two of them were fooling around, telling jokes and playing tricks on one another. Jimmy sat back and read *The Times*. He had a Cambridge degree and had won the DFC as a pilot towing glider planes over Arnhem.

At the Staff College, Haifa, 1945

Bud Flanagan leaned forward and tapped Jimmy Edwards on the knee. He said, 'You know, Jimmy, the trouble with you is you think you're doing the business a favour!'

Quite a few young officers, who had graduated from Oxford or Cambridge not long before enlisting, might, if they were honest with themselves, accept a similar accusation. Many schools in the 'thirties had an Upper Sixth for potential scholarship candidates, a Lower Sixth for those taking the Higher Certificate, the forerunner of A Levels, and an Army Class for the also-ran. There was quite a strong pacifist wave throughout those difficult years – the Peace Pledge Union had several million members – and the resulting annual Sandhurst intakes were not the cream of the crop. There was the old story about the Guards officer who was so stupid that even his fellow officers realised it; it could be replicated in quite a few county regiments. Their courage was not in question. All too many of them fought gallantly and died because of the stupid mistakes made by their seniors.

But no claims of intellectual inferiority could have been made against the Staff College in Haifa. In many ways, I learned more in six months there than I had in three years of Cambridge. They were, in fact, lessons of great benefit to my business life after the War. The directing staff drilled into their pupils the need to make 'an appreciation of the situation' before any decisions were announced.

It all started with setting down the details of 'the situation', the nature of the terrain, what one knew of the enemy's dispositions, the availability of our own troops and any other germane factors. The next step was to set out 'courses open to the enemy'. Was he likely to attack, or stay put, or withdraw? And what would be the different consequences depending on which course of action he took? Then came 'courses open to our side'. Could we attack? Was it to be by day or under cover of darkness? Had we sufficient troops and did the terrain permit a frontal attack or should it be by one flank or the other?

Above all, the objective had to be closely defined. What were we trying to achieve? It was no good coming up with a vague hope – 'Let's advance a thousand yards and see what happens.' Instead there had to be recognised targets – 'to capture Hill 50' or 'drive the enemy back across the river'. Finally, when all these factors were clear and accepted, the operation order could be written.

It began with *Information*: what we knew about the enemy forces, details of our own troops and of the terrain separating the two. Next came *Intention*: 'Eighth Army will break out from the Alamein defences, attack and destroy the Afrika Korps.' The phrasing had to be firm and specific. Now we get on to *Method*: just how was the intention to be achieved and what units would carry out which tasks. Then *Administration*: details of the back-up, where the forward dressing stations would be sited, the designated areas for spare vehicles and ammunition, routes to be taken by the l of c (lines of communication), troops and so forth. Finally came *Intercommunication*. In a fluctuating battle, it is essential for the commanders of units to be on the same RT net. The details and alternate frequencies had to be listed.

The Staff College also insisted that operational orders and instructions had to be set down in simple and sparse English. Even if read under difficult conditions, in the dark, driving rain, a mortar bombardment, they must be clear and readily understood. For anyone like myself, prone to the extra unnecessary adjective or to involved sentences, it was a salutary tonic. The Civil Service could learn a useful lesson from that teaching. And many of the general concepts could be transmuted with great benefit to present-day political and business life. In my small business years later, I often found myself thinking, what is my objective? Or, if I want to gain such-and-such, what courses are open, both to me and to the competition? Many Cabinet ministers, in my opinion, could do with an intensive Staff College course.

As a previous chapter tells, in the early months of 1943, 2nd Battalion the Buffs had been stationed near Khanaqin on the lower mountain slopes of western Iran. There were then several inches of snow on the flint-hard ground and the battalion was still licking its wounds and gradually becoming an entity again after the fairly heavy casualties endured at Alamein. Darkness fell early and there was little to do at night except huddle in our tents, arguing, drinking the sour Indian-brewed Lion beer and cracking walnuts against the tent pole.

One of my close friends was John Johnson. As the brother of Celia Johnson, the actress, and brother-in-law to Peter Fleming, the traveller-cum-writer, he had moved in artistic circles before the war and had been a junior editor at Jonathan Cape. After a post-war stint with the Arts Council in Cambridge, he was to become, partly at my urging, a discriminating literary agent, whose firm still prospers years after his death.

Books were few in Khanaqin and among the more erudite of us guarded like gold. On this occasion, he and I had just read John Brophy's *Immortal Sergeant*, a novel which featured an episode in the

Desert Campaigns and which was later filmed with Humphrey Bogart as the Canadian hero. I was holding forth in my usual dogmatic way, insisting that it was impossible to write a good war novel during wartime. Those closely involved with the action had neither the time, the inclination nor probably the ability to 'tell it how it was'. Professional novelists like John Brophy, thousands of miles away from the scene, would never get the essential details right.

John cut into my Leavis-type analysis. 'You seem to know it all,' he said. 'Here's your big chance. You talk the others down – why don't you show 'em how it's done? I bet you couldn't write a novel yourself.'

The Lion beer was beginning to hum. 'Right,' I said. 'How much?'

'Five bob.'

'Done.'

As battalion Intelligence officer, I had the use of a fifteen-hundredweight truck. There were no parades in the afternoons during our R & R (rest and recuperation) period, so the next day, I climbed into the back of the truck, sat down on a rolled up camouflage net and opened up my 'liberated' Italian typewriter, propping it on a packing case. A few pages of descriptive writing to set the scene, as it were, and then off into a plot vaguely based on fact but sufficiently altered to avoid libel. Every afternoon for a month, I bashed away until the short novel, something over 40,000 words, was finished. John Johnson read it, was polite enough to say he liked it and, further, to warn the publishers in Bedford Square by airmail that the script was on its way. I only had the one copy which went off to London by surface mail.

The Allies had just driven the Afrika Korps out of Tunisia and for the first time in three years the Mediterranean was open to other than warships. But U-boats lurked everywhere and up to one in three merchant ships were sunk. Three months after I had despatched the typescript, it came back from Jonathan Cape, accompanied by a crisp note suggesting I should break it up into a collection of short stories. Crestfallen, I chucked it into the bottom of a kitbag and decided authorship was not my bent.

Six weeks later, I left 2nd Battalion the Buffs to take up my appointment at GHQ in Baghdad. At the transit camp in Khanaqin, I had to wait a couple of days for transport to take me on the last leg of the journey. There were no books in the camp, not even a Guild paperback; all I could find was a military magazine. As a reading addict, I pored over each dreary article. I even – something I would never normally do – read every advertisement. On the next to last page there was a small notice stating that the publishing house of Macmillan was to celebrate its centenary by giving an award to the best novel and the best work of non-fiction submitted before a certain date in 1943. Submissions had, of course, to be hitherto unpublished and had to be the work of a serving member of the Forces, male or female. With nothing else to read, I dug the script of *Desert Episode*, as I had entitled it, out of the depths of the kitbag and went through it again. The hell with Jonathan Cape, I thought; it seemed to stand up fairly well as one story and not a collection. So, as soon as I had settled in at GHQ, I sent it off again on its long and dangerous journey. I had a brief acknowledgment from Macmillan in St Martin's Street – and then fifteen months' silence. I assumed they had rejected it for the award and had returned it by surface mail, along with a covering letter. After three successful trips of about 5,000 miles each way, the parcel must have run out of luck and have been consigned to full fathom five and more. Ah well, it had passed the time of day and I had at least won my bet with John Johnson. Which reminded me – I never collected the five shillings and it was now too late.

There were over a hundred students at the Staff College and only four or five daily copies of the local newspaper, *The Palestine Post*, were delivered to the mess. Immediately after breakfast, we used to rush to grab a copy or, if too late for that, try to sit next to a lucky grabber and read over his shoulder. One morning, as I was craning my neck alongside 'Red' Kelly, a half-colonel in the Green Howards, he turned and said, 'You got a brother in your regiment?'

'No,' I said. 'Haven't even got a brother.'

'Well then, who's this Captain Greenfield of the Buffs who's won the Macmillan Centenary Award for Fiction?'

And that's how they brought the good news from London to Haifa, although, to give Macmillan their due, I did receive a telegram from them next day, announcing the award. I read it through bleary eyes; the previous evening had been an expensively liquid one.

There was one interesting sequel. The routine was that each student had to write two longish essays, one during the first half of the course and the other in the second half. The subjects were never military. I was quietly proud of my essay-writing abilities and was crestfallen when the first one was given a low mark and there were scathing remarks in the margins. That was prior to the announcement of the Macmillan Award. My second essay, delivered subsequently, had suffered from lack of preparation. It was superficial and contradicted itself at its climax, a fact I spotted when it was too late to make changes. And yet it was given an 'alpha' and a complimentary remark at the foot of the last page. In the world of books, I was beginning to realise, the opposite of giving a dog a bad name may also apply.

A steep and winding road led up from the port of Haifa to the crest of the hill above it. In 1944–5, much of the hillside was occupied by a pleasant park with wooden benches where one could sit and get one's breath back from the uphill climb, all the while admiring the view spread out below and the sparkling Mediterranean. There was also an avenue of sizeable houses for the discreetly wealthy locals. At the top of the hill, if you turned right and followed another road down, you came to a tennis club and, further down, the large requisitioned hotel taken over for the College. At the end of this road, which meandered down through farms and orange groves, was a long sandy beach.

The directing staff expected us to find our own ways of keeping fit. Several, myself amongst them, would walk down to the beach on spare afternoons, have a swim, play ball-games in the bright sunshine and walk back up the hill afterwards. Half a dozen Jewish girls in their late teens or early twenties used to swim and then sunbathe near us and soon we got to chatting. There was absolutely no question of 'shalomming', as the troops called it. ('*Shalom*' is the Hebrew for 'peace' and is the common greeting when meeting a friend.) The girls were virtuous and were saving themselves with a fierce pride for the young Jewish husbands they could both love and admire. But most of us Army students had hardly spoken to a woman for perhaps a couple of years. The girls on the beach were intelligent and all of them spoke good English. Their parents had been German or Polish or Austrian before having the wit or the luck or both to emigrate to Palestine before the round-ups began. And the daughters had preconceptions about British officers. We were in the same category, although not quite so bad, as the SS and the Gestapo. Most of us had spent months, in some cases years, in actual combat with the mutual enemy and slowly the girls on the beach came to realise it.

Gradually, relationships that were chaste but in many ways all the more rewarding developed. My particular friend was a thin fair-haired girl of about twenty named Marga Hirsch. Her father was the well to do owner of a textile factory in the business area of Haifa. He owned a large house behind the park and had somehow acquired an impressive array of malt whisky. He was an affable, broad-minded man of the world and a few of us students enjoyed late afternoons, sipping his whisky and discussing the world. I had been away from a family atmosphere for well over four years, as had all my student friends, and we appreciated all the more what Mr Hirsch had to offer.

Life had slipped into a pleasant routine by the late spring of 1945. The war in Europe was almost over and we began to think vaguely about adapting to the rigours of jungle warfare. But Burma seemed more than remote in the bright sunshine and warm breezes off the Mediterranean. Meanwhile, there were tactical exercises to complete, trips to Acre and Tyre and Sidon and up into the Lebanese heights to ruined crusader castles like Krak des Chevaliers, their turrets soaring into the clear sky, studying the Crusader campaigns and approach marches towards the promised goal of Jerusalem. And in our spare time, we made our regular visits to the beach and had an occasional game of tennis with borrowed racquets at the club up the hill.

On one of the duty journeys, my syndicate stopped off for lunch at a northerly *kibbutz* in Palestine, overlooked by the Golan Heights. Set on the top of a stony, arid hill, it was a testimonial to what unremitting hard work and ingenuity can achieve. An irrigation system had been developed, vegetables grew in neat rows, even a small orange grove was beginning to blossom. The *kibbutz*, we learned, was run on communal, virtually communist, lines. Mothers handed over their babies as soon as they could walk to a communal crèche and they were reared with the community as their parents. The mothers were thus released to take up their share of work in the *kibbutz*. In the dining hall, built by the members, with its wooden tables and chairs, there was no sense of precedence, no family groupings. Anyone could and did sit anywhere.

The meal, as I recall, was simple: a bowl of soup, unleavened bread and goat's cheese. I found myself sitting next to a grey-haired, thin-faced man with slim hands and long fingers. He looked more like an artist than a farm-worker. He spoke fluent English and, after we chatted for a while, I learned that before the war, he had been first violin in the Viennese Symphony Orchestra but had fled at the time of the *Anschluss*.

'Do you still play?' I asked.

'What – with these?' He held out his hands for my closer inspection. The nails were cracked and bruised, there were calluses on his finger tips and palms, on his bowing hand the index finger had been broken and badly re-set. He gave an eloquent shrug and pointed to the platform where four musicians had just sat down in a semi-circle. As the rest of the community went on eating and chatting, they played a Beethoven quartet – to my mind, superbly but again my neighbour shrugged and said the pity of it was they lacked professional tuition and the chance to test their talents against serious competition.

So the days went pleasantly by until one afternoon when I was trudging up the steep hill out of Haifa and saw Marga Hirsch coming down towards me on the opposite footpath. I shouted and waved to catch her attention but, looking straight ahead, proud nose aloft, she walked past.

She just might be daydreaming, so I turned and shouted, 'Marga, it's me. George Greenfield.' She took no notice as she walked down the hill into the distance.

Trudging on up the hill, I wondered what on earth the matter could be. We had argued sometimes at our meetings but never to the point where rancour took over. Indeed, the last time I had seen her, a couple of days earlier, at home with her mother and father, she had been joking and friendly. Why on earth, I wondered, should she cut me dead so blatantly on this occasion?

The answer soon emerged. Next day, there was a scribbled note for me at the Staff College. The Stern Gang had telephoned her father, accusing him of letting his daughter consort with the British oppressor. A nice Jewish girl must have nothing to do with English officer scum, neo-Nazis one and all. Any repetition and they would blow up his factory. She was terribly sorry, the note added, but there was nothing she could do. The Stern Gang never made idle threats. It was the end of a pleasantly relaxed friendship.

The leader of the Gang was Menachem Begin, later to become Prime Minister of Israel. Indeed, for many years after the war, because the Stern Gang was responsible for blowing up the King David Hotel in Jerusalem and of assassinating statesmen such as Count Bernadotte and Lord Moyne, Begin was declared *persona non grata* by the British government and refused entry. The decree had to be quietly scrapped when he assumed the high office. His hit man in the Gang was the physically tiny Shamir, also destined to become Israeli Prime Minister as head of the Likud party.

Towards the end of the Staff College course, the military government of Palestine ordered the execution of a captured member of the Gang, who had been found guilty of murdering both civilians and soldiers through setting off bombs at different targets. In turn, the

Gang kidnapped two sergeants from the 6th Airborne Division and threatened to hang them if the execution went ahead. It did and they duly carried out their threat. They went further by booby-trapping the bodies so that, when they were discovered in the dark at the seaside village of Nahariya, not far from Haifa, the troops who cut them down suffered severe casualties.

It was too much for 6th Airborne. They interrogated the villagers but no one had seen anything, there had been no bumps in the night. Or so they claimed. One can sympathise with this 'three monkeys' attitude. Anyone giving information to the hated British Army would be next on the Stern Gang's hit list, along with his wife and family. The senior officers in the Division were beginning to accept the impasse but the troops had different ideas. One of which was to send a pair of tanks with armour-piercing rounds on board slowly down the main street of Nahariya and fire a round through every alternate house. A kind of *pour encourager les autres* demonstration.

Word reached Haifa that 6th Airborne was on the point of mutinying. The students were rounded up and buses ordered, the plan apparently being that the hundred students, equipped with sidearms only, would help to arrest the 12,000 and more paratroopers, armed to the teeth with sub-machine guns, self-propelled guns and heavy artillery. The power of the human eye over the beast was a truism, if unproved scientifically – but this was ridiculous. Fortunately, well before the buses arrived, the Airborne Division decided not to mutiny and each party returned to its recognised duties.

The more we got to know the Jewish settlers, the more we realised what a cauldron of hate, suspicion and contempt their community was. You would have thought that the great majority who had suffered and escaped from pogroms, expropriation of their assets at the least and genocide at the worst, would have sympathised with the native Arabs in Palestine. But, on the whole, they treated those Arabs as next to animals in understanding and spirit. But their worst enemies were among each other. The *sabra*, those actually born in Palestine, despised the johnny-come-latelies, the immigrants. The townsfolk looked down on the *kibbutz*-workers as hewers of wood and drawers of water. And the *kibbutzim*, in turn, felt they were the true sons of the soil, the builders of a promised land, while those in the towns bought and sold like any city-worker. The teenage and young adult children often disliked their parents who were living, they felt, in a past better forgotten, while those same parents were bemused and irritated by the melange of new ideas and customs.

Many of us at the College felt – and this was a good three years before the State of Israel came into being – that if the surrounding Arab states wished the new order to founder, they should step right back and leave Israel to its own resources. The one thing likely to keep all these disparate forces together was the threat of action on the frontier. Step away and they might well bash themselves to pieces.

Came 8th May and the end of the war in Europe. There was a feeling of optimism in the air. The 14th Army was advancing in Burma and if the might of the British Liberation Army (cynics maintained that the initials BLA stood for 'Burma Later Anyway') on the continent could be transhipped eastwards, along with the vast US forces, the whole shooting match might well be wrapped up in a matter of months. It had been a long war – and would be longer still – but, in Churchill's words, it was the beginning of the end. Peace was no longer a distant prospect.

For the temporary officers and gentlemen the question, 'What are you going to do after the war ?' began to arise. One evening, I was sitting over a drink with Red Kelly, the tough sandy-haired Lieutenant-Colonel who had commanded a battalion of the Green Howards with great distinction as part of 50th (Tyne and Tees) Division in prolonged desert fighting and again in Sicily and Italy. He had won the DSO and a couple of Bars for outstanding leadership in action. In a tough situation, I could imagine no one I would rather have as my leader. He was not only physically brave but had real common sense, for a fighting soldier an asset far more useful than a high IQ. He struck me as the kind of fairly senior officer, although he was only in his early thirties, the post-war army would desperately need.

He told me he had wanted to apply for a permanent commission but had been tipped off that any application would be rebuffed. He had not been to the 'right' school nor to Sandhurst. His vowel sounds were broad, not clipped as befitted a 'real' officer. The post-war Army, it seemed, wanted to go back to its narrow caste system and, in the well known phrase, Red's face would not fit. He had left school at sixteen in the Depression and had managed to get a junior job in a local bank. He had gradually worked his way up and, as soon as he was old enough, had joined the Territorial Army. Called up on the outbreak of war, he had been given a temporary commission when there was still a great shortage of infantry officers, and had literally fought for promotion all the way to Lieutenant-Colonel. I would have deemed him an ideal candidate for a permanent commission, a man who had proved himself over and over at the sharp end, someone any infantry unit would be proud to have as its leader. But it seemed I did not understand the professional military mind.

'So you see,' Red said. 'It's back to the bank. Oh yes, they have to keep a job open for me. But it won't be the kind of job I'd now have if I'd stayed on these past four or five years. Like deputy-manager, even manager, maybe. "Sorry, Mr Kelly, Miss Snooks or this fella with a bad heart filled your vacancy. Lots o' things have changed since you went away. 'Course, we appreciate what you done but you will admit there's a lot of catching up to do. So we'll give you a refresher course an' then you can go back to bein' a cashier."'

John Hershey wrote a novel in the 'seventies entitled *The War Lover*. Although it was about a US Air Force pilot, when I read it, I thought at once of Red Kelly and others like him I had known, men whose tragedy was that they were more at home in a war than in a world at peace.

Yet, alongside Red Kelly's problems when the war was over, we had a splendid example of the truth of that old, if ungrammatical saying, 'It's not a case of what you know but who you know.' In my syndicate at College there was a jolly Guards officer, Francis Legh, heir to an ancient baronetcy. He had acquitted himself well in action and was no doubt an admirable officer in the field. But as a scholar, he was a non-starter, as he was the first to admit. He could bluff his way through the oral examinations with a clearing of the throat, a joke and a vague wave in the direction of the supposed 'enemy', but he was a total loss at written papers. Jock McGregor, my New Zealand room-mate, and I liked him very much. He brought an air of gaiety to what were otherwise serious proceedings. So between us, when we had finished our own written answers, we 'ghosted' Francis's submissions, making sure that they were just that much different from our own. And he duly passed. I expected him to go on with his soldiering after the war and with luck end up as a colonel in charge of a battalion, relying on a smart adjutant for the paperwork. I was greatly surprised to read in *The Times* some years later that he had been appointed Princess Margaret's treasurer. The distinguished lineage of the Leghs had not hurt his upward progress.

As for the Regular Army's attitude towards temporary officers and gentlemen once peace was signed, I experienced an early example. Demobilised in mid-summer 1946, I decided to attend the Kent Cricket Week and Festival in Canterbury, the home of the Buffs, along with Derek Norris and Donald Whitcombe, a cool operator under any battle conditions; he was now running the Seven Stars public house not far from the cathedral. We put on our blue and buff striped regimental ties, paid our entrance fees and walked round the boundary until we came to the Buffs hospitality tent.

The first two faces we recognised were those of Lieutenant-Colonel Nicholson, he who had commanded the 2nd Battalion until wounded in the elbow from behind at the Battle of Alam Halfa, and Major Watkinson, his 2-i.c. The major had not lasted long, either. His one good eye was inflamed by the harsh sunshine and the grains of sand that blew everywhere and he was sent back to a Staff job. The three of us approached them with a cheery smile and from Donald, the joker, a quip. We had the frostiest of receptions, a slight nod, and then they turned their heads back to watching the cricket. We were clearly expendable and should by now have learned our proper place in the scheme of things.

But that was for the future. The Staff College course finished at the end of June 1945. I must have passed out reasonably well, for I was given a plum posting – promotion to major and the job of GSO 2 in Cyprus.

12

♦♦♦

Island in the Sun

♦♦♦♦♦♦

When the overnight steamer docked soon after dawn at Famagusta harbour early in July 1945, I discovered an unspoilt island. Othello's Tower loomed menacingly over the north wall of the harbour and in the city a Gothic cathedral reared its spires into a tranquil sky. A minaret had been built on to one of the spires during the period of Turkish domination and the consecrated building was still used, I learned, for Muslim worship.

The man from whom I was to take over as G II Ops Cyprus had very decently driven all the way from the HQ in Nicosia to greet me on landing. Like me, David Tregoning, a tall lanky Cornishman, had been overseas for several years. He was due to leave on the first step towards demobilisation the day after my arrival and he wanted to effect the hand-over as soon as possible. But first he suggested we should drive the short distance to the King George Hotel, on a small peninsula just south of the city, for breakfast. It was too early for the kitchens to be working full out; he proposed a swim in the sea that almost lapped the hotel verandah to wash away the overnight cobwebs.

It was a revelation. The hotel was the most south-easterly point of the island. Looking westwards, you could see nothing but miles of silvery sand. Nowadays, I believe, that stretch has become a miniature Costa Brava with concrete hotels cheek by jowl along the whole length, beach umbrellas, crowds of tourists screaming and yelling. Democracy has triumphed but a place of serene and lonely beauty has gone for ever. I swam fifty or sixty yards out to sea. Five fathoms deep, I could still see the bottom through the limpid water. A shoal of tiny fishes glinted in the refracted sun's rays deep under my feet. This was going to be quite some posting.

Driving back to Nicosia across the Messaoria Plain, David Tregoning began his briefing while I gazed out of the staff car's windows. It was obviously a horse and cart economy, or rather, a mule and cart. A blindfolded mule plodded round and round in a circle, pulling pails of water out of a deep well. And nearby a farmer was striking stalks of grain with what looked like a lacrosse racquet and then tossing the bundles into the air so that the heavier heads of grain would fall on to the threshing floor and the chaff float away on the breeze. It could have been an Old Testament scene.

Richard the Lionheart had sold the island to the de Lusignan family to help defray the expenses of one of his crusades. (There was apparently a Cypriot named Lusignan who claimed direct descent from the one-time owners. Once a year, he would write to His Excellency the Governor, asking politely if he could have his island back.) Throughout the Middle Ages ownership swopped to and fro, rather like the game of passing the parcel. At one stage, the Republic of Venice claimed ownership (*vide* Shakespeare's *Othello*). During the eighteenth and more than half the nineteenth centuries, the Turks under the Ottoman Empire were dominant until Disraeli with his political legerdemain secured a mandate for Great Britain. The island had slumbered in comparative peace ever since. There were occasional spats, Tregoning said, between the Turkish population, which accounted for a fifth to a quarter of the total, and the Cypriots but no serious clashes. Both sides tended to keep very much to themselves and there was virtually no intermarriage. Religion, apart from nationality, presented formidable barriers, the Turks being Muslim, of course, and the Greek Cypriots quite devout followers of the Greek Orthodox religion.

One political problem, he said, might develop during my time. There was an extreme party, EOKA, which was a weird mixture of rabid Communism and yet stuck on becoming Greek in every sense. Their slogan was 'Enosis – union with Greece.' The island must rise, throw off the yoke of the British oppressor and join Greece as one of its territories. Colonel Grivas, a Resistance hero during the German occupation of Greece and Crete, was said to have landed secretly in Cyprus and to be hiding out with his band of devoted supporters in the Troodos Mountains in the west of the island. Tregoning reckoned that Grivas was more nuisance value than major threat but he felt he should mark my card all the same.

He added that the Greek Cypriots were immensely proud of their descent from the ancient culture and fount of democracy. They even christened their sons after the gods and heroes – Achilles, Xenophon, Hector, Socrates. They were extremely touchy over the fact that several of the British district commissioners, having spent uncomfortable years in darkest Africa, had been given the cushy billet of a Mediterranean island by the Colonial Office. The step, they felt, equated them, the descendants of a great tradition, with the tribes of Africa.

I had good reason, a few weeks later, to experience, albeit surreptitiously, the full force of their sensitivity, when I performed one of the most stupid and childish acts in my life. I sent a typed anonymous letter to the English-language daily paper, the *Cyprus Mail*, advocating 'Sisone', which spelled out Enosis in reverse. It was right, I argued, that Cyprus should join permanently with Greece, the motherland, but Greece was poor, ravaged by years of Nazi occupation, and politically weak, whereas Cyprus was prosperous under enlightened British rule. Thus the solution I advocated was for Greece to join Cyprus and for both of them to enjoy the benefits of life under the Union Jack.

My tongue in cheek letter caused an uproar. Crowds formed outside the office of the newspaper, inflammatory speeches were made and a shoal of correspondence to the *Cyprus Mail* seemed to suggest that being torn limb from limb was too mild a punishment for the perpetrator of the scandalous proposal. And just who was this scoundrel? One of my duties was to attend government cocktail parties; I would stand at the fringe of a gathering, listening with a straight face to suggested identities. It must be someone in government circles – the inference being that the military could barely read and write. Surely not the Colonial Secretary? Too big a risk if he were found out. Ray Arthur, the District Commissioner of Nicosia? No, too stolid by half. But what about Betty Arthur, his wife and the daughter of a high-flying ambassador? She was a wit with a sharp turn of phrase. And so the controversy ran until other events overtook it. My secret has remained until now.

As the staff car neared Nicosia across the plain, David Tregoning said that the forces on the island were there to support the civil power. The archaeologist, Sir Leonard Woolley, His Excellency the Governor, was the man in charge. Protocol demanded that I should sign the Visitors' Book at Government House within a few days of my arrival and so, Tregoning suggested, I might as well get the task over with now. We drove through the city and on to its western boundary and up the well wooded drive. Some years before the war, Cyprus and the Falkland Islands happened to require new buildings for their respective governors at the same time. The architectural plans, it seems, were mixed up, with the result that the semi-tropical island received a low built heavily shuttered building, capable of with-standing blizzards and extreme cold. That was bad enough in high summer, but what of the wretched Governor of the Falkland Islands, shivering in his light airy home with high ceilings and large windows?

Life in Cyprus with the European war just ended was like straying into a Somerset Maugham short story. There were interlocking social circles with government staff and Colonial Office district com-missioners predominant. Questions of precedence loomed large at offi-cial functions. When couples marched in two by two into a formal dinner, with His Excellency in the lead, did the Second Secretary's wife take precedence over the wife of a brigadier? And did a senior lieu-tenant-general on holiday from GHQ Middle East go into dinner in front of the Colonial Secretary or after him? The order would be dis-cussed in countless cocktail parties for the next few days, mingling with the gossip of who was having an affair with whom – and was the injured party aware of it? Drink was inordinately cheap: a good bottle of Otello red wine cost a shilling (5p), a glass of pleasantly dry sherry was three-pence (a little over 1p) and a glass of three-star Hajjipavlou brandy also threepence. Thus parties were plentiful, with the same few familiar faces circulating from one location to another. Gossip flew fast. One after-noon, when I was carrying out some reconnaissance west of Kyrenia, I had a swim at Snake Island. After a rub-down, I changed into formal bush jacket and slacks and the driver of my staff car took me straight to a party in Nicosia where I had promised to put in an appearance.

The first question I was asked after arrival was, 'Did you have a good swim at Snake Island?' It was over twenty miles away and hardly an hour ago but the grapevine had got busy.

I soon learned that Cyprus was the Middle Eastern place for R & R. Senior officers from Cairo and Haifa (among them several Staff College directors of studies calling in favours) would turn up in the heat of summer, expecting a staff car to be put at their disposal for drives to the coast or up to Mount Olympus, 6,000 feet above sea level, where we kept several wooden bungalows in the cool of the pine forests. At times, I felt more like a manager at a branch of Thomas Cook than an operational soldier.

One particular visitor from London stands out in the memory. Sir Eric Speed, Permanent Under-Secretary of State for War, arrived hot-foot from Cairo. He was to take a few days off and then fly on to Singapore to see Admiral Mountbatten, C-in-C South-East Asia. It behoved us to take special care of Sir Eric. I had been in Cyprus about three weeks – it was late July – and was still finding my way around. The great man from the War Office was coming to lunch at the senior mess and we were determined to push the boat out to the far horizon. White coated mess servants kept topping up his sherry glass and when we sat down, several bottles of a good dry white wine were quickly despatched. By the time we reached the coffee stage and the port was circulating clockwise, no one was feeling any pain, least of all our distinguished guest.

He was a tallish grey-haired man, now distinctly flushed. The servants had been dismissed. Looking around the table, he said, 'I know I can trust you chaps. I'm on a rather delicate mission, you know. I've just been briefing General Wilson and in a couple of days I'm off to Singapore to brief Lord Louis. This next bit is top, top secret. You see, we and the Americans have come up with a special new kind of bomb. It's called an atom bomb. It's no bigger than a traditional big bomb – smaller, in fact – but it's so powerful, one atom bomb could blow up a complete city. And very soon we're going to drop it on Japan. That should put a quick end to the war in the Far East.'

He rattled on for a bit until the staff car arrived to take him up to Troodos near the top of Mount Olympus. We shook hands and waved him goodbye, then went back to finish our coffee. 'Pull the other one' was the general feeling. One bomb that could blow up a town. And the rest. The fellow must be smashed out of his mind, thanks to our hospitality. We were not even shocked by his indiscretion, it sounded so inane.

Two weeks later, Hiroshima and Nagasaki exploded in turn – and a frightful new weapon had entered the armoury of war. Sir Eric was proven right, but he should by his age and experience have learned to avoid putting an enemy in his mouth to steal away his brains.

The authorities back home were determined not to repeat the follies and problems of demob at the end of the Great War. Then, the forces were sent home en masse within a few weeks of the Armistice. There were far too many men chasing too few jobs, unemployment was rife, crime flourished. It took many months, even years, to regulate things but by then the damage had been done. This time round, the release flow was properly adjusted. Every man, and woman, was given a demob number depending on the date of joining the forces, age, time spent abroad, special skills – qualified teachers, for example, had an accelerated release date – and so forth. My number, I recall, was 29 and my provisional 'get-out' date was set for March 1946, nine months away. As things turned out, knowing that I would never again in my lifetime enjoy the services of a valet (a batman), a big car and a chauffeur (military driver) and live on a sunny island where grapes fresh off the vine or pleasantly fermented would be in such abundance, I opted to postpone my release by three months to the end of June 1946.

There were still a couple of infantry battalions stationed in Cyprus and an Indian Army tank regiment. In addition, there were several Cyprus Volunteer Force squads, as well as a training centre for the CVF at Polymedia, near Limassol. Somehow these units had to be kept busy and reasonably content while awaiting the end of their service. Square-bashing was out, except for a few solemn occasions like the Armistice Day parade. Many of the troops had seen action and they were not going to spend their daylight hours marching up and down a parade ground and being shouted at by the RSM. As G II Ops, my job was to devise a series of exercises to keep them busy and, if possible, interested. A chat with the Chief of Police, a burly Londoner with gleaming black hair and a bushy black moustache, at one of the interminable Nicosia parties, gave me the clue. The Chief was telling me that, a year earlier, some of the more rabid EOKA followers set up a demonstration. The Army was called out and made a complete cock-up. It was a total shambles. The troops had never before encountered that kind of situation and they were useless in the face of a shouting, jeering mob.

Next morning, I studied the relevant bits of *The Manual of Military Law*. There was an exact drill to be followed. When a riot started, the local mayor or chief civilian was in charge. If he could disperse the rioters by his force of personality or whatever, well and good. But if he deemed it would shortly lead to physical attack and possibly bloodshed, his next step was to hand over to the military. He did so by reading out a lengthy address. Presumably, the rioters were so fascinated by this development that they stood by peaceably for the five or ten minutes the reading required.

Once the military had taken over, the senior officer ordered a blast or two on the bugle and told a trained sniper to load up with one round. Then he ordered the mob to disperse and gave them a minute or two in which to obey his order. If they failed to do so, he ordered the sniper to shoot to kill the leading inciter of the mob. According to the book of rules, the leaders would be urging their men on from the front. In practice, the wily mob leaders would be urging them on from well to the rear. 'Those in the rear cried "Onward" and those at the front cried "Back!"' The sniper was more likely to shoot some innocent bystander who had been swept up in the onrush.

Between us, the Chief of Police and I drafted a scenario. With their CO's permission, I borrowed one company, about a hundred men, from a neighbouring battalion. They were dressed up in *kefiyehs* and flowing robes and had their faces and arms darkened. They were to be our tame rioters. There were some outbuildings and a paved area, an abandoned camp site, near B Military Hospital on a hill south of Nicosia. This was to be the operational zone. In turn, the COs and company commanders of the different battalions were called into HQ and briefed by me. The camp site was to be the Mayor's office and the streets leading to it. The Mayor had passed an edict banning Communists from taking up membership of the town council, even though they had amassed sufficient votes to win their seats. Outraged, they decided to hold a demonstration outside the town council building and the mayoral offices. The Mayor tried to pacify them by making a speech from his balcony but the act had made them even angrier. Missiles were thrown at him and the crowd seemed on the point of storming the official building. The senior police officer present told the Mayor bluntly that his men would be unable to control the masses; the Army should be called in at once.

That's the scenario, I said to the first CO. Positively no live rounds. You will be issued with some blanks. Now it's up to you to disperse the rioting mob and save the civil power.

Our 'rioters' tried all the tricks in the book and a few more of their own devising. They sneaked around the back of the buildings where there were no guards and caused a hullabaloo. The ringleaders had been drilled to hang about in the rear of the mob, inciting them to surge forwards. They made a frantic din by beating old pots and pans together when the officer in charge of mob control tried to issue an order. After half an hour's bedlam, greatly enjoyed by the 'rioters' and even by the defending troops, I blew a whistle to halt the activity. The men were given a break, while the CO and his senior officers concerned with holding the fort adjourned for a discussion with the Chief of Police, myself and our Lieutenant-Colonel, DA & QMG. We had all learned some important lessons; in an effervescent, flaring up situation, you could not go by the book. The civil authority must learn to hand over to the military the moment an unlawful assembly took place. The defending CO must get his men round to the flanks and to the rear just as fast as possible, to control the movements of the crowd and put a scare into the leaders. When and if to open fire would be the most fraught decision. The Amritsar Massacre must never be repeated but to pick off the chief ringleader would cut one of two ways. The crowd might disperse in shock and fear; equally, the killing might lead to enflamed anger and an urge for revenge.

One after another, the battalions in Cyprus underwent the test. Each CO agreed that it was valuable and had straightened out his thinking on the subject. A decade or so later, the British forces in Cyprus found themselves in the same situation for real against screaming, murderous EOKA mobs. By then, our immediate post-war training had probably been long forgotten.

The average reader may wonder why a mere major virtually ran the Army side of an important Mediterranean colony. The simple answer was I had the ear of the Brigadier commanding the island. My office was next to his in the HQ building at Tres Elias, 'halfway between the leper colony and the lunatic asylum', as the local saying put it. We dined together, we played bridge in the evenings. Brigadier Jack Anstice, who was in overall charge during the last nine months of my stay was not a desk-general. He was a cavalryman and had won a DSO with General Slim in the 1941 retreat from Burma. Later, in the Western Desert, he had won a Bar to his medal for conspicuous gallantry. And, a regular soldier who had been a half-colonel at least two years earlier, he was still only one rank higher. What rankled with him most was that he was the eldest of three brothers, one of whom had ended as a Lord of the Admiralty and the other an air marshal in the RAF. He spent half his time off duty bemoaning his fate and what a bloody outfit the Regular Army was and the other half trying to persuade me to stay on and become a regular.

Yet again it was a case of his face not fitting. Too often the old phrase has tumbled out to excuse a lack of promotion which was wholly undeserved. But in Anstice's case, it was all too true. Handsome, lean, with chestnut-coloured hair and moustache and pale grey eyes, he was the very model of a dashing cavalry officer but he was desperately competitive with a fiendish temper. Before his arrival, some of us in the senior mess would play a few rubbers of bridge after dinner. It was a light-hearted game with modest stakes. There was more chitchat and joking than strict adherence to Ely Cuthbertson's laws. But when Brigadier Anstice joined in, the whole tenor of the evening changed. He was determined to win at all costs and became extremely angry, almost offensive, in hinting at cheating from his opponents, if he lost a rubber. My partner was Godfrey Somerfield, a witty Scottish major. We became so fed up with Anstice's behaviour that we deliberately tried to lose. As soon as he had sorted his hand, Godfrey would call 'Two spades'. I would bid that up to 'Three no trumps' and the Brigadier would double. As soon as Godfrey put his hand down as dummy, I would give an internal groan. He had just the right court cards to fit in with my hand and a long line of diamonds to score, once we had squeezed the opposition's few diamonds. Jack Anstice would almost yell with rage and shout that we must have a secret code for bidding, which was tantamount to cheating. I had enjoyed playing friendly bridge since the age of fifteen but I was so put off by these nightly sessions that I vowed never to play again – a pledge I have kept for over fifty years.

It was the same with tennis. Having been in the finals of the Fenner's Hard Court Tournament at Cambridge, I was above average as a club player. The Brigadier was all bash and dash. I used to play against him at doubles and would deliberately aim to hit a return into the top of the net. He would be smart enough to spot a too obvious throwing of the point. But, time after time, the result would be an ace that skimmed the net and flew low and fast to the back of the court. He would scream and yell and then stand close to the net, glowering like a sulky child as the set ran against him and his reluctant partner.

Anstice was deeply in love with his wife and kept a silver-framed photograph of her on his office desk. More often than not, when I would knock and enter with some query, he would be scribbling away at page after page of a love letter to her back in England. He was pulling all the strings he could for her to join him on the island. Finally, he succeeded. She was then in her mid-to late forties but you could see that she must have been a real beauty in her youth. There was a sense of calm and repose about her, valuable qualities for a woman whose husband's temper might blaze at the slightest, or indeed no, provocation. They had a daughter who joined them on leaving boarding school. By then, I had left the island, but I heard that she was even more beautiful than her mother had been.

The daughter, it seems, met and fell in love with a Turkish harbourmaster at Kyrenia. After a brief courtship, she married him. This was a great social come-down for the Anstices and the cause of much muttering behind gloved hands on the part of the feminine party-goers in Nicosia. And then, some months later, a much-married duke on a cruise of the eastern Mediterranean in his yacht put in at Kyrenia harbour for revictualling. He saw the daughter, he was ravished by her beauty, he had to have her. A divorce was arranged and the harbourmaster's wife ended up as a duchess. I would have given much to attend the next big party and watch the reactions of the catty set when the news broke.

In an early chapter, I mentioned how the adjutant at the Lincolnshire Regimental Depot had taken a sudden, and to my mind quite unwarranted, dislike of me and had gone out of his way to have me placed on extra guard duties, usually at weekends, and cookhouse fatigues. I had never cheeked Captain Darwall or shown what the Army calls dumb insolence. Doing a lonely stretch of sentry-go from two till four a.m. on a cold night on the north Lincoln hill made me feel murderous. If the slight figure of Captain Darwall had come along, I would happily have fixed my bayonet and plunged it into him over and over. I used to pass the time thinking how one day I might get my revenge. Revenge, according to the Italian saying, is a meal best eaten cold.

We had a system in Cyprus where officers of any status transferred to the island paid their respects to the senior A & Q officer and the G II Ops on arriving in Nicosia. I would try to make them feel at home, give them a rundown on the military situation and tell them something about the unit they were being posted to. We found it helped to break the ice and on both sides put a face to a name they might hear quite often in the coming weeks.

Late one afternoon in the winter months, with dusk creeping in, I had just switched on my desk lamp when there were a couple of discreet taps on the closed door. I yelled, 'Come in'. The door opened and an officer, of medium height, a captain, entered, took three paces forward, halted and slung me a smart salute. Being bare-headed, I could only nod in reply. I could not see him in any detail and it would have been rude to tip up the desk light like a searchlight.

'Would you mind switching on the main lights?' I asked. 'On the wall, just by the door.'

'Sir,' he said. He did an about turn, marched over to the wall, switched on the lights and then returned to his position in front of my desk. He stood rigidly to attention.

Now I could see him full face, as indeed he could see me. Christ, I thought, it's Captain Darwall. Still a captain five years after we had first met; something must have gone hideously wrong with his career as a regular. By odds, he should have been a brigadier by now, even a major-general.

We looked hard at each other. Perhaps it was the brightness of the main lighting but his face seemed to have gone somewhat pale.

'We've met before, I think,' I said.

Still stiffly to attention: 'Yessir.'

'At the Lincolnshire Regimental Depot, I recall.'

'Yessir.'

'All right, stand at ease, man. Now what are we going to do with you?'

I could have posted him on his own to the northernmost tip of the Panhandle with a bivouac but no rations and the orders to live off the stony land as best he could. Or posted him alone in the forest on the far side of Kykkos Monastery as a one-man unit to track the bandits thought to be holed up there. This was operational, I would not need the Brigadier's signature on the order. But it had all gone. That cold meal of revenge had congealed. In fact, I felt strangely sorry for the man. After all, a war is often the only chance a regular soldier has to prove himself and gain promotion. Here was one who had missed out on his chances. And again, perhaps that represented my best retaliation.

So we chatted quite amiably for a few minutes and I arranged for him to be posted to an infantry battalion which needed a replacement company commander.

The Area Commander, stationed in Beirut, had gone on leave and Brigadier Anstice, as the senior District Commander, went to replace him for a few weeks. He still retained nominal control of Cyprus and after several days various issues had cropped up on which I needed his 'chop'. That, at least, was the official story. Beirut at the time was the Monte Carlo and Cannes combined of the Middle East. Two great hotels, the Normandie and the St Georges overlooked the placid bay, edged with yachts and sailing boats. The boulevards sparkled, the streets in the city were clean, the restaurants provided a blend of the best in French and Arab cooking. It was a privileged playpen for the Levantine rich. Even though I was being spoiled in Cyprus, whenever I thought of my elderly parents with their coupon books and ration cards, I still fancied an excuse for a couple of days' R & R in that sophisticated milieu.

At a party in the RAF Mess at Nicosia, I happened to be chatting to the Group Captain in charge, a bemedalled warrior, and told him I had to go to Beirut shortly.

'Great idea!' he said. 'I mean, I've just had a great idea. Look, the Air Ministry has issued an order that all officers qualified as pilots have to put in X hours up there' – he pointed to the ceiling with his free hand – 'by this time next month, or something. I've been a bit chairborne of late. Why don't I fly you over? We have an Anson trainer. Seats five but you can fly it with two, I guess. Piece of cake. What d'you say?'

I thought, great. To be flown as sole passenger by a senior officer with two DFCs and a DSO, that was something in itself. And we'd be there within an hour of take-off, whereas the steamer took almost the whole day and you had to drive all the way to Famagusta to board her. I accepted smartly.

On the morning, my driver took me out to the RAF runway and pulled up alongside the red-painted Anson. I climbed aboard and dumped my overnight bag on a rear seat. The Group Captain was fiddling around with the controls, turning at times to an instruction book. 'Never flown one of these beasts before,' he announced, 'but after a Spit, it should be a piece of cake, what?'

He fiddled around some more and then said, 'I don't really need you to navigate, George.' He waved a map sheet in his spare hand. 'I've taken a bearing on Beirut – 138°E I make it – and that should see us home and dry. But I will need your help. According to the book of words, when we're airborne a red light should come on at the top of the panel. That means the wheels are still down. Seems they don't work hydraulically. That lever down by the spare pilot's seat – the one you're sitting in – got it? If you work that forwards and backwards, it should raise the wheels. But for Christ's sake, not till we're airborne. Otherwise, we'll do the dying swan act right here on the runway. My name will be mud.'

Eventually, we took off and flew eastwards, with the dazzling sun still rising on our starboard side. At first, we bumped around a bit in the limpid air, which I took to be atmospheric problems but which were in fact due to my pilot's getting used to flying again after a long spell on the ground. After about an hour, we arrived over the coast – but where was Beirut? There were sandy beaches, woods and fields with the occasional cottage dotted about the landscape but no sign of a major town.

'Reckon we must have shot a bit too far north,' declared the Group Captain. 'Frankly, I never was all that hot as a navigator. Tell you what, let's work our way south down the coastline. Bound to hit Beirut that way.'

So southwards we flew for about ten minutes. And then a familiar sight came into view, an oil installation, a busy harbour, buildings tucked hard against the bottom of the slope with a steep hill and parkland above.

I coughed. 'Excuse me,' I said, 'but down there, that's Haifa.'

'You sure?'

'Hell, I spent six months there, not so long back. I'd know it anywhere.'

'OK, you win. Let's do an about turn and go back up the coast north.'

Back we went, past Tyre and Sidon until Beirut loomed into view. Then I suddenly remembered from past flights. The airfield was on top of a cliff. The regular breeze blew in off the sea and so aircraft landing ran towards the edge of the cliff on the rather short runway. The only barrier to prevent an overshoot was a coil of double dannert barbed wire, which would hardly stop a bicycle in full flight. And I was about to make a landing in the hands of an out of practice pilot. Having survived two blowings-up in one morning and the disease of typhus, I felt it was rather a silly way to die, months after the end of hostilities.

The Group Captain got clearance from the tower, did a wide U-turn and approached the runway from the land side. If you have ever watched a small boy skimming a pebble over the surface of a lake, you can guess how it felt like to land. I had waggled the lever to lock the wheels down. They bumped on the tarmac, the plane shot up a few feet in the air, down again, another bump, another lift and so on until, as the cliff loomed near, the pilot yanked with all his strength on the brake and the plane shuddered to a halt with its nose about a yard from the barbed wire on the cliff's edge. I could feel the sweat trickling down from my shoulder blades to the small of my back.

I retrieved the overnight bag and we both climbed out. A jeep from Beirut HQ drove up to collect me. The Group Captain was due to fly back to Cyprus on his own, provided he did not overshoot and end up in Rhodes or Crete.

We shook hands and I thanked him for the flight. 'Forget it,' he said, 'all in the day's work. Tell you what, George, you send me a signal when you're ready to come back and I'll pop over and get you.'

'Sounds great,' I said. Not in a million years, I thought.

On the locomotion front I myself was able to benefit from a Ministry of Transport-issued edict that any soldier who passed an Army driving test would get an automatic civilian licence if he applied after leaving the service. It was a great opportunity. I arranged for a junior RASC officer, one of several attached to HQ, to appear on parade, along with a jeep, at 0900 hours sharp the following morning.

I turned up in full service dress, Sam Browne belt shining in the sun, which glinted off my major's crowns. The lieutenant flung me a smart salute.

'Right,' I said in as sharp a tone as I could muster, 'let's get on with it.'

'Yes, sir. I take it, sir, you've had some driving experience?'

'I learned on a fifteen-hundredweight truck in the Welsh mountains in 1940. Since then, I've driven most types of Army vehicle, including jeeps in the Western Desert and staff cars here in Cyprus.'

'That's fine, sir.' He made a note on a buff-coloured form he was carrying. 'Would you mind getting into the jeep, sir – in the driver's seat. Thank you, sir.'

I sat down behind the steering wheel and waited.

'Now, sir, would you please switch on the engine.'

I switched on.

'Please, sir, would you engage first gear and drive forward slowly. If you would listen to my next – excuse me –word of command, sir.'

'Right.' I put it into gear and rolled forward four, five yards. The lieutenant called out, 'Stop!' I applied the foot brake and flicked the gear lever into neutral.

He came over. 'Excellent, sir, you've passed the driving test. If you'd care to come back to the office, I'll make out the chitty.'

'Good. Thanks for your help. But I've got an important conference due in half an hour, back at the HQ building. Sign the form, will you, and have it sent up to my room.'

'Of course, sir. Thank you, sir.' He saluted again and I acknowledged with a good 'longest way up, shortest way down' one of my own.

And that's how I gained my UK driver's licence. I can only say, in my defence, that was over fifty years ago and, touch wood, I still have a fairly clean licence.

Life rolled pleasantly along until the second week of June 1946. My demobilisation papers had come through and I was due to leave in a couple of weeks by ship to Port Said and then on down the Canal to a transit camp near Port Suez before embarkation and a leisurely voyage through the Mediterranean. Then it happened.

I was woken in the small hours one morning by a signaller with a TOP SECRET MOST IMMEDIATE signal from the War Office (copy to the Admiralty) via GHQ MEF. The gist of it was that the unscrupulous skippers of various rust-buckets, aged ships with clapped out engines and holds wallowing in filth, had extorted large sums from various European Jewish exiles to ship them safely to the Promised Land. Similar vessels had attempted the illegal run before from ports like Bari in southern Italy and had sailed south of Cyprus towards Haifa. They had been rounded up by the Royal Navy. This time, two rusty old ships, liable to sink in a real storm, were attempting to creep through to the north, in the narrow stretch of sea between the Kyrenia coastline and the shores of Turkey, hardly twenty miles across. The Navy expected to intercept them in turn, the first in three days' time, and 'sheepdog' them into Famagusta harbour, which would take another day. The signal ordered HQ Cyprus to erect a secure camp to accommodate the passengers.

My colleagues and I knew that entry into Palestine for Jewish immigrants was, like many post-war desirables, strictly rationed. In many ways, this was a sensible step. The Foreign Office had to keep a balance between the aspirations of the immigrants and the rights of the Arabs who had lived there for centuries before it became a homeland for the Jews. Besides, typhus and other fell diseases had ravaged the concentration camps themselves and the slums of European cities. Thus all Jewish immigrants had to be medically screened before receiving their papers, a process needing time and calm conditions. If 'illegals' were dumped on some lonely shore by a skipper in it for the money, they would disperse. Infectious diseases could spread like a bush fire.

And, perhaps the most telling point of all, it was widely realised that Ernest Bevin, the union hard man who had fought his way up to the post of Foreign Secretary, was pro-Arab and anti-semitic. A fellow politician said to Bevin about Herbert Morrison, another leading Labour minister, 'He's his own worst enemy.'

'Not while I'm alive, he ain't,' was Bevin's riposte. Some might think that his feelings about the Jews fell into the same category.

At dawn that morning, a Royal Engineers major and I drove to Famagusta at some speed. The camp had to be built close to that point in the harbour wall where the ship would come alongside. There would have to be a kind of funnel, posts and barbed wire, leading from the edge of the wall to the camp's entrance, to steer the disembarking passengers in. Latrines would need to be dug, tents erected, a medical centre set apart, and twenty-four-hour-a-day look-out posts established at the four corners of the camp. Beds and bedding would also have to be ferried in. Fortunately, the steady rundown of troops in the Famagusta area meant that surplus gear had built up in a neighbouring ordnance store but there was still the problem of shifting it into the camp at very short notice.

The sapper major and I finished our reconnaissance, sited the perimeter fences, compared notes. Then we drove back at speed to Nicosia. I still needed to consult the medicos and the DAAG before drafting the operational instruction, which would have to go out to the participating battalions that same day. I managed to complete it by the late afternoon. It stressed that the immigrants must be treated with proper consideration. They were not enemy nor prisoners of war. The troops would carry bayonets, which must be sheathed at all times, unless in a real emergency a senior officer gave the order to fix bayonets. Rifles would also be carried but kept slung over the shoulder, both for safety and to allow the soldier freedom of both arms. If any passenger from the ship resisted, only reasonable force could be used in moving him or her into the camp.

Late the following morning, a Royal Navy frigate caught up with the leading rust-bucket north-west of the Panhandle. She was wallowing deep in the water and making only three or four knots at best. At first, it seems, the skipper refused to heave to but a warning shot across his bows appeared to concentrate his mind. Now ship and 'sheepdog' had rounded the peninsula of the Panhandle and were sailing erratically southwards towards Famagusta. The ETA would be about thirty-six hours ahead.

I could not stay away; partly because I wanted to make sure that the operational instruction, drafted in a hurry, stood up in all its detail and partly because I was curious to see the men and women who were symbols of what we had been fighting for over nearly six years. The camp was virtually complete. What three days before had been an open expanse was now filled with neat rows of tents. Even a wooden bath-house had been erected. The sappers and the infantry battalion had done a great job; I made a mental note to send their CO a congratulatory signal, officially signed by the Brigadier.

At last, the high-sided steamer crept into the harbour and amid gushing of steam and groaning of the engines was tied up alongside the harbour. The gangway was hauled into place and an Army MO with a team of stretcher-bearers went on board to evacuate the sick and the very elderly first. They were ragged, faces ravaged with pain and fear, dark eyes darting to and fro. Then troops went in to help the walking wounded ashore. One old crone stood at the top of the gangway, refusing to leave the ship. She was clearly overwrought, beside herself. A soldier went forward and gently put an arm round her shoulders. She whirled around, raised her arm and raked him right down the cheek with the claws of her hand. Two red stripes ran down his cheek.

Christ, I thought, he'll knock her down with the flat of his butt. If we're lucky. But all he said was 'There, there, mum – no panic.' Slowly, he helped her down the gangway. With men like that, I thought – even our generals can't lose wars.

And then it hit me. They were so close to their Promised Land and now, at the last minute, diverted into a camp in another land. All right, it was not a concentration camp; there were no gas chambers, no furnaces for corpses. But it was still a kind of prison, outlined by barbed wire and with security posts. What a greeting. Politicians, even the ones held to be statesmen, talked gravely about justice for all and freedom for the oppressed but expedience was really their private goal.

Nearly seven years before, when Chamberlain made his sombre radio speech on a Sunday morning, announcing we were at war with Germany, many thousands of young men, myself included, had volunteered to enlist. We had seen Hitler marching first into the Ruhr, then Austria, then Czechoslovakia and now Poland. It was time to say, 'No further', to strike a blow for men's right to live in peace and freedom – for democracy, indeed.

I had been chasing the beast for all those years, often from a considerable distance, but somehow we must have come full circle. Now the beast was chasing me. Was this to be my memorial, this barbed wire camp? Was my defence to be, 'I was only obeying orders?'

It was time to go.

Index

Index

Page numbers in *italics* refer to illustrations.